CURTAIN CALL

WRITTEN BY
WILFRID LUPANO

ILLUSTRATED BY
RODGUEN

COLORS BY
OHAZAR

Translation, Layout, and Editing by Mike Kennedy

ISBN: 978-1-942367-48-2
Library of Congress Control Number: 2018941031

10 9 8 7 6 5 4 3 2 1

This book is dedicated to all the funny night owls, barflies, mobsters, deviants, dreamers, and the lost who felt the need, for reasons that still escape me, to tell their heroic stories to the bartender or doorman I was at the time. I have always taken this trust as a mark of honor. With all of the many stories they had the goodness to share or live with me, I composed this story as a boastful tribute to their interconnected fates.

Thanks also to Henri Guaino, for transcribing the speech on page 17 about the legacy of the events and riots of May '68 as delivered by Nicolas Sarkozy during his presidential campaign in 2007. I have rarely been so angry at a political speech, but this little nugget of rhetoric and bad faith didn't have me laughing for very long...

Thank you with all my heart to Rodguen for his warrior spirit on this long journey. It is with gratitude and a feeling of accomplishment that I give him back to his family, almost in the state in which I found him.

And thanks to Ohazar for his total involvement on the colors of this book.

— Wilfrid Lupano

A huge thank-you to Wilfrid for this wonderful gift and this long and ideal collaboration.

A special thank-you to my wife and sons, who didn't see me much during the four years of weekends it took me to make this book.

I dedicate this book to my brother, Philippe, who loved the script and would have loved having this book in his hands now.

— Rodguen

A huge thank-you to Wilfrid, Rodguen, and Grégoire for pulling me into the loop of colorist testing for this wonderful story. And thank you three for choosing me and entrusting me with your baby at the end of the process, for a collaboration that can only be described as idyllic. Your choice in technique is neither obvious nor forgiving, but truly freeing and full of atmosphere.

Wilfrid, everything you write is just awesome.

Rod, thank you for your trust.

Grégoire, thank you for your relevant and constructive exchanges.

And thanks to Laetitia, Rebecca, and Eleonore for supporting me during these three months.

— Ohazar

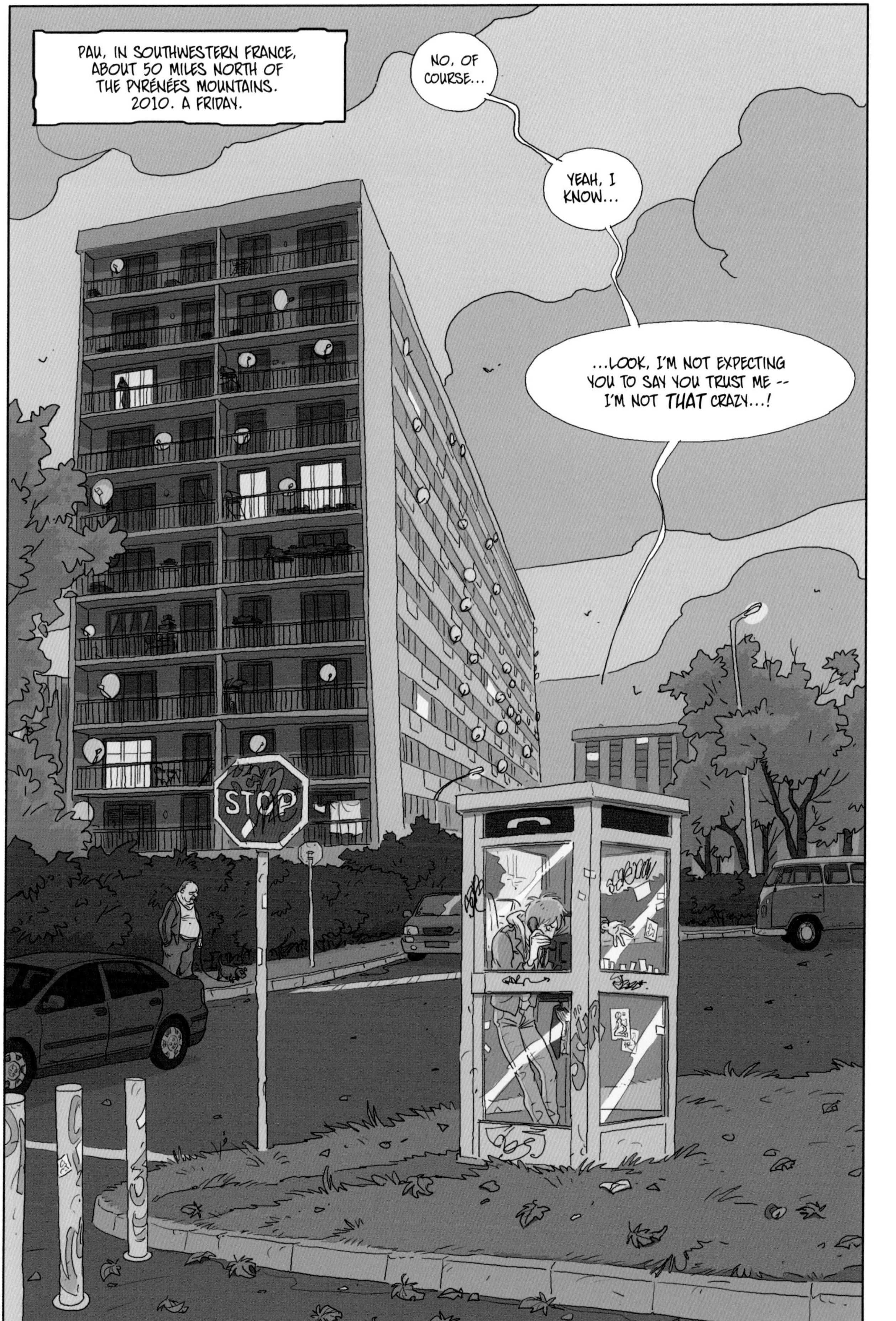
PAU, IN SOUTHWESTERN FRANCE, ABOUT 50 MILES NORTH OF THE PYRÉNÉES MOUNTAINS. 2010. A FRIDAY.
NO, OF COURSE...
YEAH, I KNOW...
...LOOK, I'M NOT EXPECTING YOU TO SAY YOU TRUST ME -- I'M NOT THAT CRAZY...!
STOP

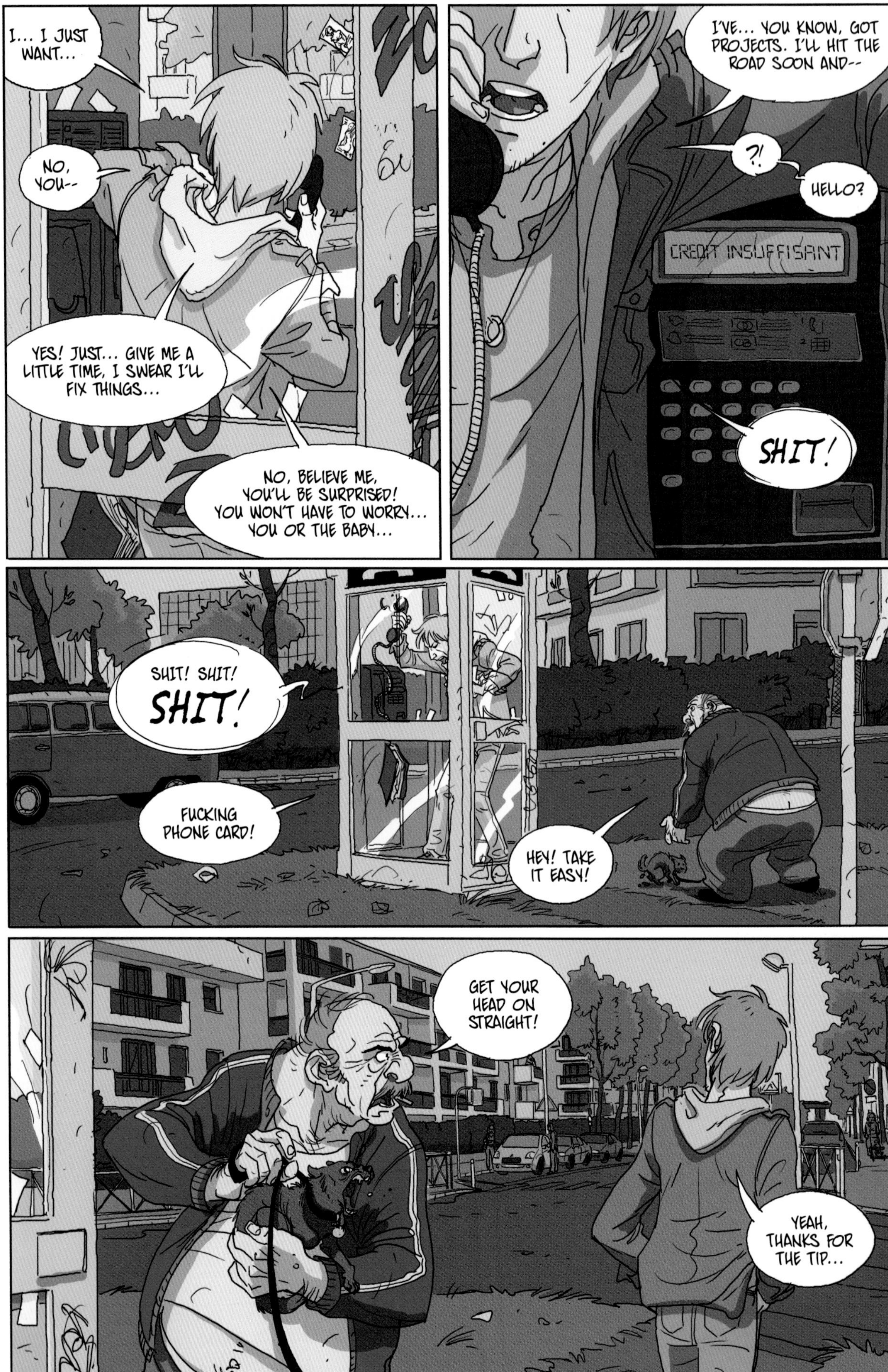
I... I JUST WANT...
NO, YOU--
YES! JUST... GIVE ME A LITTLE TIME, I SWEAR I'LL FIX THINGS...
NO, BELIEVE ME, YOU'LL BE SURPRISED! YOU WON'T HAVE TO WORRY... YOU OR THE BABY...
I'VE... YOU KNOW, GOT PROJECTS. I'LL HIT THE ROAD SOON AND--
?!
HELLO?
CREDIT INSUFFISANT
SHIT!
SHIT! SHIT! SHIT!
FUCKING PHONE CARD!
HEY! TAKE IT EASY!
GET YOUR HEAD ON STRAIGHT!
YEAH, THANKS FOR THE TIP...

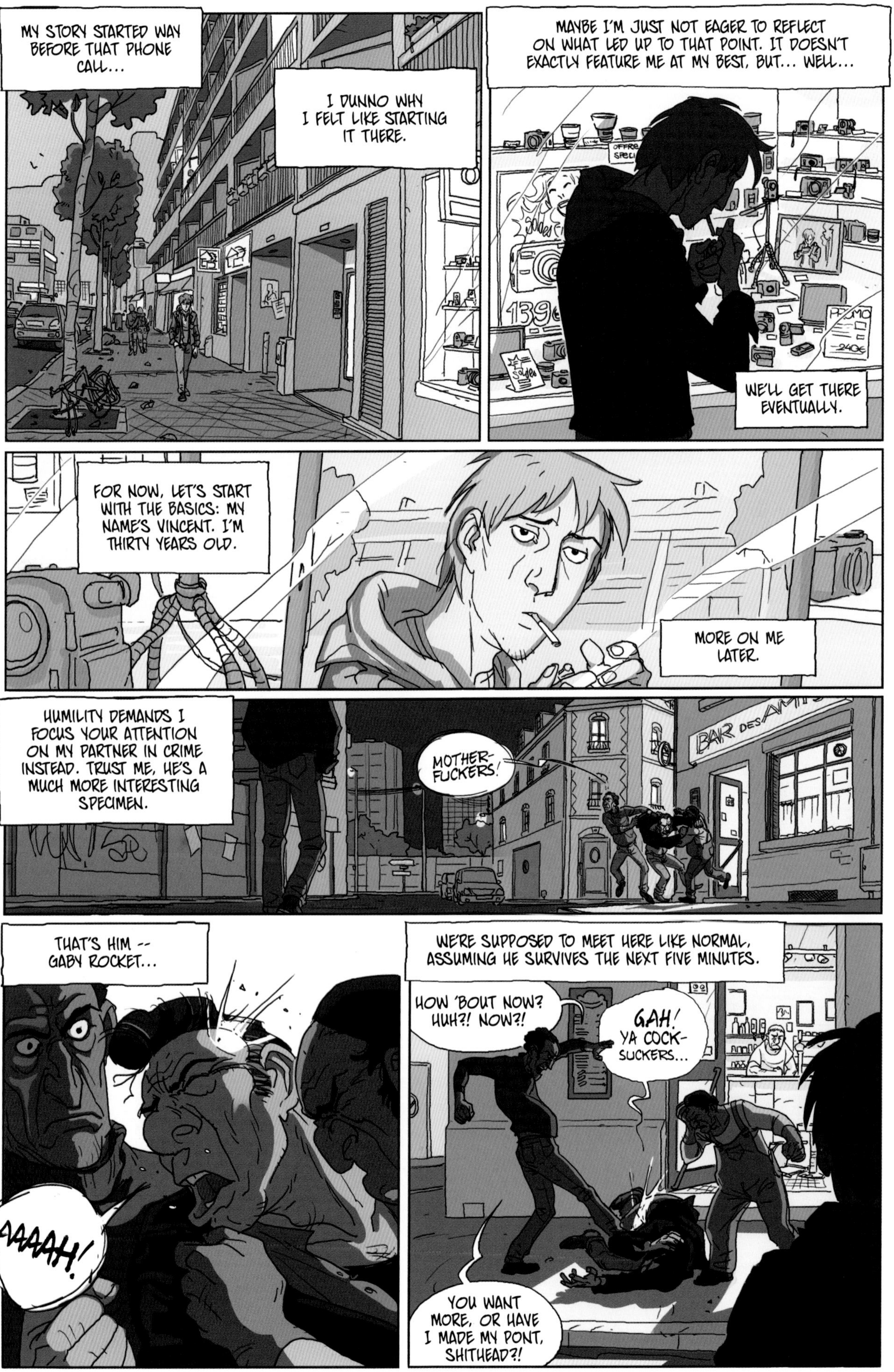
MY STORY STARTED WAY BEFORE THAT PHONE CALL...
I DUNNO WHY I FELT LIKE STARTING IT THERE.
MAYBE I'M JUST NOT EAGER TO REFLECT ON WHAT LED UP TO THAT POINT. IT DOESN'T EXACTLY FEATURE ME AT MY BEST, BUT... WELL...
WE'LL GET THERE EVENTUALLY.
FOR NOW, LET'S START WITH THE BASICS: MY NAME'S VINCENT. I'M THIRTY YEARS OLD.
MORE ON ME LATER.
HUMILITY DEMANDS I FOCUS YOUR ATTENTION ON MY PARTNER IN CRIME INSTEAD. TRUST ME, HE'S A MUCH MORE INTERESTING SPECIMEN.
MOTHER-FUCKERS!
THAT'S HIM -- GABY ROCKET...
AAAAH!
WE'RE SUPPOSED TO MEET HERE LIKE NORMAL, ASSUMING HE SURVIVES THE NEXT FIVE MINUTES.
HOW 'BOUT NOW? HUH?! NOW?!
GAH! YA COCK-SUCKERS...
YOU WANT MORE, OR HAVE I MADE MY PONT, SHITHEAD?!

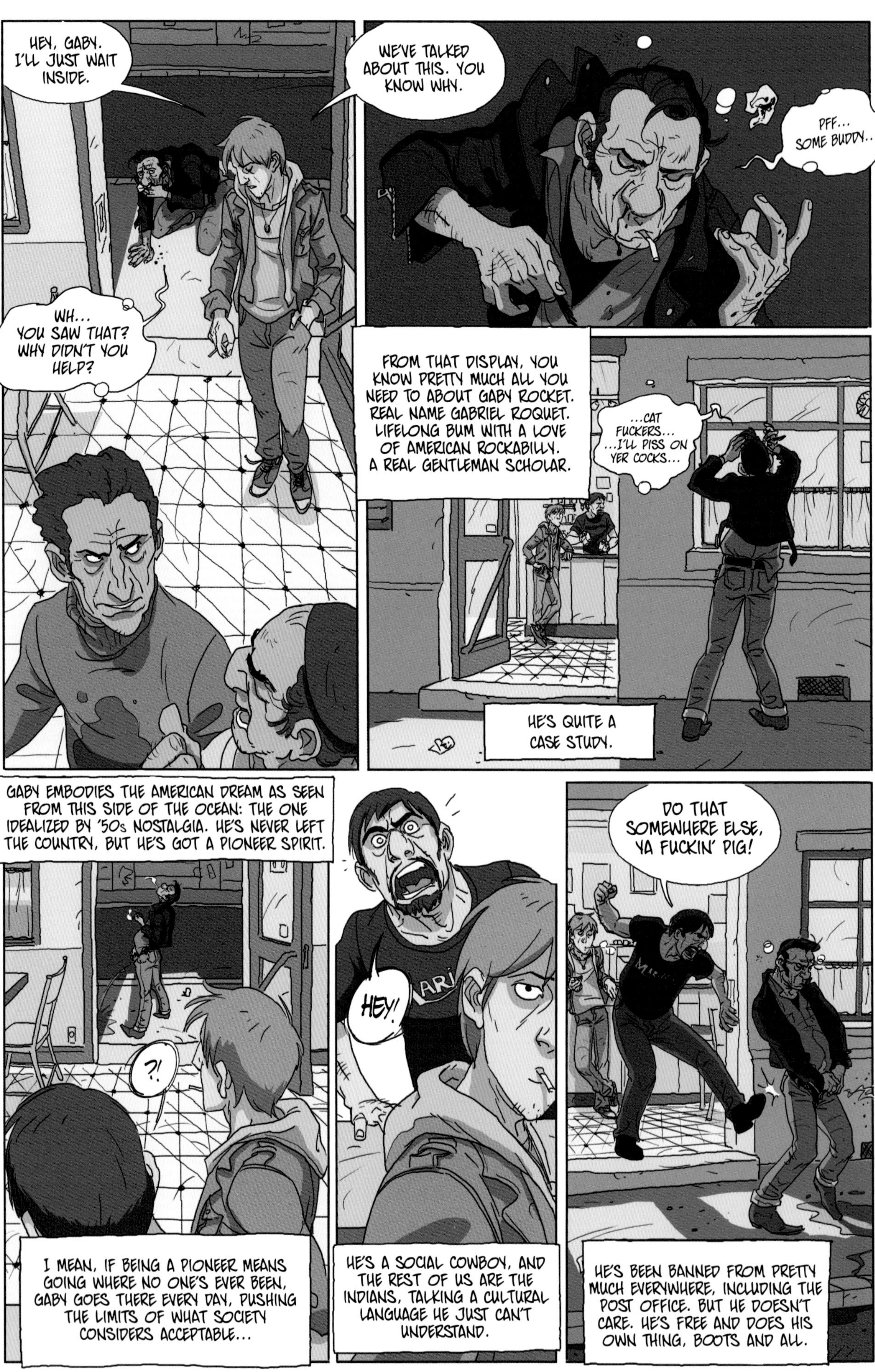
HEY, GABY. I'LL JUST WAIT INSIDE.
WE'VE TALKED ABOUT THIS. YOU KNOW WHY.
WH... YOU SAW THAT? WHY DIDN'T YOU HELP?
PFF... SOME BUDDY...
FROM THAT DISPLAY, YOU KNOW PRETTY MUCH ALL YOU NEED TO ABOUT GABY ROCKET. REAL NAME GABRIEL ROQUET. LIFELONG BUM WITH A LOVE OF AMERICAN ROCKABILLY. A REAL GENTLEMAN SCHOLAR.
...CAT FUCKERS... ...I'LL PISS ON YER COCKS...
HE'S QUITE A CASE STUDY.
GABY EMBODIES THE AMERICAN DREAM AS SEEN FROM THIS SIDE OF THE OCEAN: THE ONE IDEALIZED BY '50s NOSTALGIA. HE'S NEVER LEFT THE COUNTRY, BUT HE'S GOT A PIONEER SPIRIT.
?!
I MEAN, IF BEING A PIONEER MEANS GOING WHERE NO ONE'S EVER BEEN, GABY GOES THERE EVERY DAY, PUSHING THE LIMITS OF WHAT SOCIETY CONSIDERS ACCEPTABLE...
HEY!
HE'S A SOCIAL COWBOY, AND THE REST OF US ARE THE INDIANS, TALKING A CULTURAL LANGUAGE HE JUST CAN'T UNDERSTAND.
DO THAT SOMEWHERE ELSE, YA FUCKIN' PIG!
HE'S BEEN BANNED FROM PRETTY MUCH EVERYWHERE, INCLUDING THE POST OFFICE. BUT HE DOESN'T CARE. HE'S FREE AND DOES HIS OWN THING, BOOTS AND ALL.

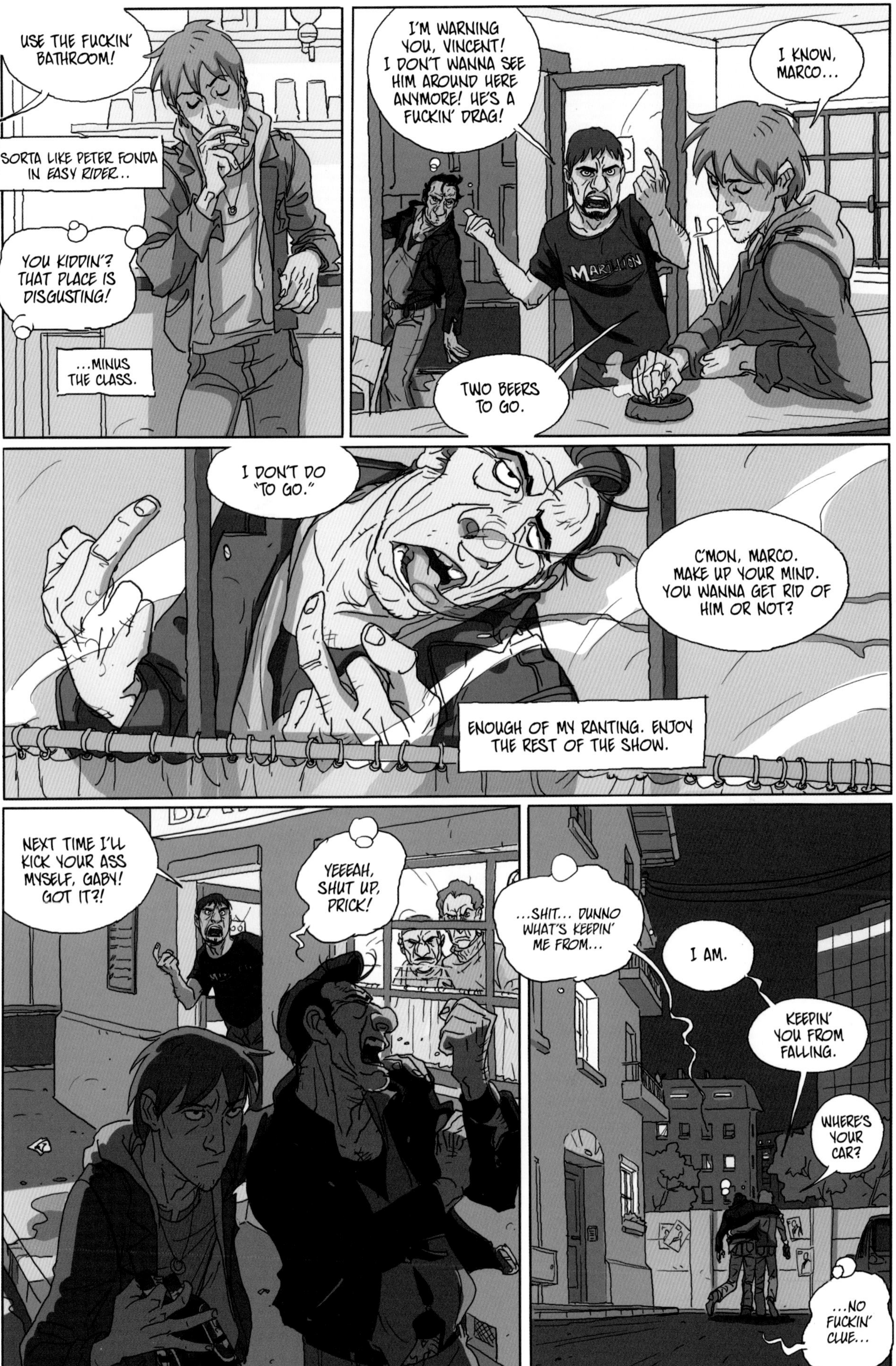
USE THE FUCKIN' BATHROOM!
SORTA LIKE PETER FONDA IN EASY RIDER...
YOU KIDDIN'? THAT PLACE IS DISGUSTING!
...MINUS THE CLASS.
I'M WARNING YOU, VINCENT! I DON'T WANNA SEE HIM AROUND HERE ANYMORE! HE'S A FUCKIN' DRAG!
I KNOW, MARCO...
TWO BEERS TO GO.
I DON'T DO "TO GO."
C'MON, MARCO. MAKE UP YOUR MIND. YOU WANNA GET RID OF HIM OR NOT?
ENOUGH OF MY RANTING. ENJOY THE REST OF THE SHOW.
NEXT TIME I'LL KICK YOUR ASS MYSELF, GABY! GOT IT?!
YEEEAH, SHUT UP, PRICK!
...SHIT... DUNNO WHAT'S KEEPIN' ME FROM...
I AM.
KEEPIN' YOU FROM FALLING.
WHERE'S YOUR CAR?
...NO FUCKIN' CLUE...

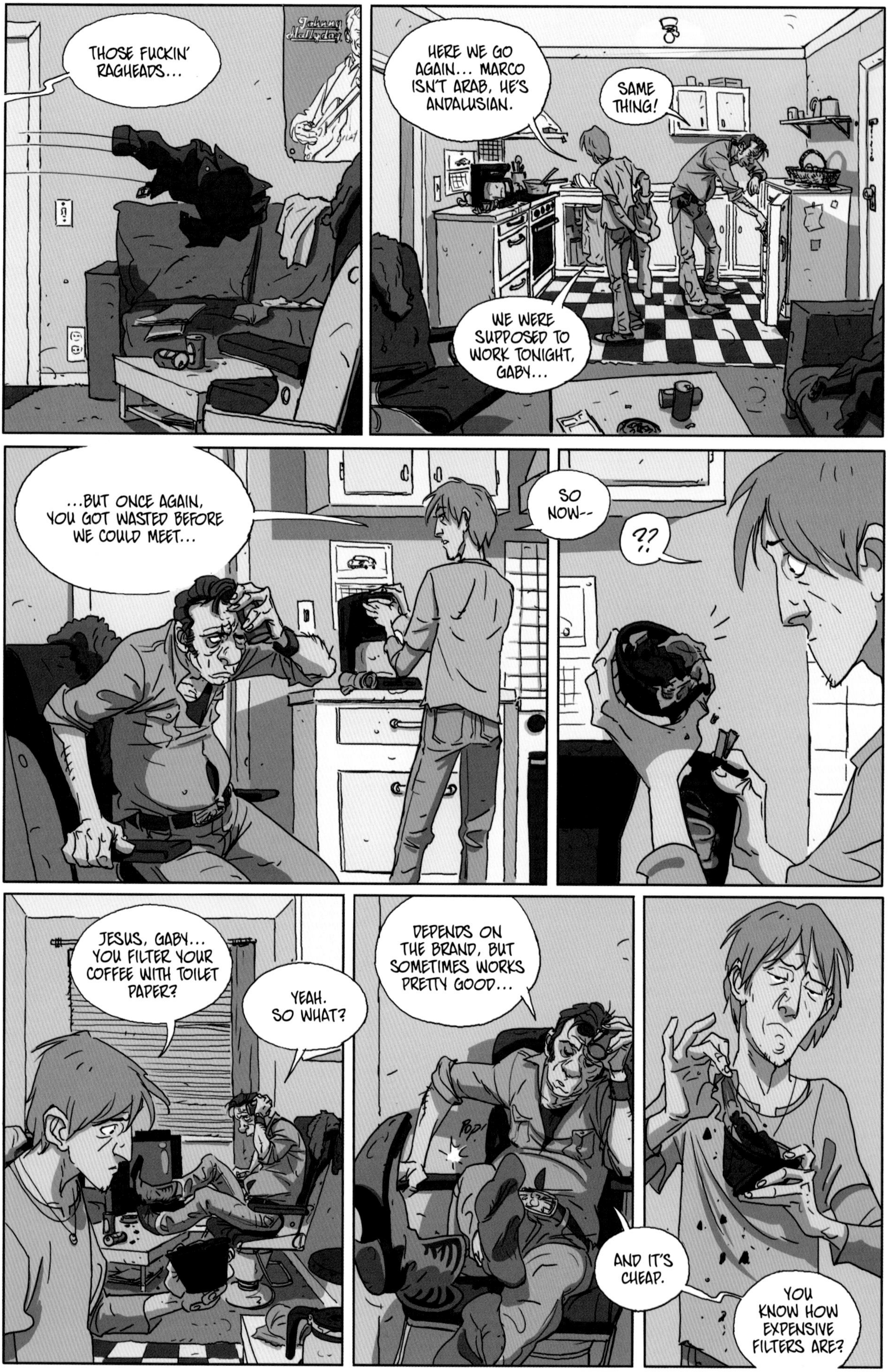
Johnny Hallyday
THOSE FUCKIN' RAGHEADS...
HERE WE GO AGAIN... MARCO ISN'T ARAB, HE'S ANDALUSIAN.
SAME THING!
WE WERE SUPPOSED TO WORK TONIGHT, GABY...
...BUT ONCE AGAIN, YOU GOT WASTED BEFORE WE COULD MEET...
SO NOW--
??
JESUS, GABY... YOU FILTER YOUR COFFEE WITH TOILET PAPER?
YEAH. SO WHAT?
DEPENDS ON THE BRAND, BUT SOMETIMES WORKS PRETTY GOOD...
AND IT'S CHEAP.
YOU KNOW HOW EXPENSIVE FILTERS ARE?

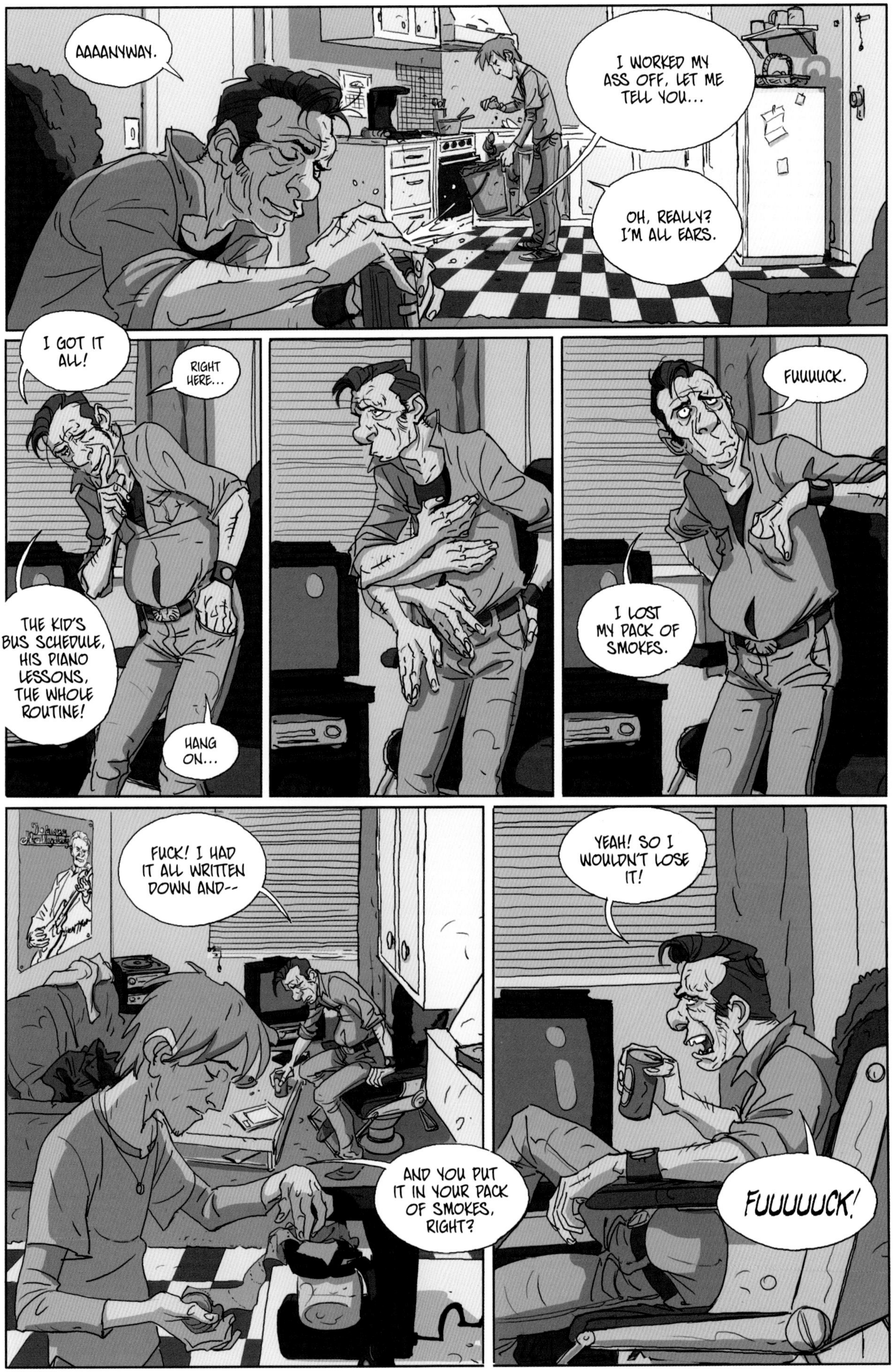
AAAANYWAY.
I WORKED MY ASS OFF, LET ME TELL YOU...
OH, REALLY? I'M ALL EARS.
I GOT IT ALL!
RIGHT HERE...
THE KID'S BUS SCHEDULE, HIS PIANO LESSONS, THE WHOLE ROUTINE!
HANG ON...
FUUUUCK.
I LOST MY PACK OF SMOKES.
FUCK! I HAD IT ALL WRITTEN DOWN AND--
AND YOU PUT IT IN YOUR PACK OF SMOKES, RIGHT?
YEAH! SO I WOULDN'T LOSE IT!
FUUUUUCK!

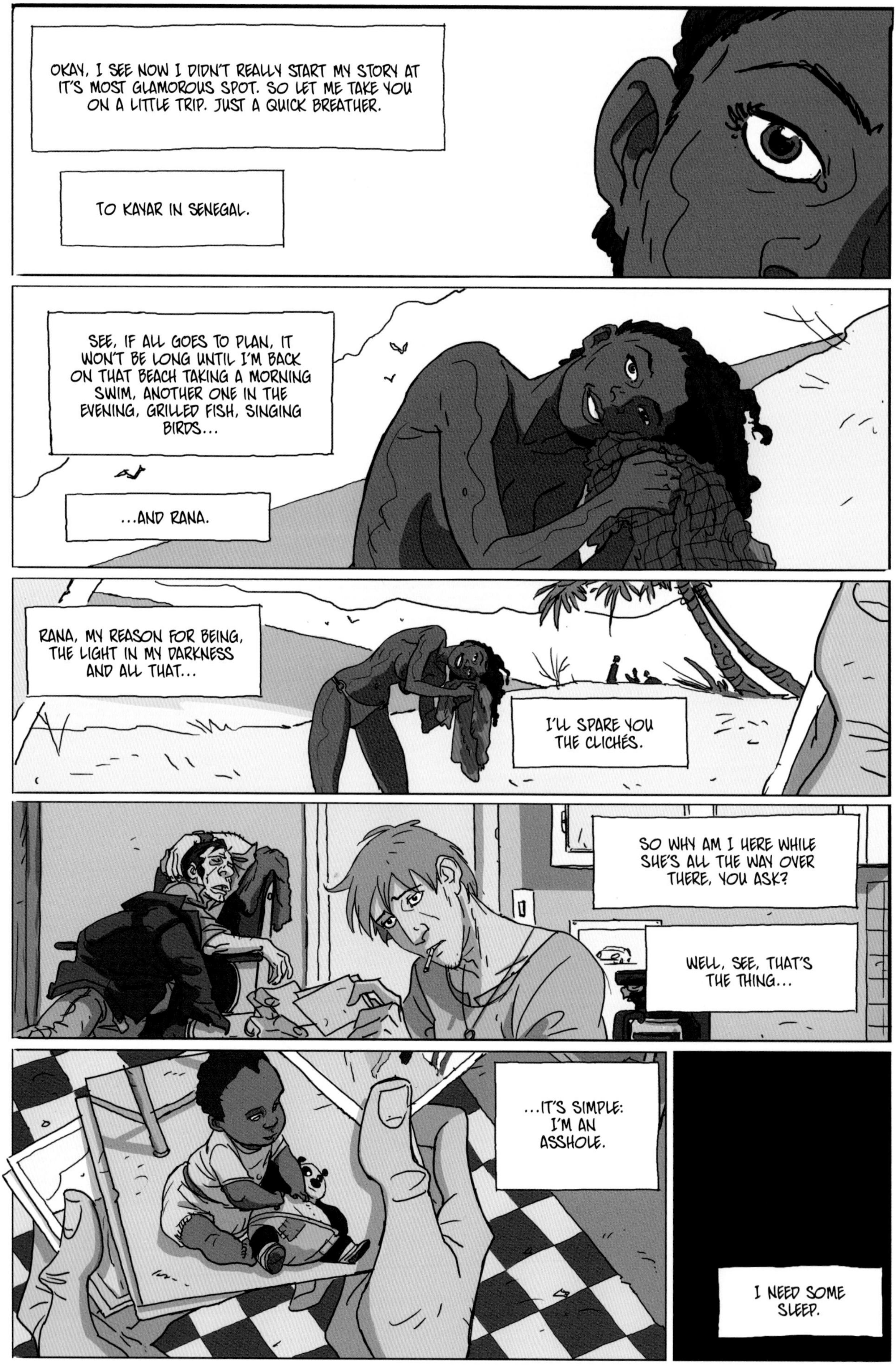
OKAY, I SEE NOW I DIDN'T REALLY START MY STORY AT IT'S MOST GLAMOROUS SPOT. SO LET ME TAKE YOU ON A LITTLE TRIP. JUST A QUICK BREATHER.
TO KAYAR IN SENEGAL.
SEE, IF ALL GOES TO PLAN, IT WON'T BE LONG UNTIL I'M BACK ON THAT BEACH TAKING A MORNING SWIM, ANOTHER ONE IN THE EVENING, GRILLED FISH, SINGING BIRDS...
...AND RANA.
RANA, MY REASON FOR BEING, THE LIGHT IN MY DARKNESS AND ALL THAT...
I'LL SPARE YOU THE CLICHÉS.
SO WHY AM I HERE WHILE SHE'S ALL THE WAY OVER THERE, YOU ASK?
WELL, SEE, THAT'S THE THING...
...IT'S SIMPLE: I'M AN ASSHOLE.
I NEED SOME SLEEP.

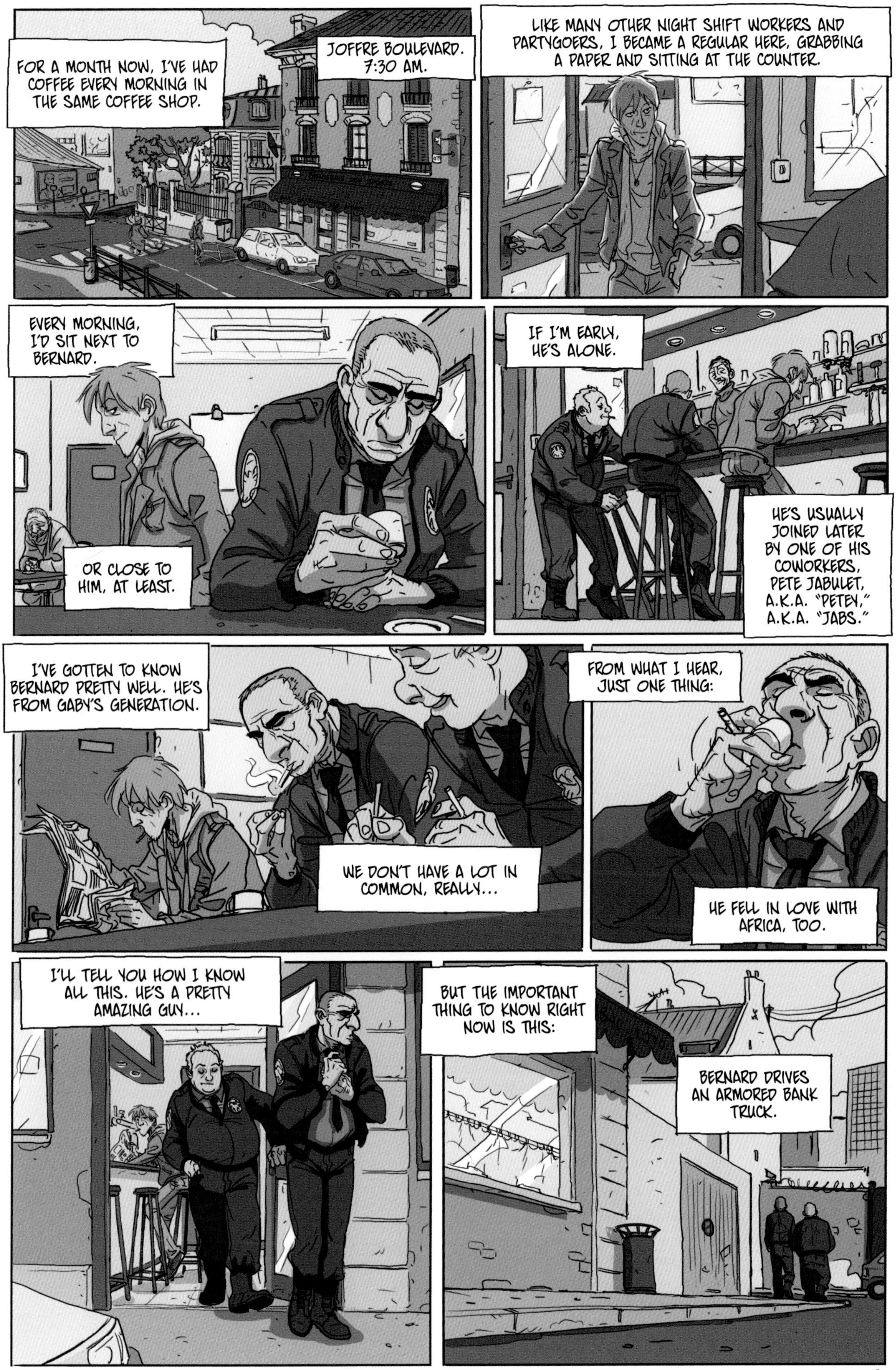
FOR A MONTH NOW, I'VE HAD COFFEE EVERY MORNING IN THE SAME COFFEE SHOP.
JOFFRE BOULEVARD. 7:30 AM.
LIKE MANY OTHER NIGHT SHIFT WORKERS AND PARTYGOERS, I BECAME A REGULAR HERE, GRABBING A PAPER AND SITTING AT THE COUNTER.
EVERY MORNING, I'D SIT NEXT TO BERNARD.
OR CLOSE TO HIM, AT LEAST.
IF I'M EARLY, HE'S ALONE.
HE'S USUALLY JOINED LATER BY ONE OF HIS COWORKERS, PETE JABULET, A.K.A. "PETEY," A.K.A. "JABS."
I'VE GOTTEN TO KNOW BERNARD PRETTY WELL. HE'S FROM GABY'S GENERATION.
WE DON'T HAVE A LOT IN COMMON, REALLY...
FROM WHAT I HEAR, JUST ONE THING:
HE FELL IN LOVE WITH AFRICA, TOO.
I'LL TELL YOU HOW I KNOW ALL THIS. HE'S A PRETTY AMAZING GUY...
BUT THE IMPORTANT THING TO KNOW RIGHT NOW IS THIS:
BERNARD DRIVES AN ARMORED BANK TRUCK.

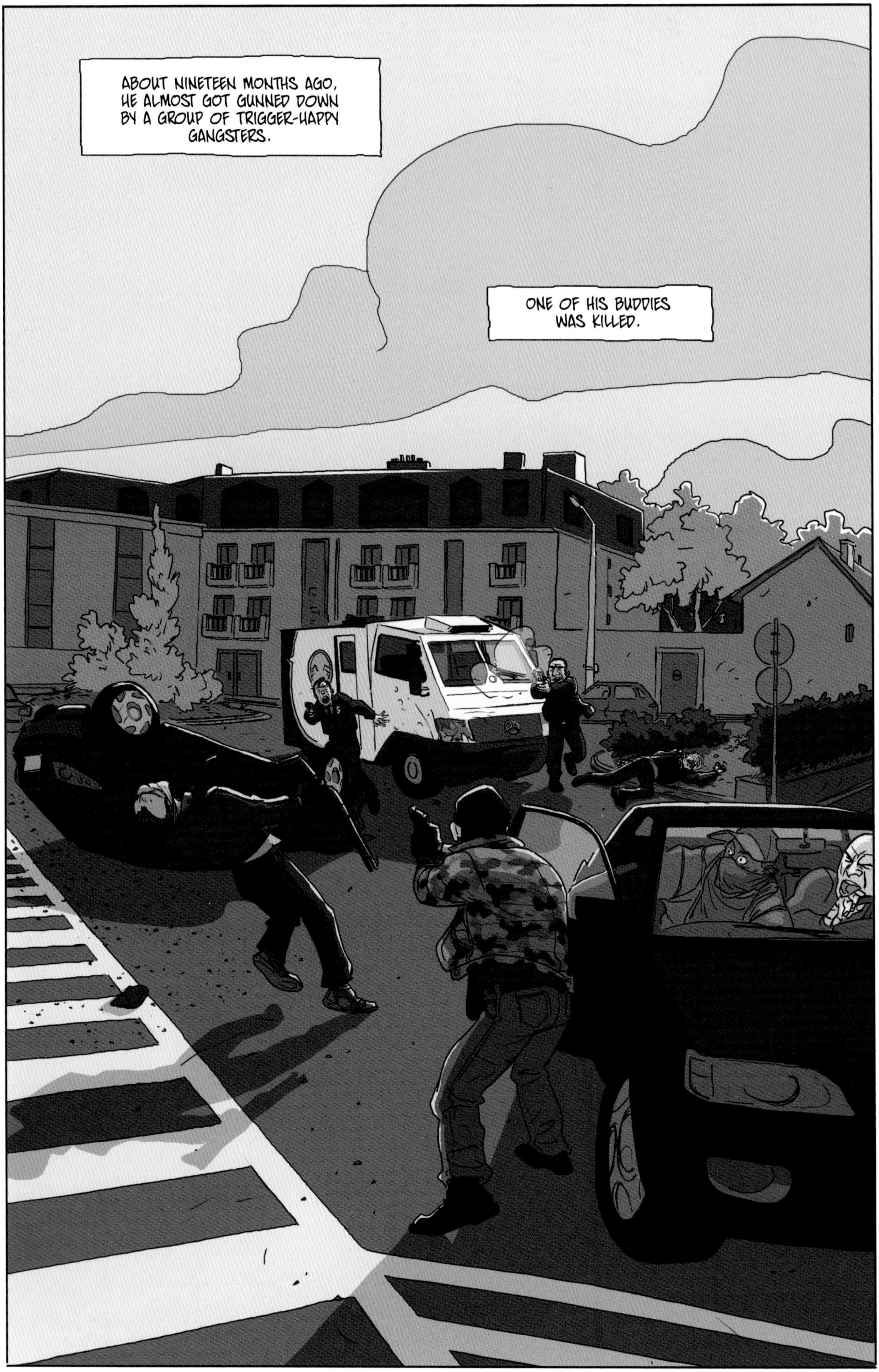
ABOUT NINETEEN MONTHS AGO, HE ALMOST GOT GUNNED DOWN BY A GROUP OF TRIGGER-HAPPY GANGSTERS.
ONE OF HIS BUDDIES WAS KILLED.

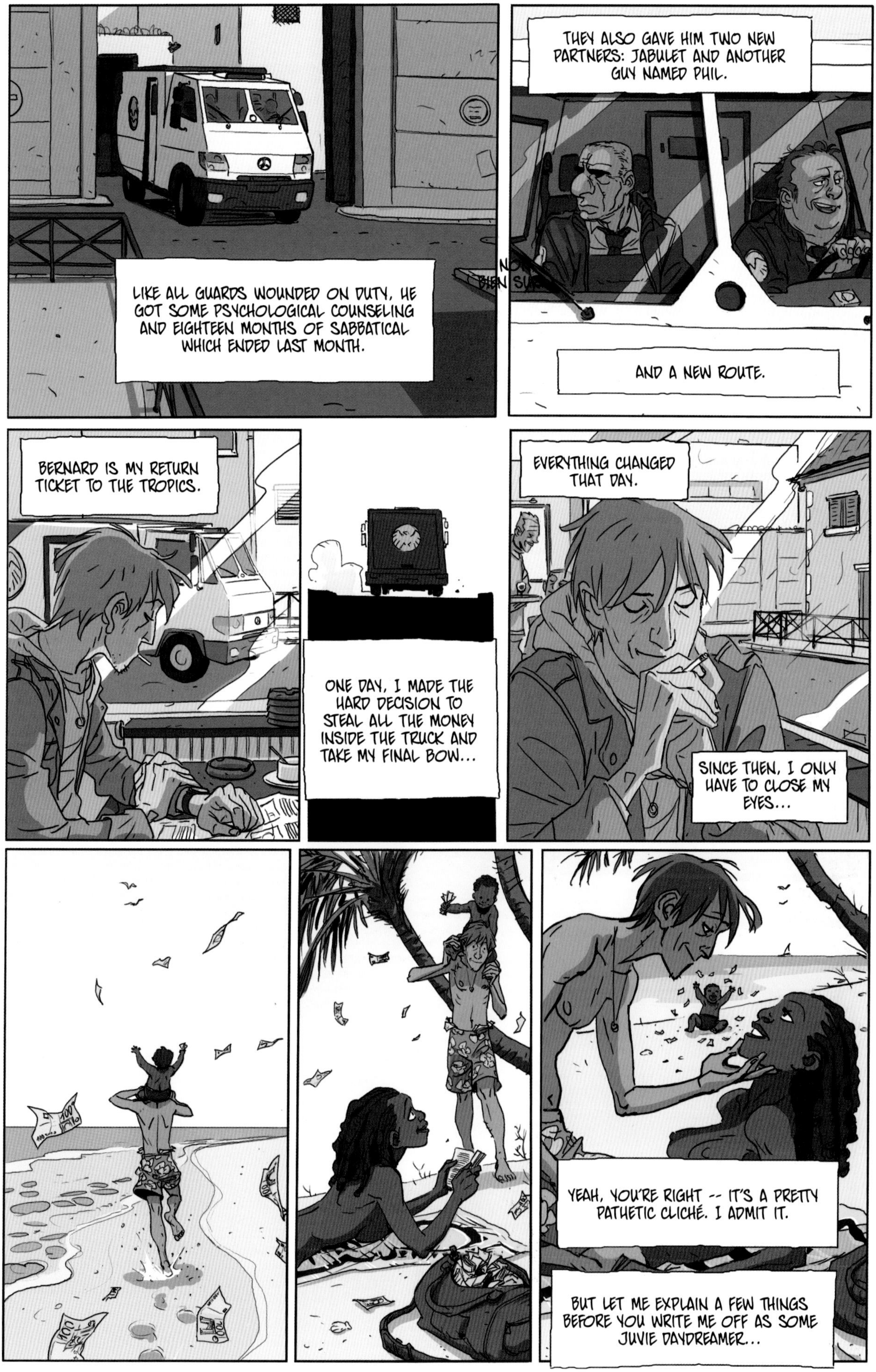
LIKE ALL GUARDS WOUNDED ON DUTY, HE GOT SOME PSYCHOLOGICAL COUNSELING AND EIGHTEEN MONTHS OF SABBATICAL WHICH ENDED LAST MONTH.
THEY ALSO GAVE HIM TWO NEW PARTNERS: JABULET AND ANOTHER GUY NAMED PHIL.
AND A NEW ROUTE.
BERNARD IS MY RETURN TICKET TO THE TROPICS.
ONE DAY, I MADE THE HARD DECISION TO STEAL ALL THE MONEY INSIDE THE TRUCK AND TAKE MY FINAL BOW...
EVERYTHING CHANGED THAT DAY.
SINCE THEN, I ONLY HAVE TO CLOSE MY EYES...
YEAH, YOU'RE RIGHT -- IT'S A PRETTY PATHETIC CLICHÉ. I ADMIT IT.
BUT LET ME EXPLAIN A FEW THINGS BEFORE YOU WRITE ME OFF AS SOME JUVIE DAYDREAMER...

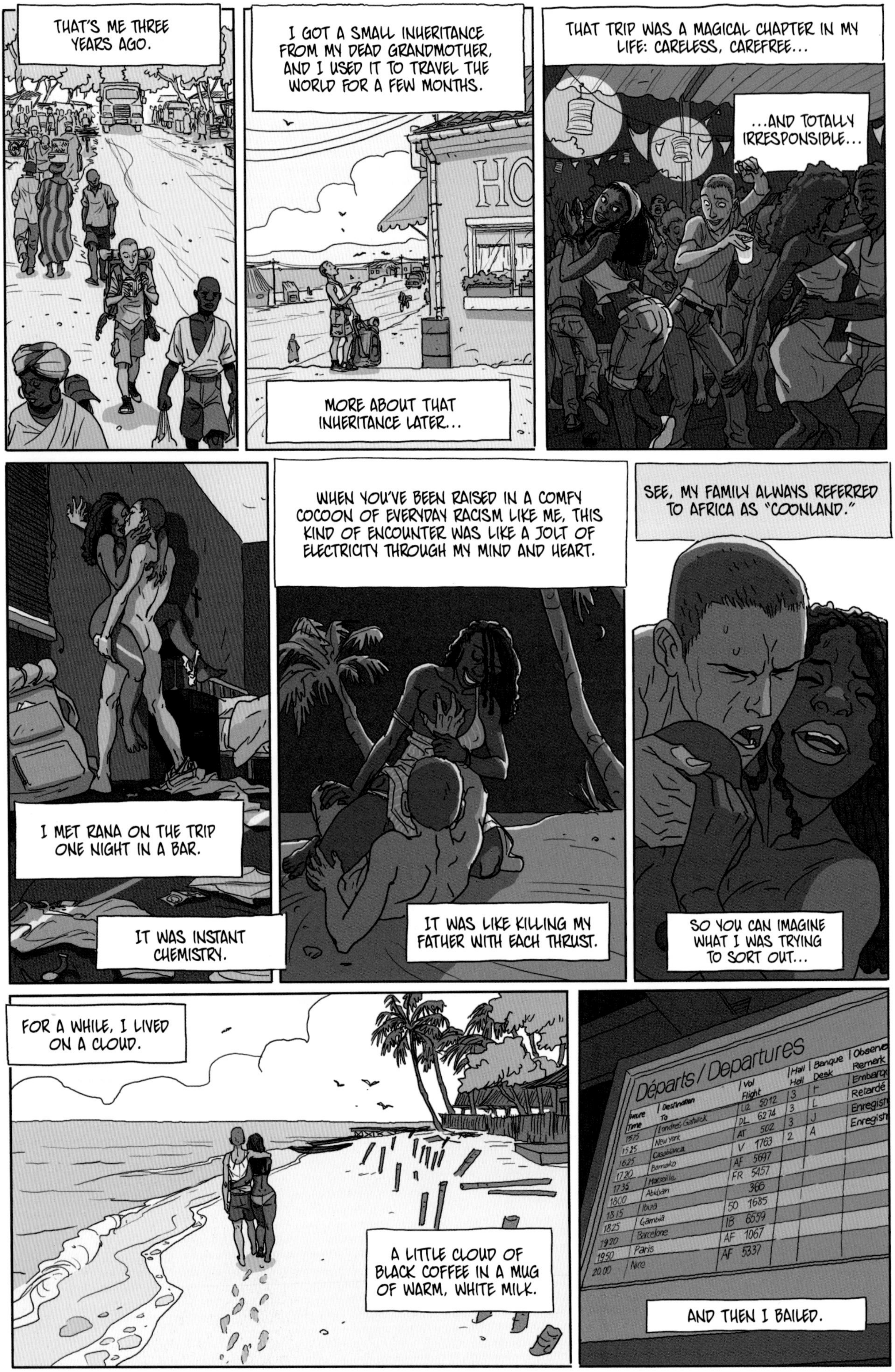
THAT'S ME THREE YEARS AGO.
I GOT A SMALL INHERITANCE FROM MY DEAD GRANDMOTHER, AND I USED IT TO TRAVEL THE WORLD FOR A FEW MONTHS.
MORE ABOUT THAT INHERITANCE LATER...
THAT TRIP WAS A MAGICAL CHAPTER IN MY LIFE: CARELESS, CAREFREE...
...AND TOTALLY IRRESPONSIBLE...
I MET RANA ON THE TRIP ONE NIGHT IN A BAR.
IT WAS INSTANT CHEMISTRY.
WHEN YOU'VE BEEN RAISED IN A COMFY COCOON OF EVERYDAY RACISM LIKE ME, THIS KIND OF ENCOUNTER WAS LIKE A JOLT OF ELECTRICITY THROUGH MY MIND AND HEART.
IT WAS LIKE KILLING MY FATHER WITH EACH THRUST.
SEE, MY FAMILY ALWAYS REFERRED TO AFRICA AS "COONLAND."
SO YOU CAN IMAGINE WHAT I WAS TRYING TO SORT OUT...
FOR A WHILE, I LIVED ON A CLOUD.
A LITTLE CLOUD OF BLACK COFFEE IN A MUG OF WARM, WHITE MILK.
Départs / Departures
AND THEN I BAILED.

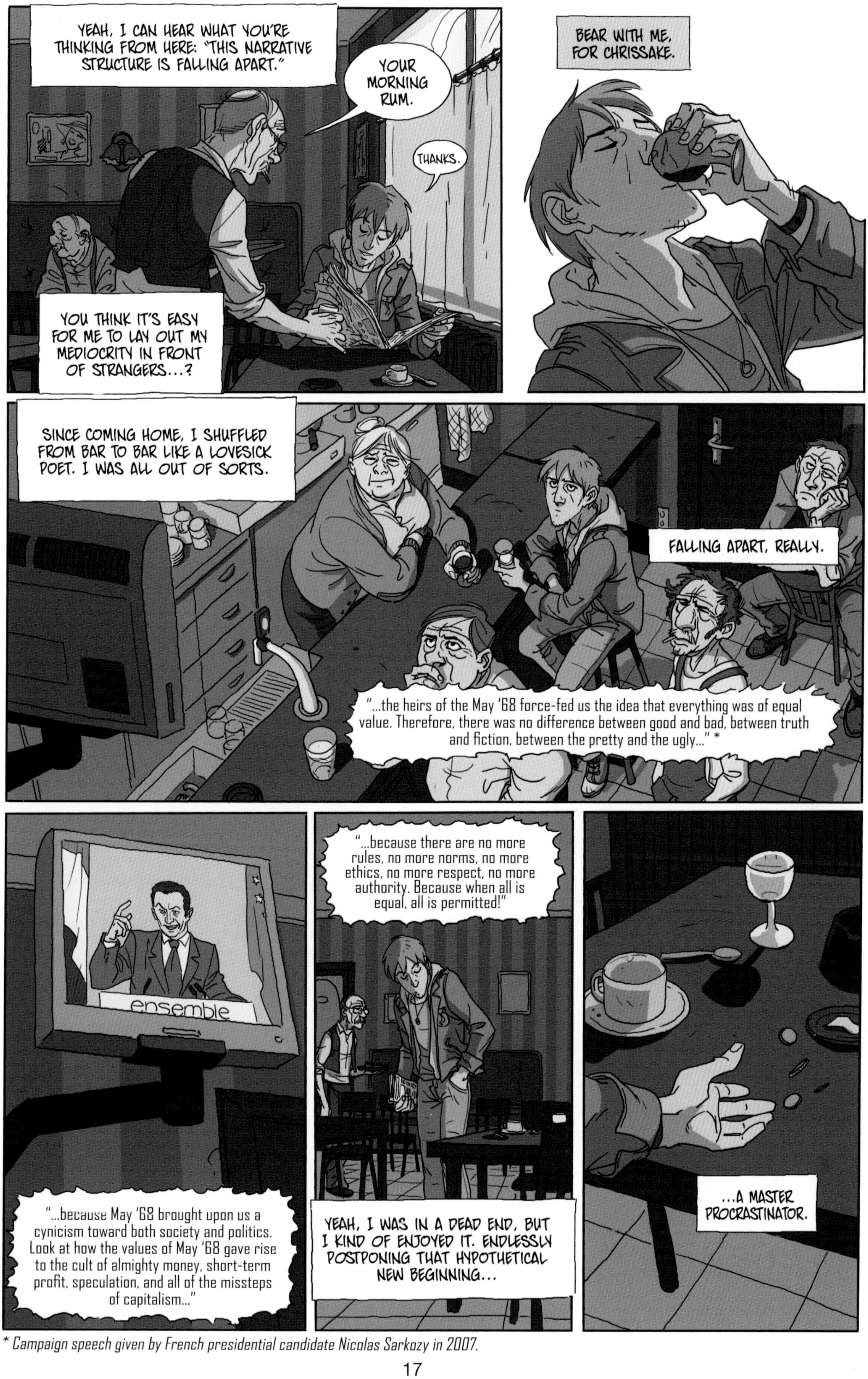

YEAH, I CAN HEAR WHAT YOU'RE THINKING FROM HERE: "THIS NARRATIVE STRUCTURE IS FALLING APART."
YOUR MORNING RUM.
THANKS.
YOU THINK IT'S EASY FOR ME TO LAY OUT MY MEDIOCRITY IN FRONT OF STRANGERS...?
BEAR WITH ME, FOR CHRISSAKE.
SINCE COMING HOME, I SHUFFLED FROM BAR TO BAR LIKE A LOVESICK POET. I WAS ALL OUT OF SORTS.
FALLING APART, REALLY.
"...the heirs of the May '68 force-fed us the idea that everything was of equal value. Therefore, there was no difference between good and bad, between truth and fiction, between the pretty and the ugly..." *
ensemble
"...because May '68 brought upon us a cynicism toward both society and politics. Look at how the values of May '68 gave rise to the cult of almighty money, short-term profit, speculation, and all of the missteps of capitalism..."
"...because there are no more rules, no more norms, no more ethics, no more respect, no more authority. Because when all is equal, all is permitted!"
YEAH, I WAS IN A DEAD END, BUT I KIND OF ENJOYED IT. ENDLESSLY POSTPONING THAT HYPOTHETICAL NEW BEGINNING...
...A MASTER PROCRASTINATOR.

* *Campaign speech given by French presidential candidate Nicolas Sarkozy in 2007.*

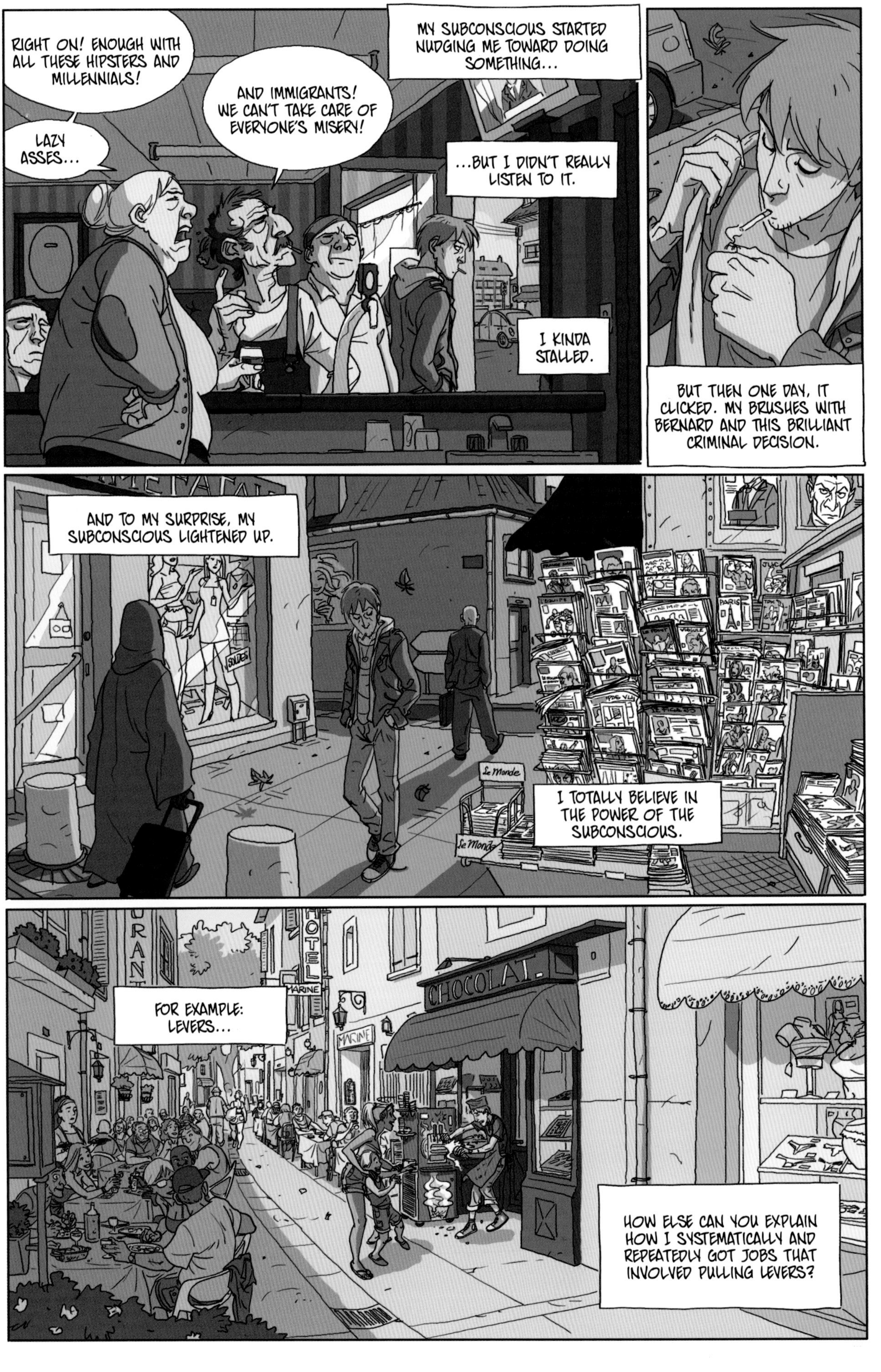
RIGHT ON! ENOUGH WITH ALL THESE HIPSTERS AND MILLENNIALS!
LAZY ASSES...
AND IMMIGRANTS! WE CAN'T TAKE CARE OF EVERYONE'S MISERY!
MY SUBCONSCIOUS STARTED NUDGING ME TOWARD DOING SOMETHING...
...BUT I DIDN'T REALLY LISTEN TO IT.
I KINDA STALLED.
BUT THEN ONE DAY, IT CLICKED. MY BRUSHES WITH BERNARD AND THIS BRILLIANT CRIMINAL DECISION.
AND TO MY SURPRISE, MY SUBCONSCIOUS LIGHTENED UP.
I TOTALLY BELIEVE IN THE POWER OF THE SUBCONSCIOUS.
FOR EXAMPLE: LEVERS...
CHOCOLAT.
HOTEL
MARINE
HOW ELSE CAN YOU EXPLAIN HOW I SYSTEMATICALLY AND REPEATEDLY GOT JOBS THAT INVOLVED PULLING LEVERS?

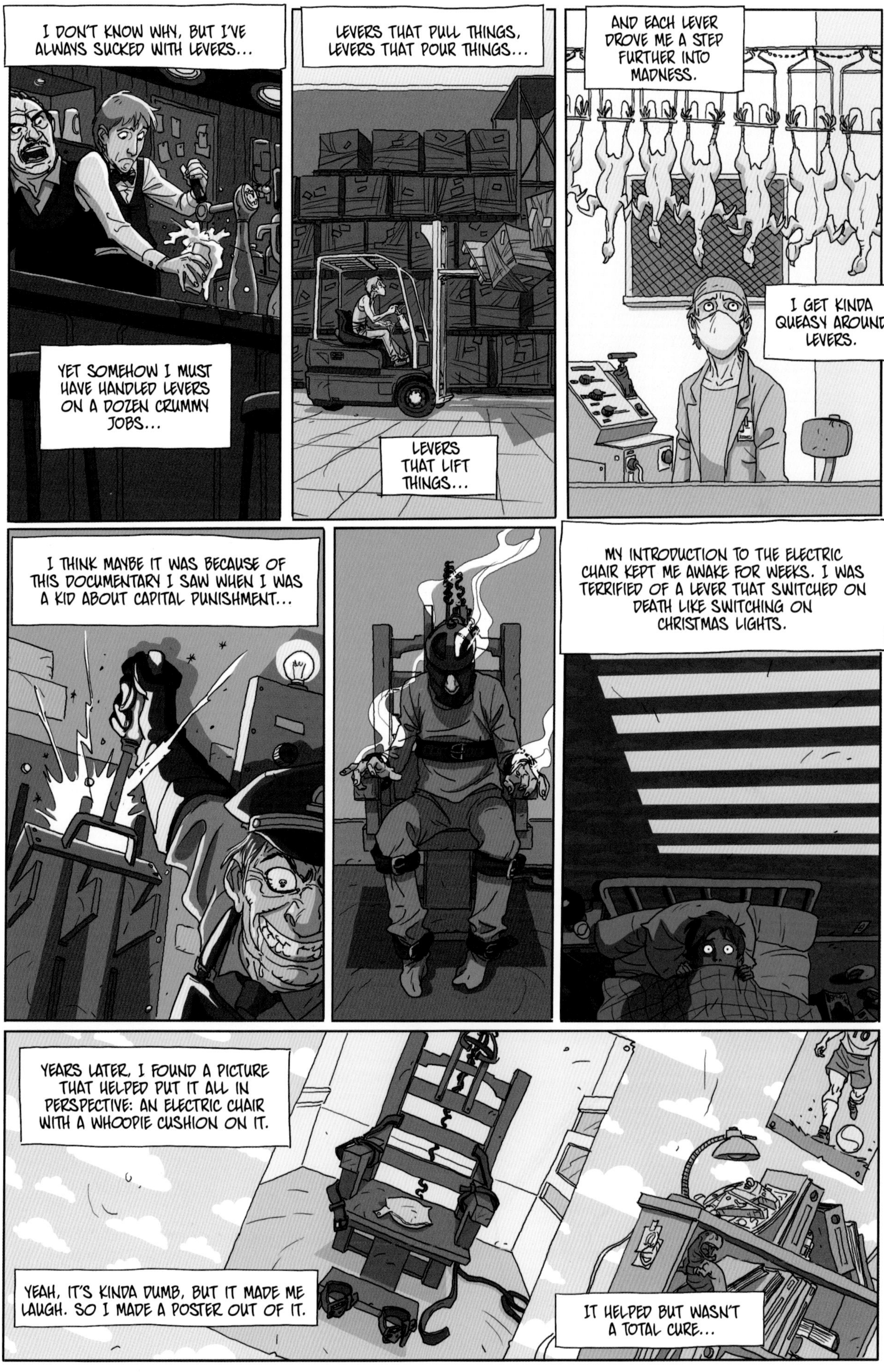
I DON'T KNOW WHY, BUT I'VE ALWAYS SUCKED WITH LEVERS...
YET SOMEHOW I MUST HAVE HANDLED LEVERS ON A DOZEN CRUMMY JOBS...
LEVERS THAT PULL THINGS, LEVERS THAT POUR THINGS...
LEVERS THAT LIFT THINGS...
AND EACH LEVER DROVE ME A STEP FURTHER INTO MADNESS.
I GET KINDA QUEASY AROUND LEVERS.
I THINK MAYBE IT WAS BECAUSE OF THIS DOCUMENTARY I SAW WHEN I WAS A KID ABOUT CAPITAL PUNISHMENT...
MY INTRODUCTION TO THE ELECTRIC CHAIR KEPT ME AWAKE FOR WEEKS. I WAS TERRIFIED OF A LEVER THAT SWITCHED ON DEATH LIKE SWITCHING ON CHRISTMAS LIGHTS.
YEARS LATER, I FOUND A PICTURE THAT HELPED PUT IT ALL IN PERSPECTIVE: AN ELECTRIC CHAIR WITH A WHOOPIE CUSHION ON IT.
YEAH, IT'S KINDA DUMB, BUT IT MADE ME LAUGH. SO I MADE A POSTER OUT OF IT.
IT HELPED BUT WASN'T A TOTAL CURE...

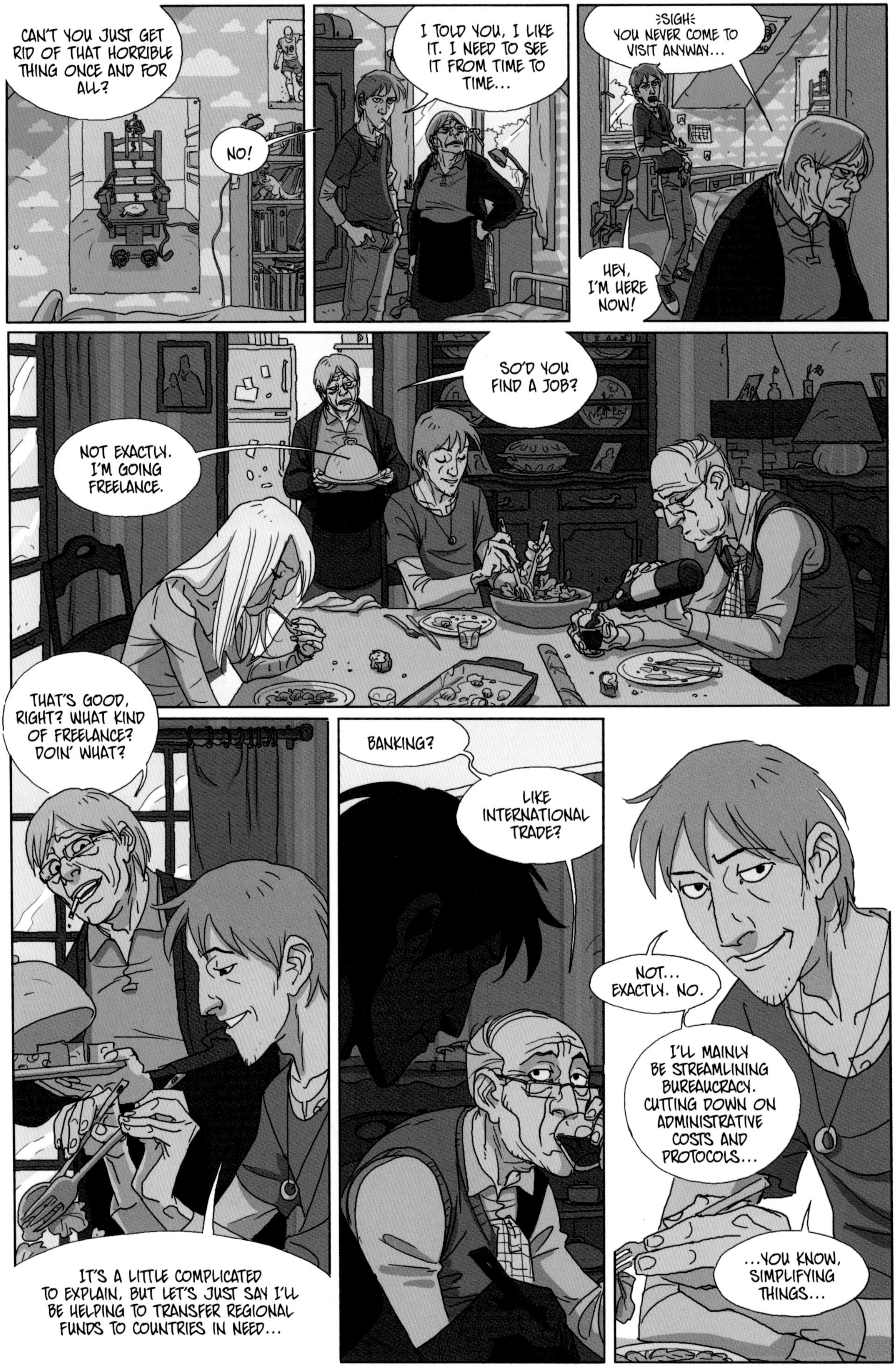
CAN'T YOU JUST GET RID OF THAT HORRIBLE THING ONCE AND FOR ALL?
NO!
I TOLD YOU, I LIKE IT. I NEED TO SEE IT FROM TIME TO TIME...
SIGH
YOU NEVER COME TO VISIT ANYWAY...
HEY, I'M HERE NOW!
SO'D YOU FIND A JOB?
NOT EXACTLY. I'M GOING FREELANCE.
THAT'S GOOD, RIGHT? WHAT KIND OF FREELANCE? DOIN' WHAT?
IT'S A LITTLE COMPLICATED TO EXPLAIN, BUT LET'S JUST SAY I'LL BE HELPING TO TRANSFER REGIONAL FUNDS TO COUNTRIES IN NEED...
BANKING?
LIKE INTERNATIONAL TRADE?
NOT... EXACTLY. NO.
I'LL MAINLY BE STREAMLINING BUREAUCRACY. CUTTING DOWN ON ADMINISTRATIVE COSTS AND PROTOCOLS...
...YOU KNOW, SIMPLIFYING THINGS...

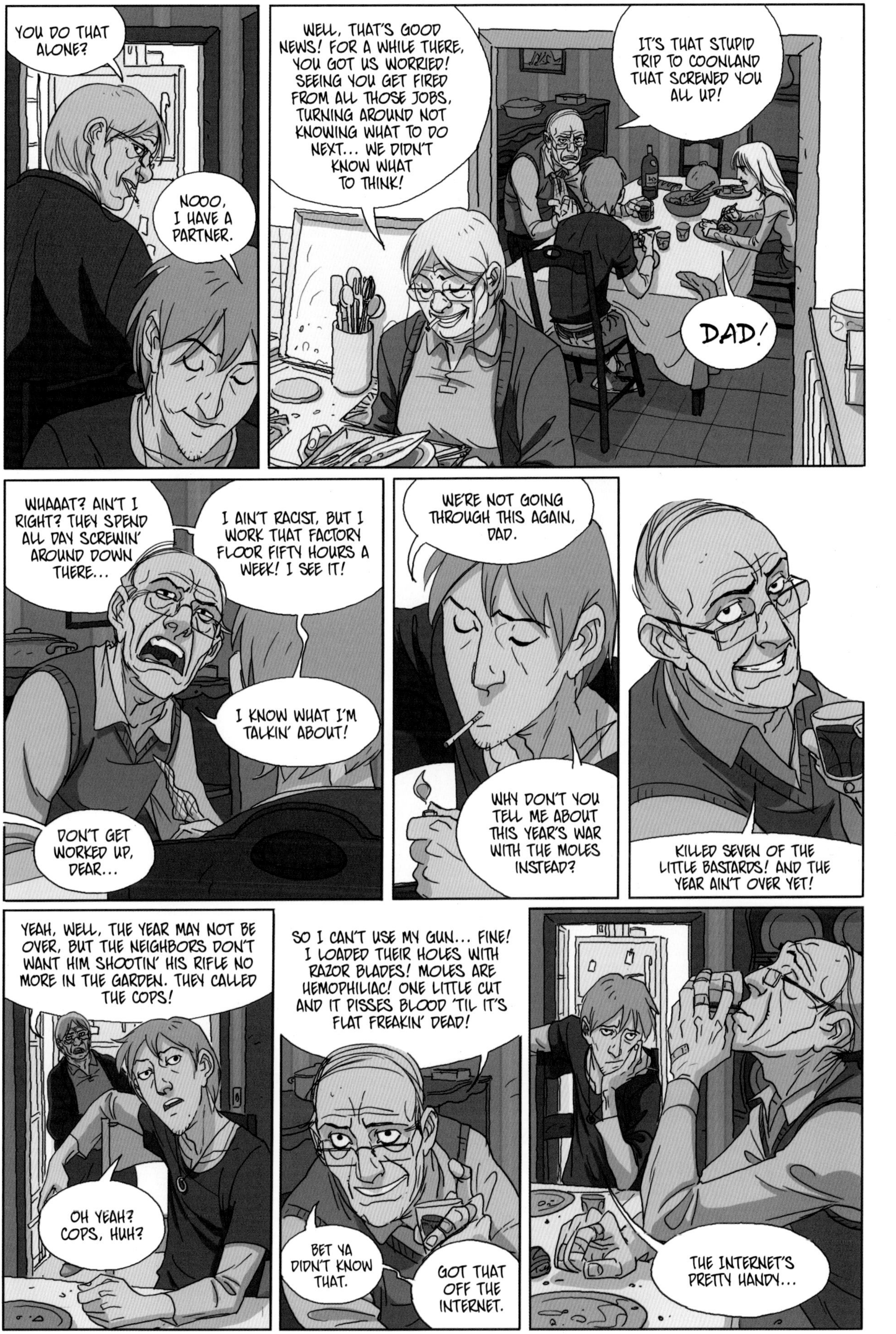

YOU DO THAT ALONE?
NOOO, I HAVE A PARTNER.
WELL, THAT'S GOOD NEWS! FOR A WHILE THERE, YOU GOT US WORRIED! SEEING YOU GET FIRED FROM ALL THOSE JOBS, TURNING AROUND NOT KNOWING WHAT TO DO NEXT... WE DIDN'T KNOW WHAT TO THINK!
IT'S THAT STUPID TRIP TO COONLAND THAT SCREWED YOU ALL UP!
DAD!
WHAAAT? AIN'T I RIGHT? THEY SPEND ALL DAY SCREWIN' AROUND DOWN THERE...
I AIN'T RACIST, BUT I WORK THAT FACTORY FLOOR FIFTY HOURS A WEEK! I SEE IT!
I KNOW WHAT I'M TALKIN' ABOUT!
DON'T GET WORKED UP, DEAR...
WE'RE NOT GOING THROUGH THIS AGAIN, DAD.
WHY DON'T YOU TELL ME ABOUT THIS YEAR'S WAR WITH THE MOLES INSTEAD?
KILLED SEVEN OF THE LITTLE BASTARDS! AND THE YEAR AIN'T OVER YET!
YEAH, WELL, THE YEAR MAY NOT BE OVER, BUT THE NEIGHBORS DON'T WANT HIM SHOOTIN' HIS RIFLE NO MORE IN THE GARDEN. THEY CALLED THE COPS!
OH YEAH? COPS, HUH?
SO I CAN'T USE MY GUN... FINE! I LOADED THEIR HOLES WITH RAZOR BLADES! MOLES ARE HEMOPHILIAC! ONE LITTLE CUT AND IT PISSES BLOOD 'TIL IT'S FLAT FREAKIN' DEAD!
BET YA DIDN'T KNOW THAT.
GOT THAT OFF THE INTERNET.
THE INTERNET'S PRETTY HANDY...

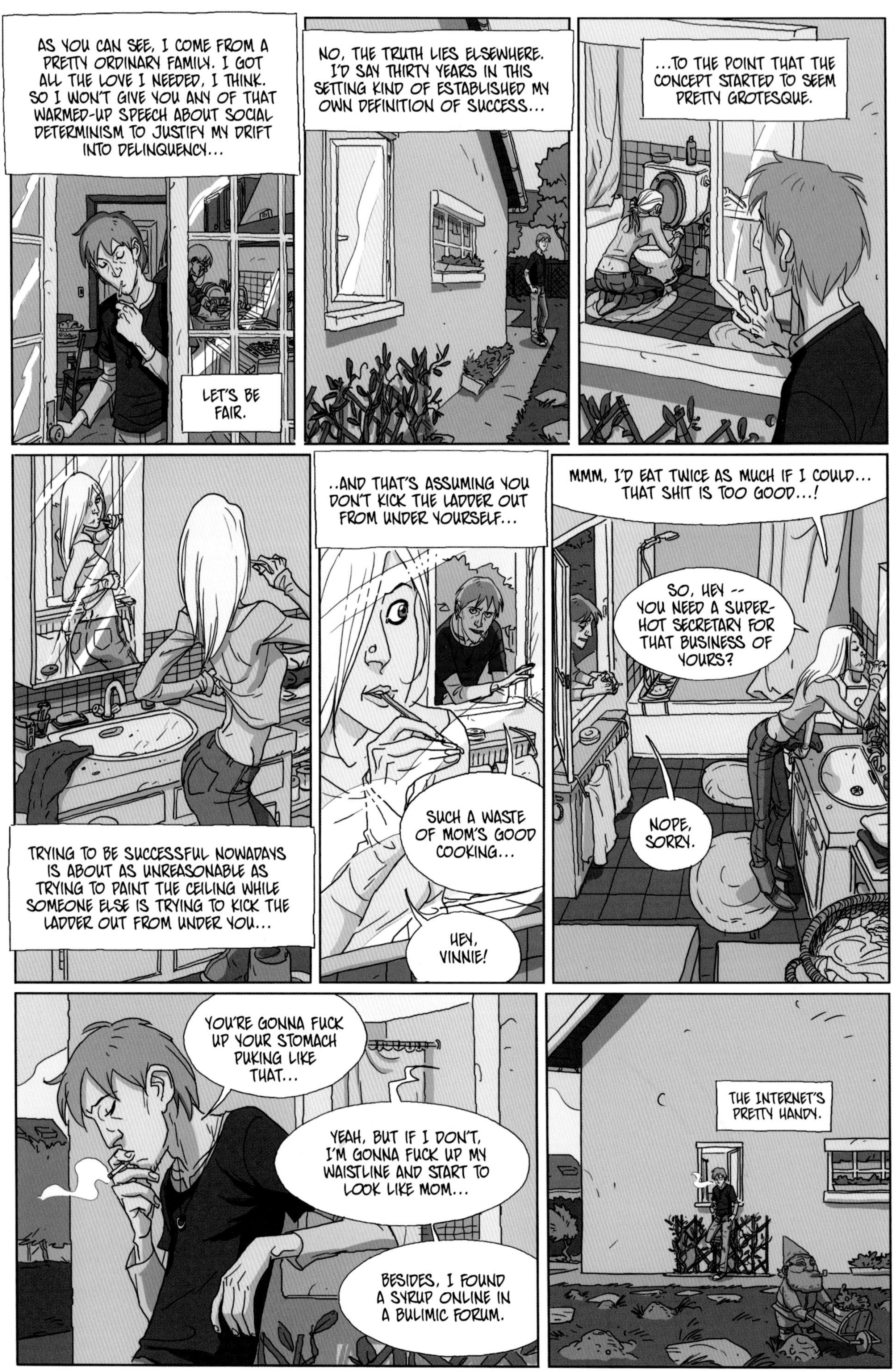
AS YOU CAN SEE, I COME FROM A PRETTY ORDINARY FAMILY. I GOT ALL THE LOVE I NEEDED, I THINK. SO I WON'T GIVE YOU ANY OF THAT WARMED-UP SPEECH ABOUT SOCIAL DETERMINISM TO JUSTIFY MY DRIFT INTO DELINQUENCY...
LET'S BE FAIR.
NO, THE TRUTH LIES ELSEWHERE. I'D SAY THIRTY YEARS IN THIS SETTING KIND OF ESTABLISHED MY OWN DEFINITION OF SUCCESS...
...TO THE POINT THAT THE CONCEPT STARTED TO SEEM PRETTY GROTESQUE.
TRYING TO BE SUCCESSFUL NOWADAYS IS ABOUT AS UNREASONABLE AS TRYING TO PAINT THE CEILING WHILE SOMEONE ELSE IS TRYING TO KICK THE LADDER OUT FROM UNDER YOU...
..AND THAT'S ASSUMING YOU DON'T KICK THE LADDER OUT FROM UNDER YOURSELF...
SUCH A WASTE OF MOM'S GOOD COOKING...
HEY, VINNIE!
MMM, I'D EAT TWICE AS MUCH IF I COULD... THAT SHIT IS TOO GOOD...!
SO, HEY -- YOU NEED A SUPER-HOT SECRETARY FOR THAT BUSINESS OF YOURS?
NOPE, SORRY.
YOU'RE GONNA FUCK UP YOUR STOMACH PUKING LIKE THAT...
YEAH, BUT IF I DON'T, I'M GONNA FUCK UP MY WAISTLINE AND START TO LOOK LIKE MOM...
BESIDES, I FOUND A SYRUP ONLINE IN A BULIMIC FORUM.
THE INTERNET'S PRETTY HANDY.

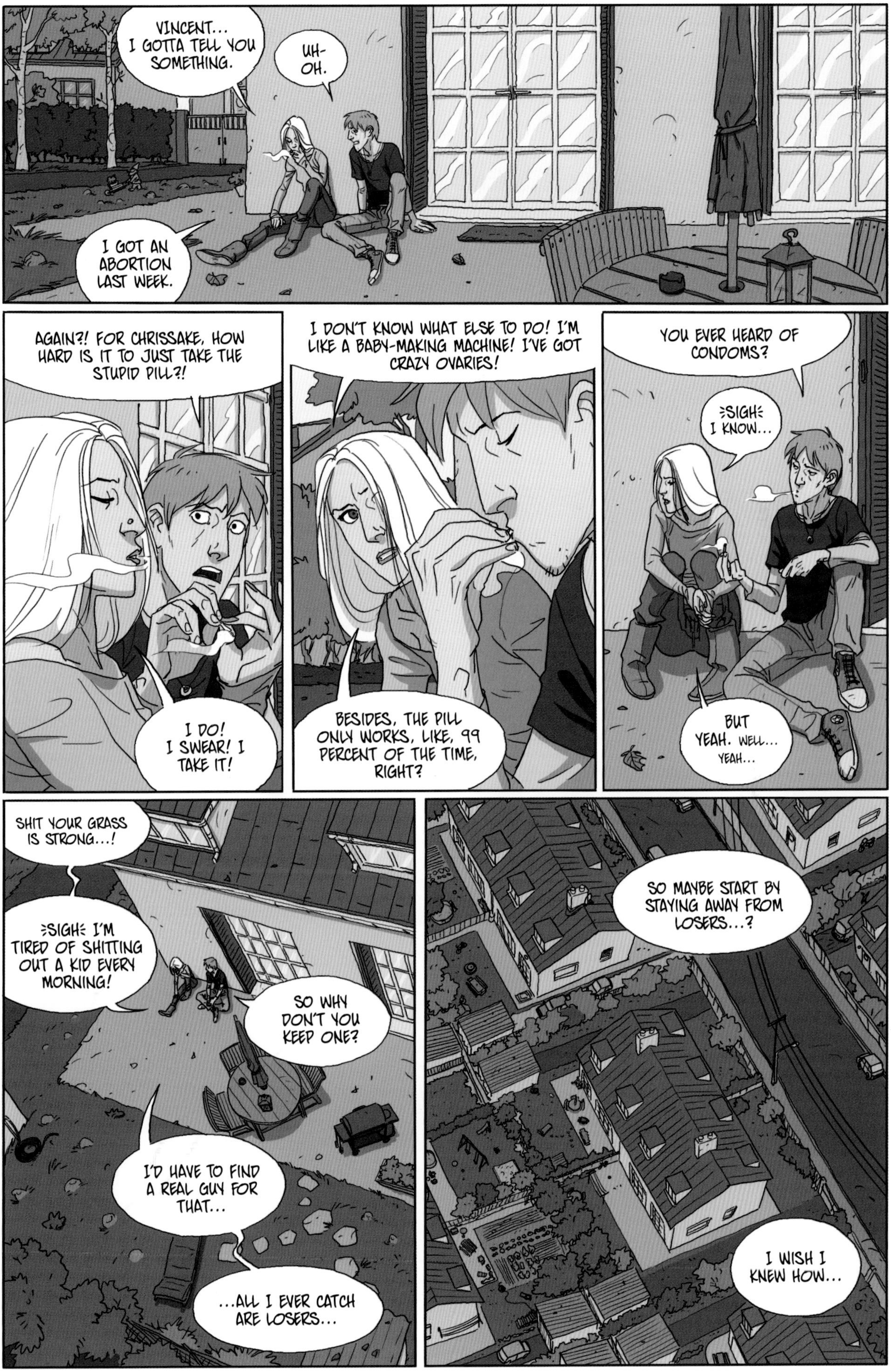
VINCENT... I GOTTA TELL YOU SOMETHING.
UH-OH.
I GOT AN ABORTION LAST WEEK.
AGAIN?! FOR CHRISSAKE, HOW HARD IS IT TO JUST TAKE THE STUPID PILL?!
I DO! I SWEAR! I TAKE IT!
I DON'T KNOW WHAT ELSE TO DO! I'M LIKE A BABY-MAKING MACHINE! I'VE GOT CRAZY OVARIES!
BESIDES, THE PILL ONLY WORKS, LIKE, 99 PERCENT OF THE TIME, RIGHT?
YOU EVER HEARD OF CONDOMS?
SIGH I KNOW...
BUT YEAH. WELL... YEAH...
SHIT YOUR GRASS IS STRONG...!
SIGH I'M TIRED OF SHITTING OUT A KID EVERY MORNING!
SO WHY DON'T YOU KEEP ONE?
I'D HAVE TO FIND A REAL GUY FOR THAT...
...ALL I EVER CATCH ARE LOSERS...
SO MAYBE START BY STAYING AWAY FROM LOSERS...?
I WISH I KNEW HOW...

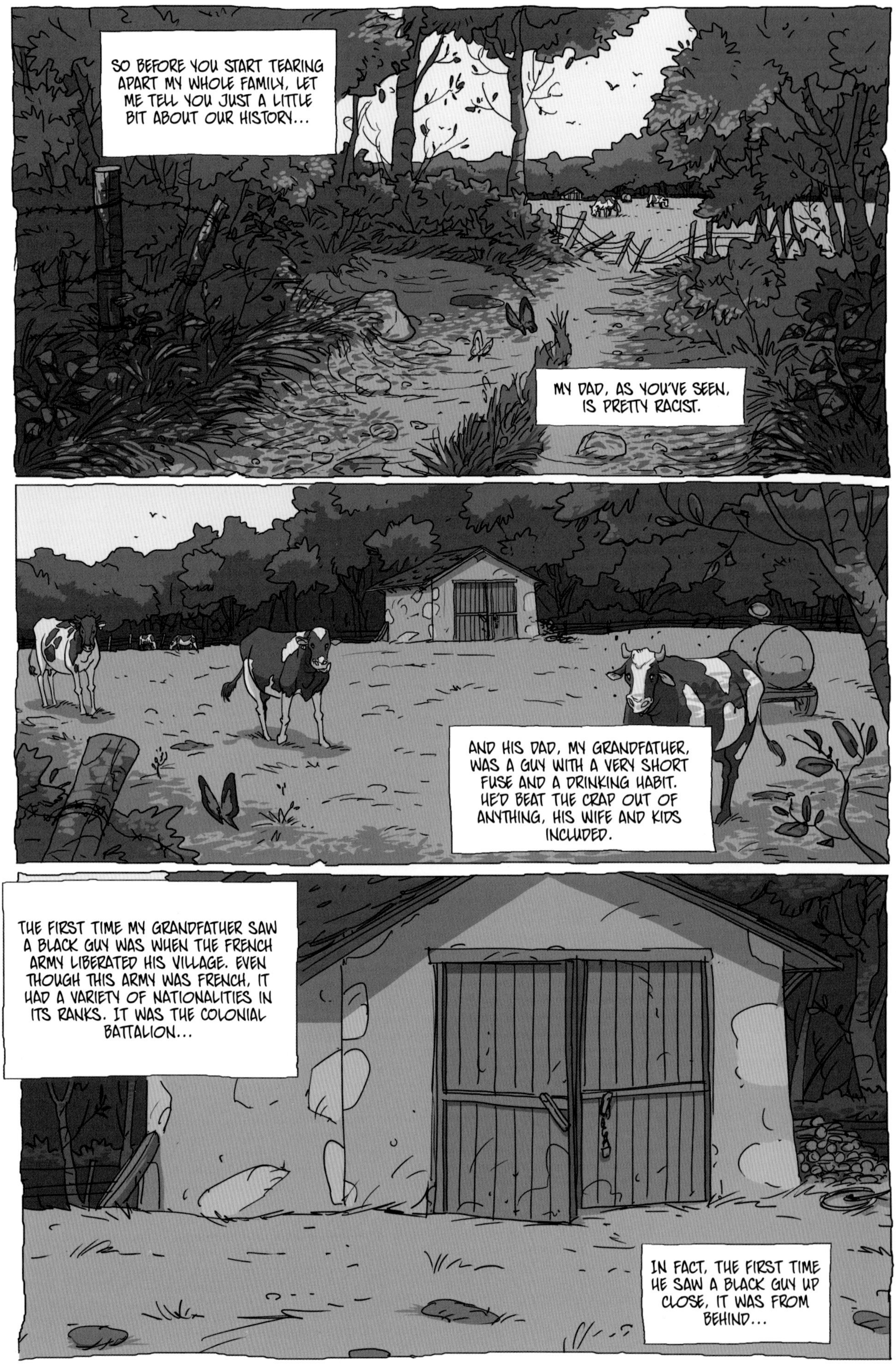
SO BEFORE YOU START TEARING APART MY WHOLE FAMILY, LET ME TELL YOU JUST A LITTLE BIT ABOUT OUR HISTORY...
MY DAD, AS YOU'VE SEEN, IS PRETTY RACIST.
AND HIS DAD, MY GRANDFATHER, WAS A GUY WITH A VERY SHORT FUSE AND A DRINKING HABIT. HE'D BEAT THE CRAP OUT OF ANYTHING, HIS WIFE AND KIDS INCLUDED.
THE FIRST TIME MY GRANDFATHER SAW A BLACK GUY WAS WHEN THE FRENCH ARMY LIBERATED HIS VILLAGE. EVEN THOUGH THIS ARMY WAS FRENCH, IT HAD A VARIETY OF NATIONALITIES IN ITS RANKS. IT WAS THE COLONIAL BATTALION...
IN FACT, THE FIRST TIME HE SAW A BLACK GUY UP CLOSE, IT WAS FROM BEHIND...

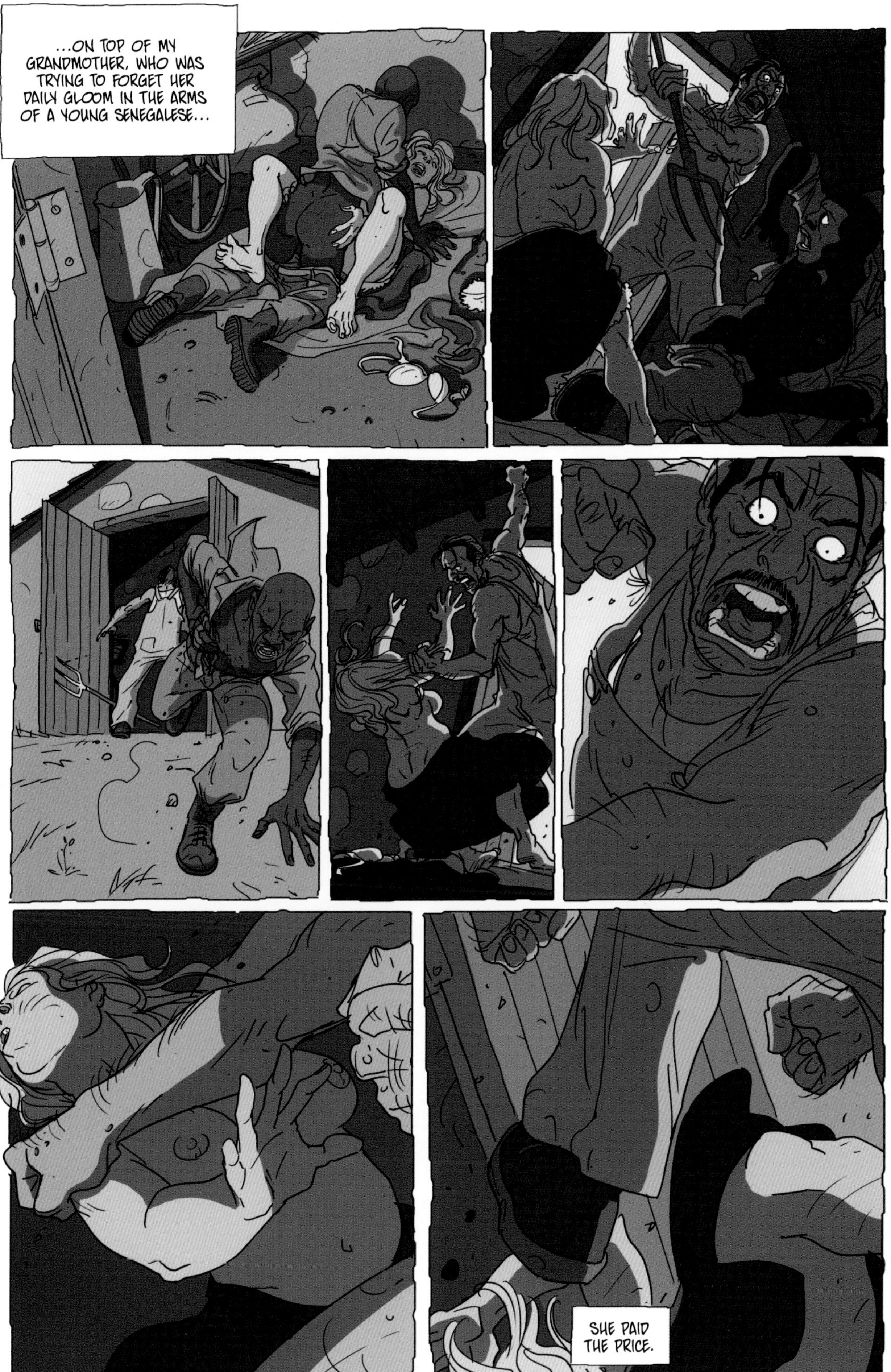
...ON TOP OF MY GRANDMOTHER, WHO WAS TRYING TO FORGET HER DAILY GLOOM IN THE ARMS OF A YOUNG SENEGALESE...
SHE PAID THE PRICE.

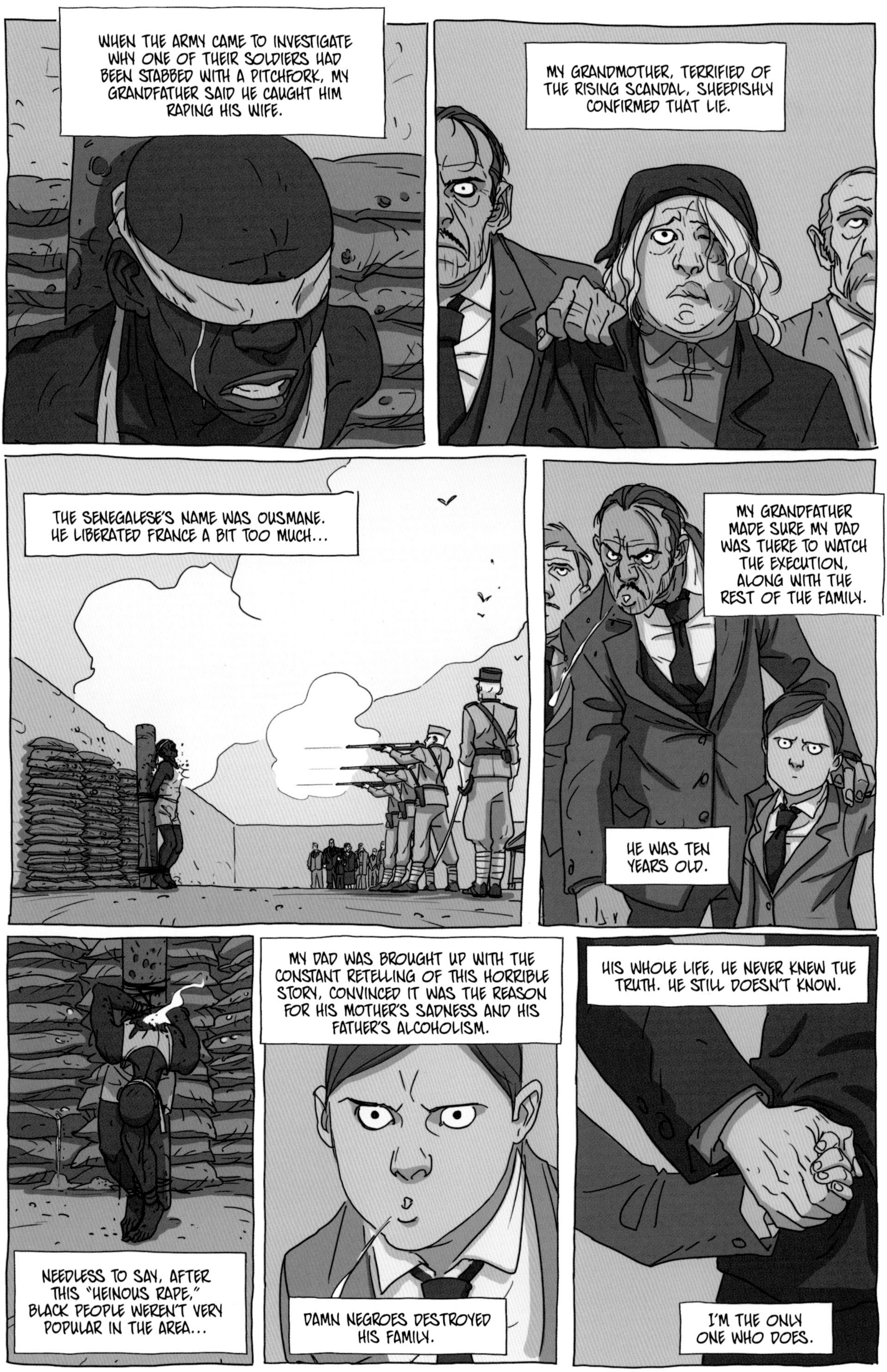
WHEN THE ARMY CAME TO INVESTIGATE WHY ONE OF THEIR SOLDIERS HAD BEEN STABBED WITH A PITCHFORK, MY GRANDFATHER SAID HE CAUGHT HIM RAPING HIS WIFE.
MY GRANDMOTHER, TERRIFIED OF THE RISING SCANDAL, SHEEPISHLY CONFIRMED THAT LIE.
THE SENEGALESE'S NAME WAS OUSMANE. HE LIBERATED FRANCE A BIT TOO MUCH...
MY GRANDFATHER MADE SURE MY DAD WAS THERE TO WATCH THE EXECUTION, ALONG WITH THE REST OF THE FAMILY.
HE WAS TEN YEARS OLD.
NEEDLESS TO SAY, AFTER THIS "HEINOUS RAPE," BLACK PEOPLE WEREN'T VERY POPULAR IN THE AREA...
MY DAD WAS BROUGHT UP WITH THE CONSTANT RETELLING OF THIS HORRIBLE STORY, CONVINCED IT WAS THE REASON FOR HIS MOTHER'S SADNESS AND HIS FATHER'S ALCOHOLISM.
DAMN NEGROES DESTROYED HIS FAMILY.
HIS WHOLE LIFE, HE NEVER KNEW THE TRUTH. HE STILL DOESN'T KNOW.
I'M THE ONLY ONE WHO DOES.

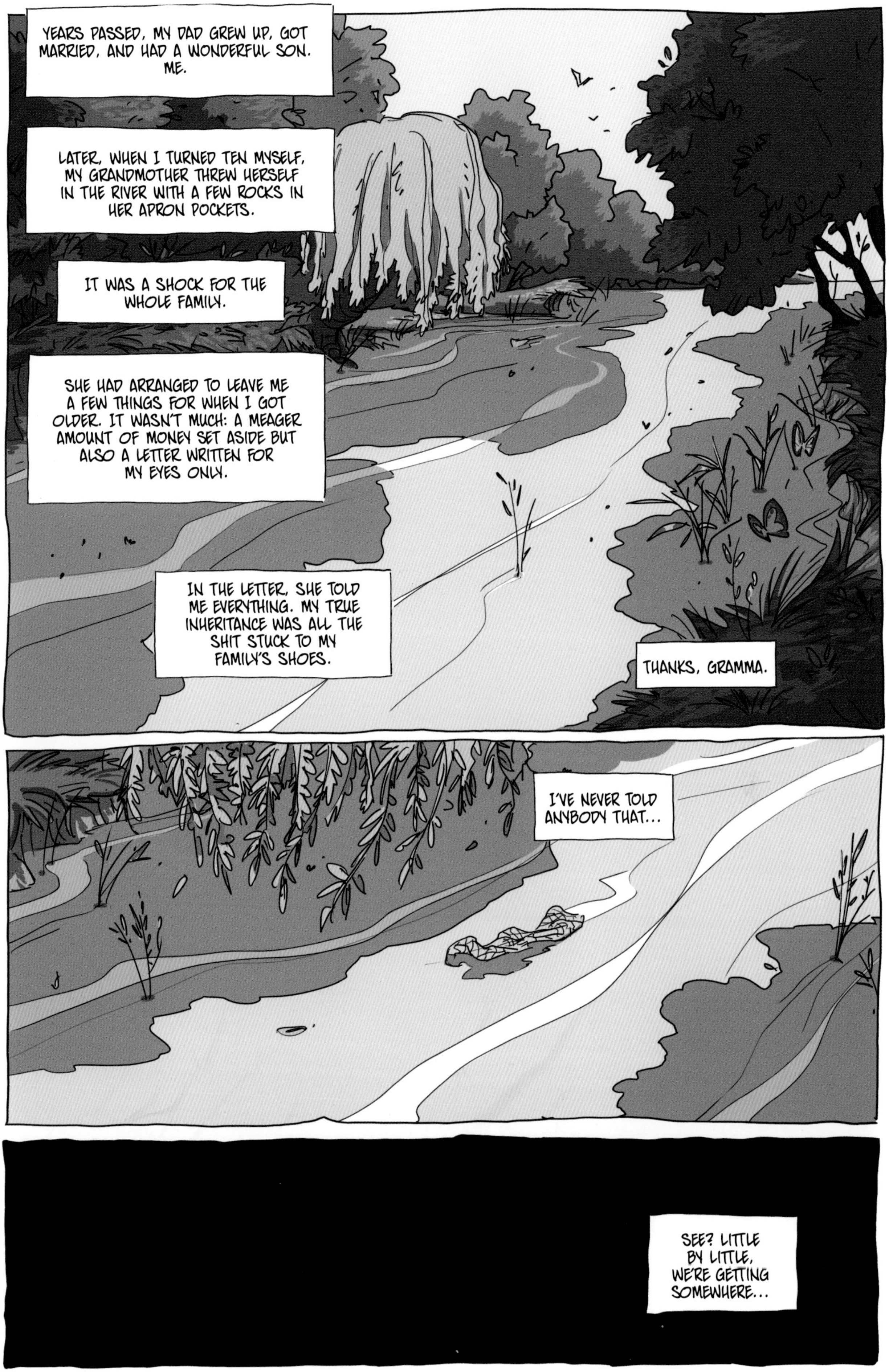
YEARS PASSED, MY DAD GREW UP, GOT MARRIED, AND HAD A WONDERFUL SON. ME.
LATER, WHEN I TURNED TEN MYSELF, MY GRANDMOTHER THREW HERSELF IN THE RIVER WITH A FEW ROCKS IN HER APRON POCKETS.
IT WAS A SHOCK FOR THE WHOLE FAMILY.
SHE HAD ARRANGED TO LEAVE ME A FEW THINGS FOR WHEN I GOT OLDER. IT WASN'T MUCH: A MEAGER AMOUNT OF MONEY SET ASIDE BUT ALSO A LETTER WRITTEN FOR MY EYES ONLY.
IN THE LETTER, SHE TOLD ME EVERYTHING. MY TRUE INHERITANCE WAS ALL THE SHIT STUCK TO MY FAMILY'S SHOES.
THANKS, GRAMMA.
I'VE NEVER TOLD ANYBODY THAT...
SEE? LITTLE BY LITTLE, WE'RE GETTING SOMEWHERE...

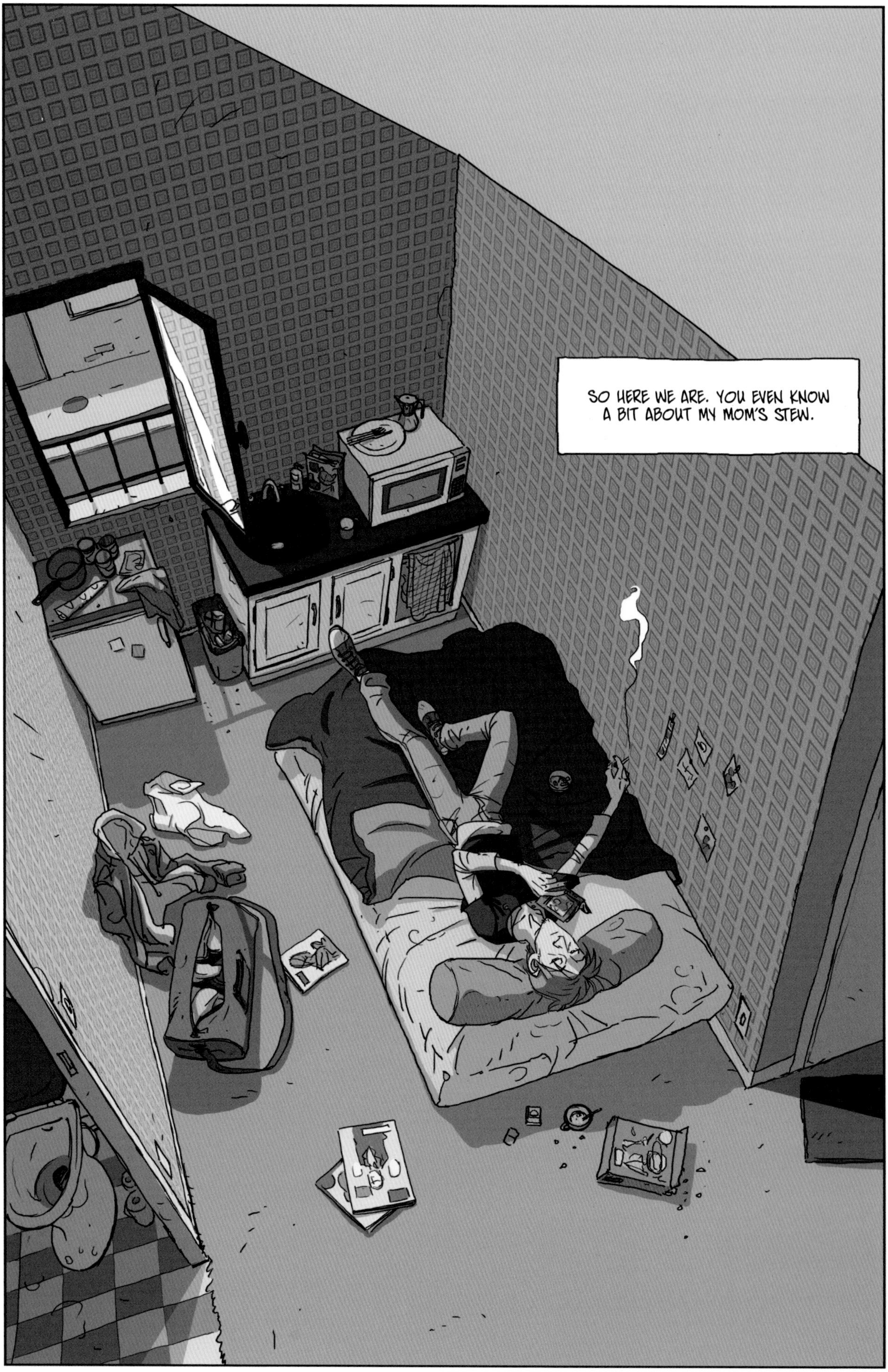
SO HERE WE ARE. YOU EVEN KNOW A BIT ABOUT MY MOM'S STEW.

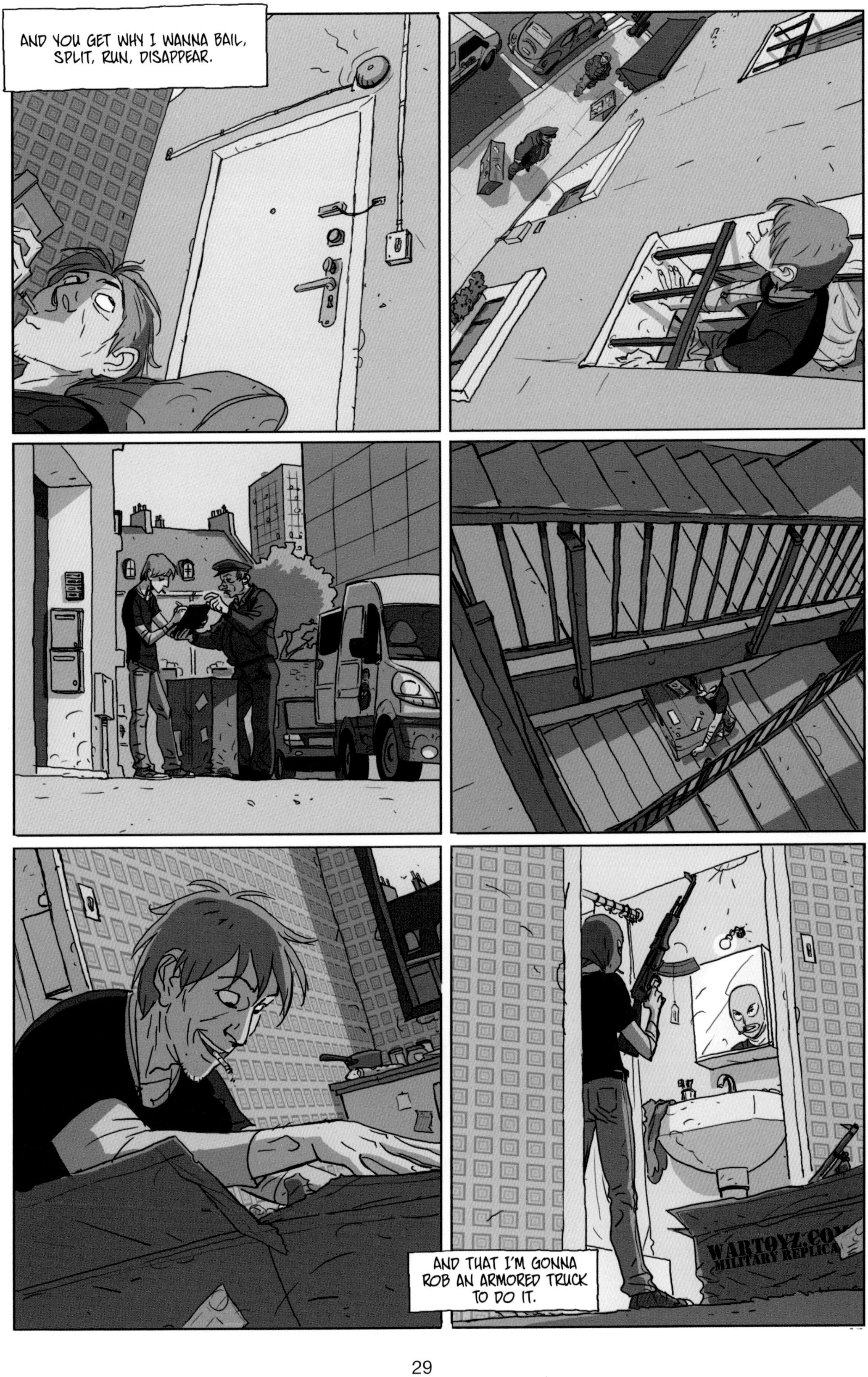
AND YOU GET WHY I WANNA BAIL, SPLIT, RUN, DISAPPEAR.
WARTOYZ.COM
MILITARY REPLICA
AND THAT I'M GONNA ROB AN ARMORED TRUCK TO DO IT.

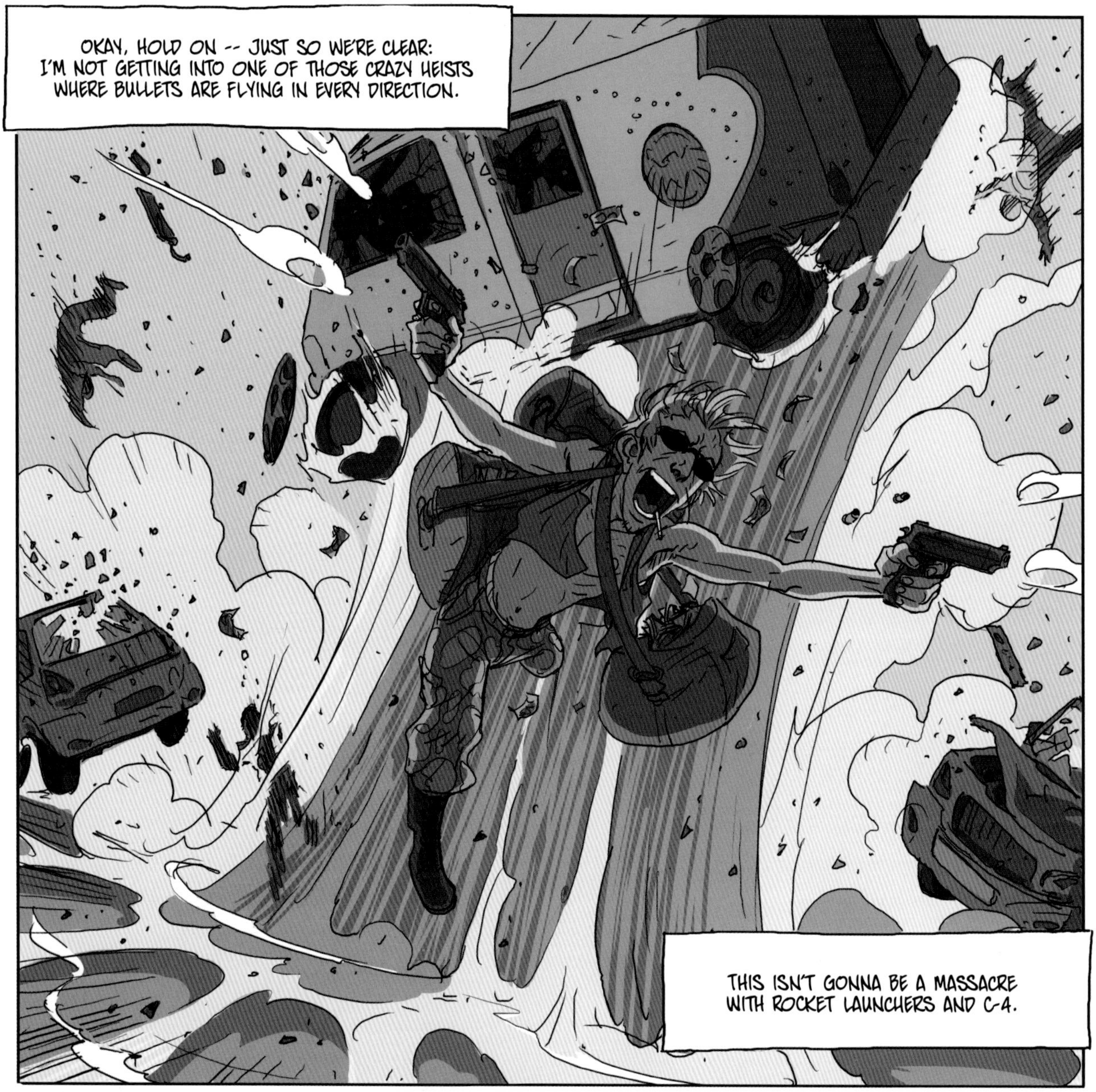
OKAY, HOLD ON -- JUST SO WE'RE CLEAR:
I'M NOT GETTING INTO ONE OF THOSE CRAZY HEISTS
WHERE BULLETS ARE FLYING IN EVERY DIRECTION.
THIS ISN'T GONNA BE A MASSACRE
WITH ROCKET LAUNCHERS AND C-4.

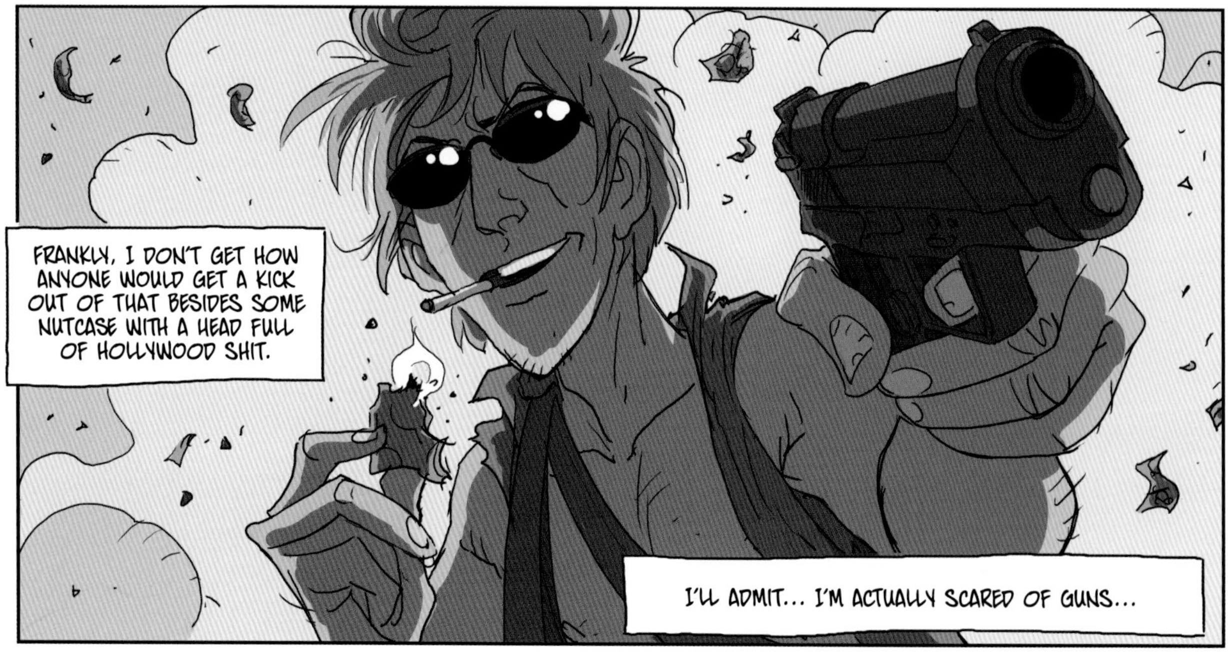
FRANKLY, I DON'T GET HOW ANYONE WOULD GET A KICK OUT OF THAT BESIDES SOME NUTCASE WITH A HEAD FULL OF HOLLYWOOD SHIT.
I'LL ADMIT... I'M ACTUALLY SCARED OF GUNS...

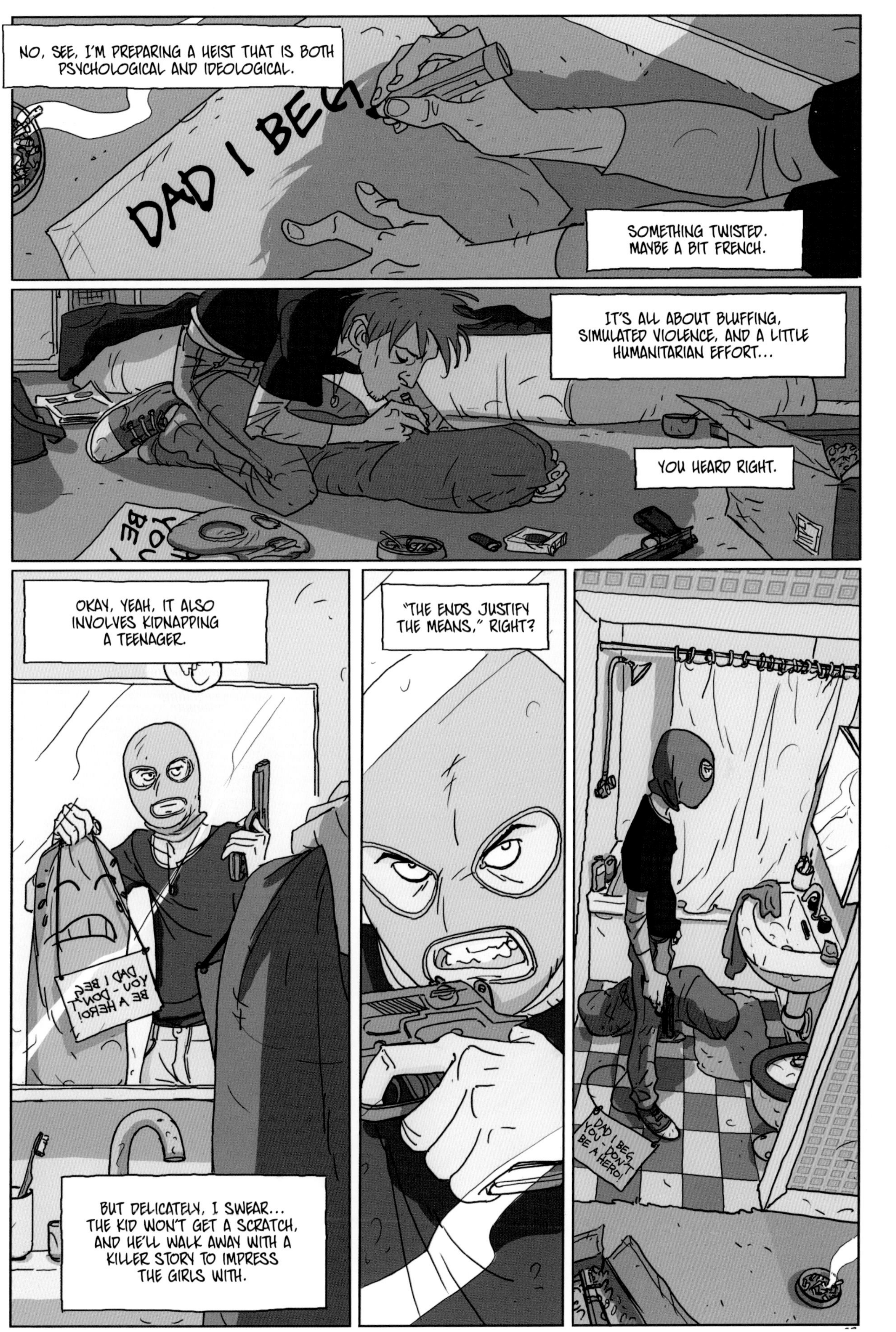
NO, SEE, I'M PREPARING A HEIST THAT IS BOTH PSYCHOLOGICAL AND IDEOLOGICAL.
DAD I BEG
SOMETHING TWISTED. MAYBE A BIT FRENCH.
IT'S ALL ABOUT BLUFFING, SIMULATED VIOLENCE, AND A LITTLE HUMANITARIAN EFFORT...
YOU HEARD RIGHT.
OKAY, YEAH, IT ALSO INVOLVES KIDNAPPING A TEENAGER.
DAD I BEG YOU - DON'T BE A HERO!
BUT DELICATELY, I SWEAR... THE KID WON'T GET A SCRATCH, AND HE'LL WALK AWAY WITH A KILLER STORY TO IMPRESS THE GIRLS WITH.
"THE ENDS JUSTIFY THE MEANS," RIGHT?
DAD I BEG YOU - DON'T BE A HERO!

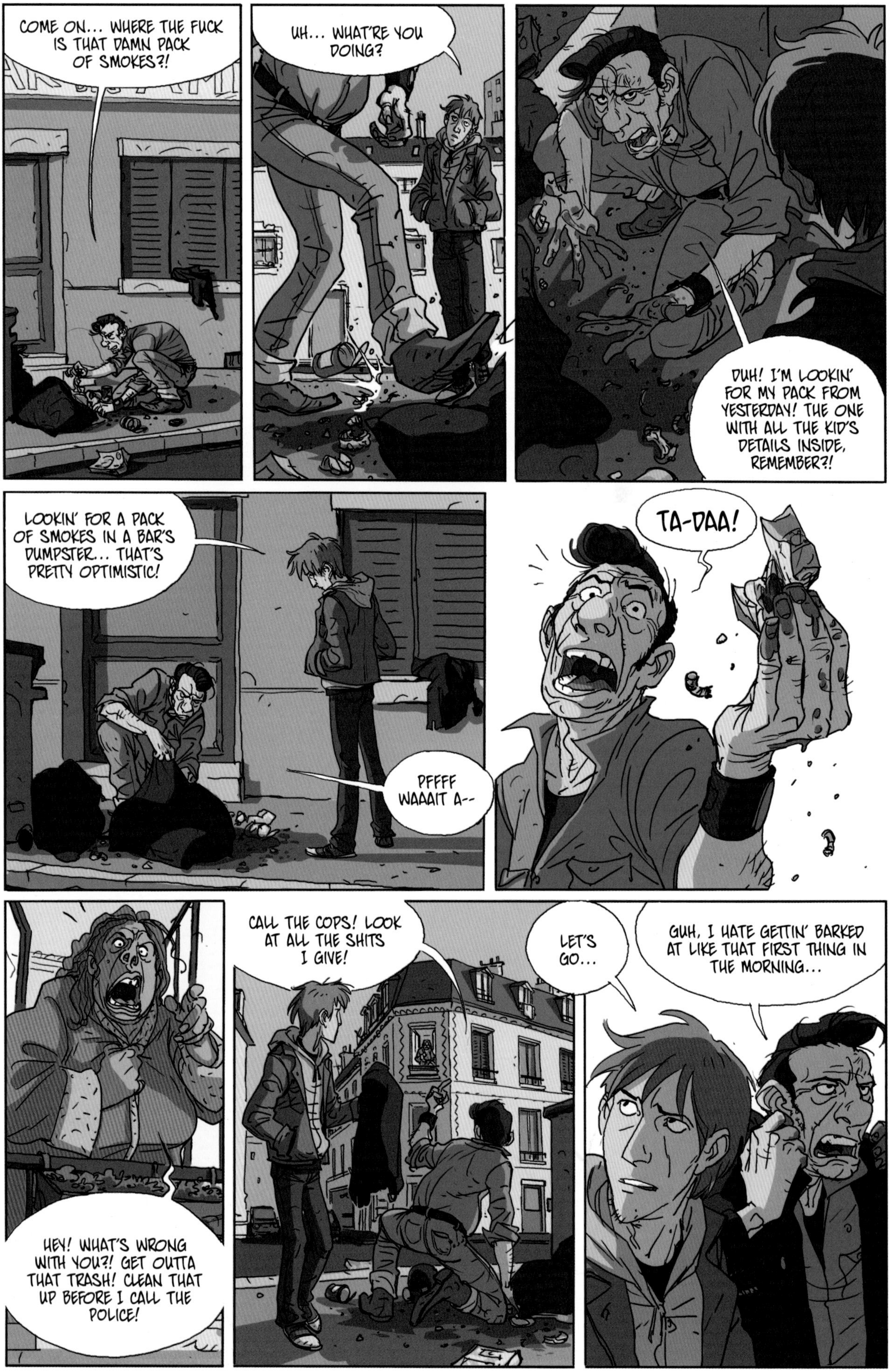
COME ON... WHERE THE FUCK IS THAT DAMN PACK OF SMOKES?!
UH... WHAT'RE YOU DOING?
DUH! I'M LOOKIN' FOR MY PACK FROM YESTERDAY! THE ONE WITH ALL THE KID'S DETAILS INSIDE, REMEMBER?!
LOOKIN' FOR A PACK OF SMOKES IN A BAR'S DUMPSTER... THAT'S PRETTY OPTIMISTIC!
PFFFF WAAAIT A--
TA-DAA!
HEY! WHAT'S WRONG WITH YOU?! GET OUTTA THAT TRASH! CLEAN THAT UP BEFORE I CALL THE POLICE!
CALL THE COPS! LOOK AT ALL THE SHITS I GIVE!
LET'S GO...
GUH, I HATE GETTIN' BARKED AT LIKE THAT FIRST THING IN THE MORNING...

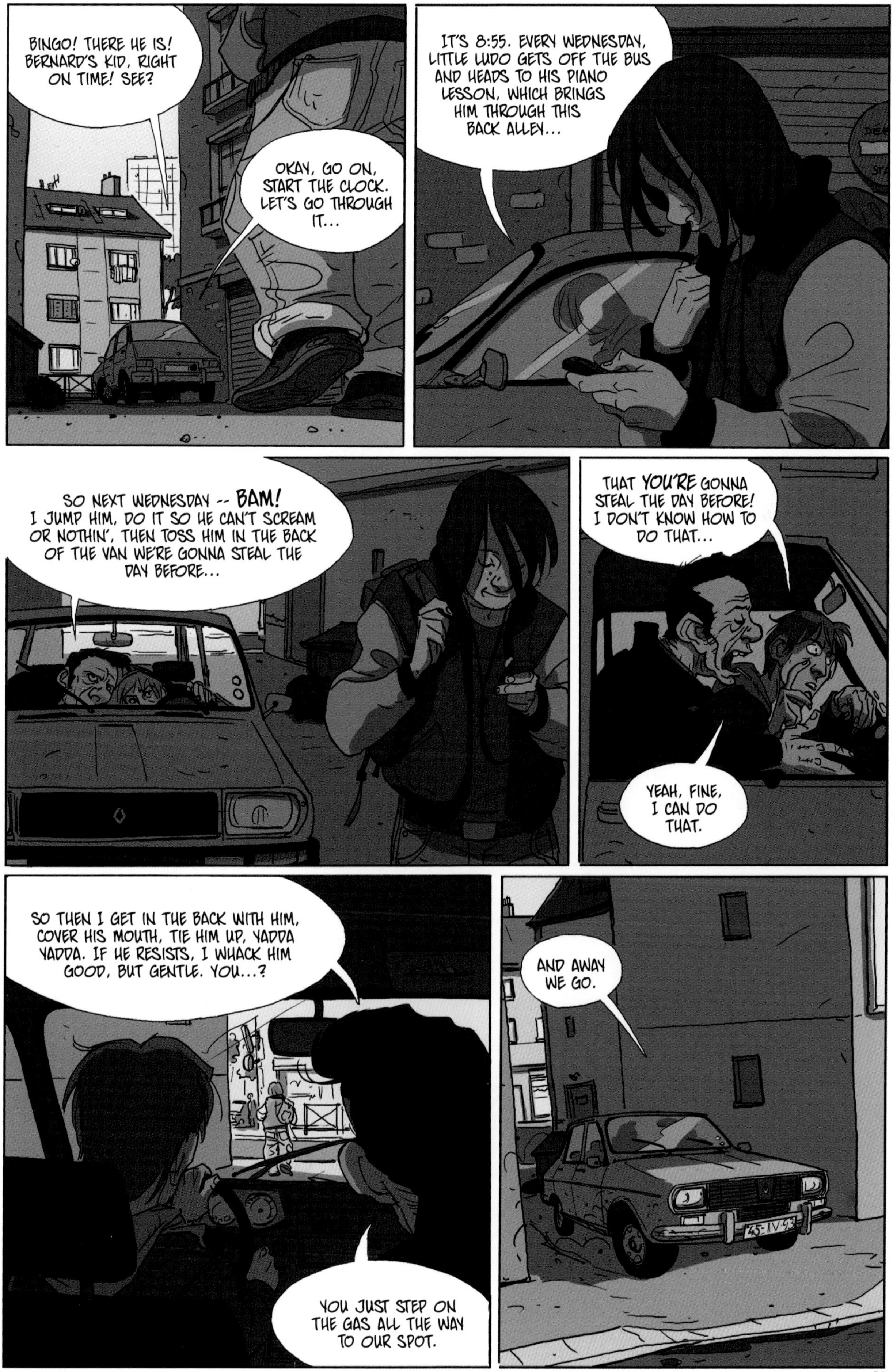
BINGO! THERE HE IS! BERNARD'S KID, RIGHT ON TIME! SEE?
OKAY, GO ON, START THE CLOCK. LET'S GO THROUGH IT...
IT'S 8:55. EVERY WEDNESDAY, LITTLE LUDO GETS OFF THE BUS AND HEADS TO HIS PIANO LESSON, WHICH BRINGS HIM THROUGH THIS BACK ALLEY...
SO NEXT WEDNESDAY -- BAM! I JUMP HIM, DO IT SO HE CAN'T SCREAM OR NOTHIN', THEN TOSS HIM IN THE BACK OF THE VAN WE'RE GONNA STEAL THE DAY BEFORE...
THAT YOU'RE GONNA STEAL THE DAY BEFORE! I DON'T KNOW HOW TO DO THAT...
YEAH, FINE, I CAN DO THAT.
SO THEN I GET IN THE BACK WITH HIM, COVER HIS MOUTH, TIE HIM UP, YADDA YADDA. IF HE RESISTS, I WHACK HIM GOOD, BUT GENTLE. YOU...?
YOU JUST STEP ON THE GAS ALL THE WAY TO OUR SPOT.
AND AWAY WE GO.

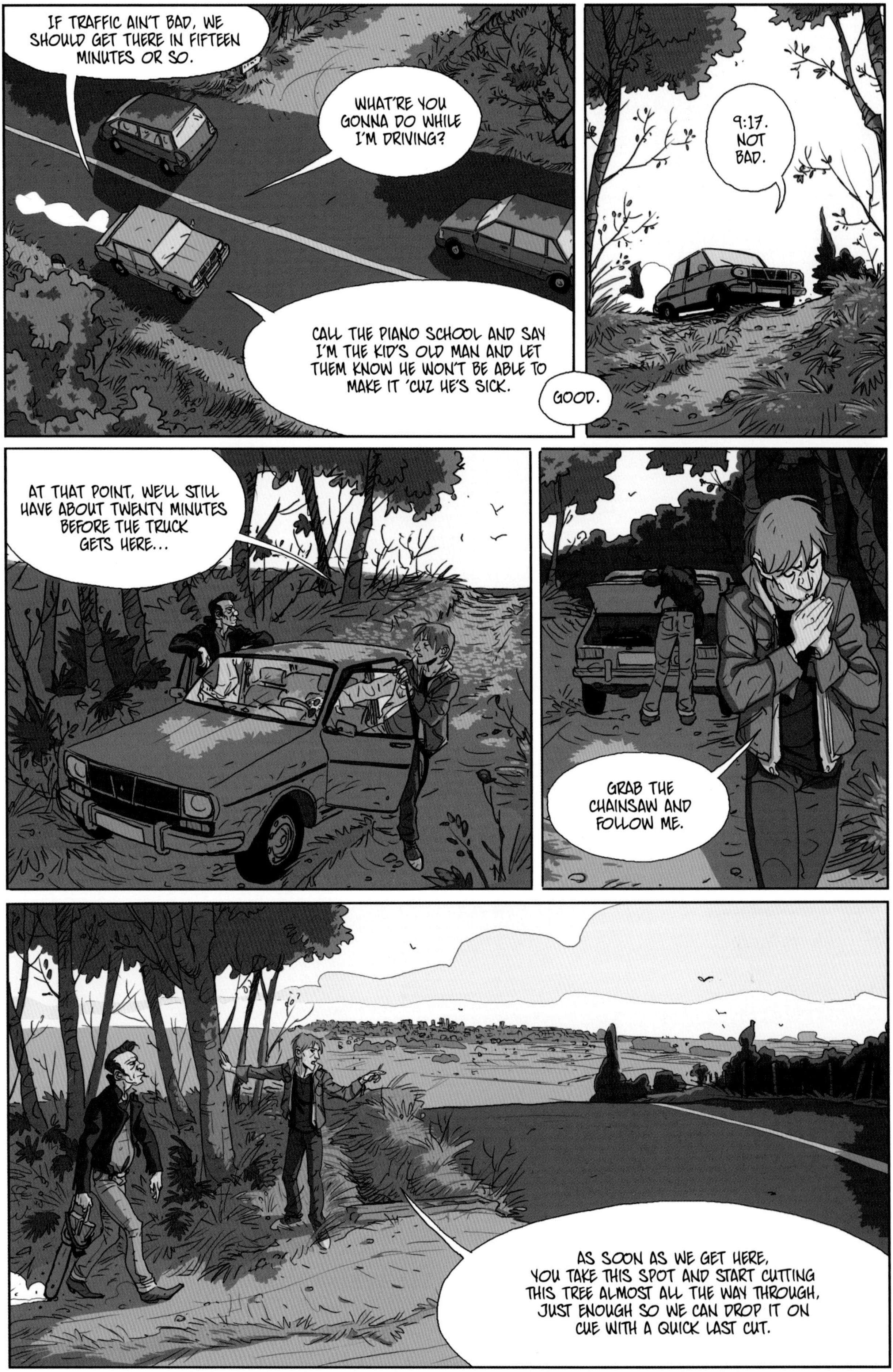
IF TRAFFIC AIN'T BAD, WE SHOULD GET THERE IN FIFTEEN MINUTES OR SO.
WHAT'RE YOU GONNA DO WHILE I'M DRIVING?
CALL THE PIANO SCHOOL AND SAY I'M THE KID'S OLD MAN AND LET THEM KNOW HE WON'T BE ABLE TO MAKE IT 'CUZ HE'S SICK.
GOOD.
9:17. NOT BAD.
AT THAT POINT, WE'LL STILL HAVE ABOUT TWENTY MINUTES BEFORE THE TRUCK GETS HERE...
GRAB THE CHAINSAW AND FOLLOW ME.
AS SOON AS WE GET HERE, YOU TAKE THIS SPOT AND START CUTTING THIS TREE ALMOST ALL THE WAY THROUGH, JUST ENOUGH SO WE CAN DROP IT ON CUE WITH A QUICK LAST CUT.

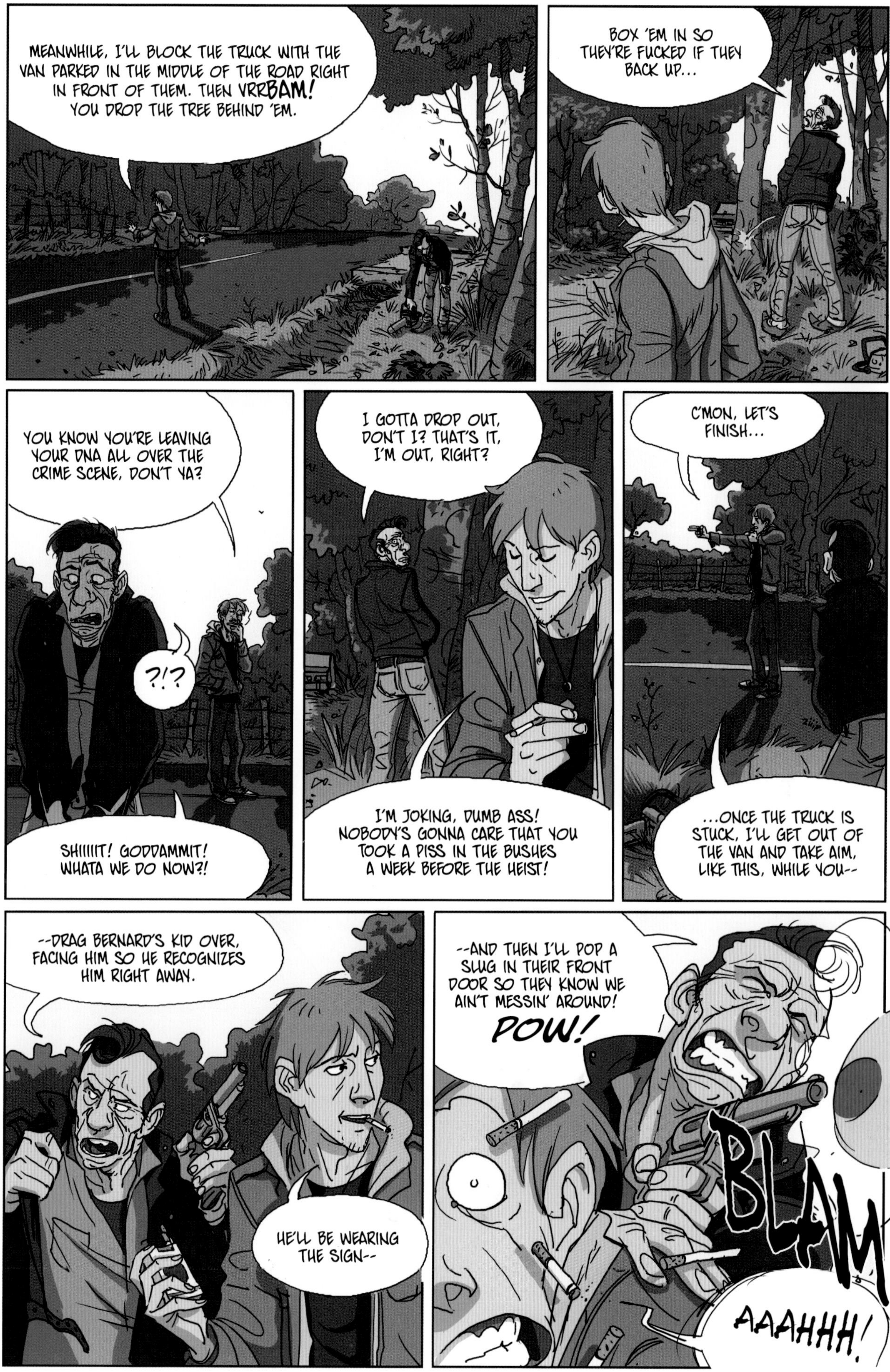
MEANWHILE, I'LL BLOCK THE TRUCK WITH THE VAN PARKED IN THE MIDDLE OF THE ROAD RIGHT IN FRONT OF THEM. THEN VRRBAM! YOU DROP THE TREE BEHIND 'EM.
BOX 'EM IN SO THEY'RE FUCKED IF THEY BACK UP...
YOU KNOW YOU'RE LEAVING YOUR DNA ALL OVER THE CRIME SCENE, DON'T YA?
?!?
SHIIIIIT! GODDAMMIT! WHATA WE DO NOW?!
I GOTTA DROP OUT, DON'T I? THAT'S IT, I'M OUT, RIGHT?
I'M JOKING, DUMB ASS! NOBODY'S GONNA CARE THAT YOU TOOK A PISS IN THE BUSHES A WEEK BEFORE THE HEIST!
C'MON, LET'S FINISH...
ZIIIP
...ONCE THE TRUCK IS STUCK, I'LL GET OUT OF THE VAN AND TAKE AIM, LIKE THIS, WHILE YOU--
--DRAG BERNARD'S KID OVER, FACING HIM SO HE RECOGNIZES HIM RIGHT AWAY.
HE'LL BE WEARING THE SIGN--
--AND THEN I'LL POP A SLUG IN THEIR FRONT DOOR SO THEY KNOW WE AIN'T MESSIN' AROUND! POW!
BLAM!
AAAHHH!

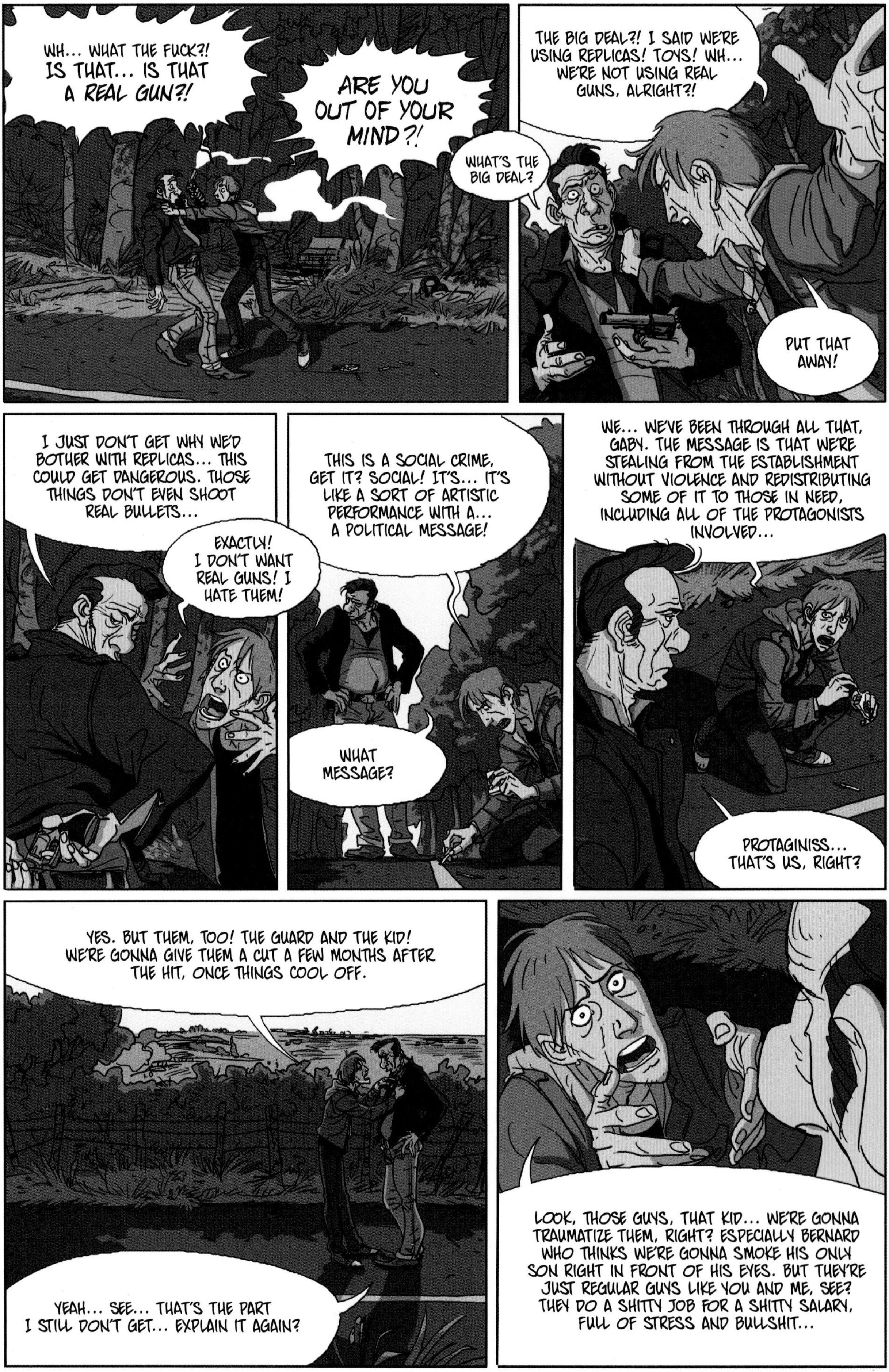

WH... WHAT THE FUCK?! IS THAT... IS THAT A REAL GUN?!
ARE YOU OUT OF YOUR MIND?!
WHAT'S THE BIG DEAL?
THE BIG DEAL?! I SAID WE'RE USING REPLICAS! TOYS! WH... WE'RE NOT USING REAL GUNS, ALRIGHT?!
PUT THAT AWAY!
I JUST DON'T GET WHY WE'D BOTHER WITH REPLICAS... THIS COULD GET DANGEROUS. THOSE THINGS DON'T EVEN SHOOT REAL BULLETS...
EXACTLY! I DON'T WANT REAL GUNS! I HATE THEM!
THIS IS A SOCIAL CRIME, GET IT? SOCIAL! IT'S... IT'S LIKE A SORT OF ARTISTIC PERFORMANCE WITH A... A POLITICAL MESSAGE!
WHAT MESSAGE?
WE... WE'VE BEEN THROUGH ALL THAT, GABY. THE MESSAGE IS THAT WE'RE STEALING FROM THE ESTABLISHMENT WITHOUT VIOLENCE AND REDISTRIBUTING SOME OF IT TO THOSE IN NEED, INCLUDING ALL OF THE PROTAGONISTS INVOLVED...
PROTAGINISS... THAT'S US, RIGHT?
YES. BUT THEM, TOO! THE GUARD AND THE KID! WE'RE GONNA GIVE THEM A CUT A FEW MONTHS AFTER THE HIT, ONCE THINGS COOL OFF.
YEAH... SEE... THAT'S THE PART I STILL DON'T GET... EXPLAIN IT AGAIN?
LOOK, THOSE GUYS, THAT KID... WE'RE GONNA TRAUMATIZE THEM, RIGHT? ESPECIALLY BERNARD WHO THINKS WE'RE GONNA SMOKE HIS ONLY SON RIGHT IN FRONT OF HIS EYES. BUT THEY'RE JUST REGULAR GUYS LIKE YOU AND ME, SEE? THEY DO A SHITTY JOB FOR A SHITTY SALARY, FULL OF STRESS AND BULLSHIT...

SO AFTER THE HOLDUP, WHEN WE'RE BOTH SAFE AND COOL, THEY'LL GET THEIR SHARE. 30 PERCENT AS COMPENSATION FOR HELPING US REDISTRIBUTE THOSE FUNDS.

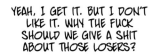

YEAH, I GET IT. BUT I DON'T LIKE IT. WHY THE FUCK SHOULD WE GIVE A SHIT ABOUT THOSE LOSERS?

THAT'S WHY IT'S SO BEAUTIFUL! IT'S A NONVIOLENT AND NOBLE HOLDUP! ONE OF A KIND! OTHERWISE IT DOESN'T MAKE ANY SENSE!

IT'S LIKE THEY'RE ACCOMPLICES, BUT THEY DON'T KNOW IT, GET IT?

DO I LOOK LIKE MOTHER TERESA?

NO! WE'RE LIKE ROBIN HOOD!

YEAH, BUT 30 PERCENT... DAMN!

LISTEN, WE'RE DONE TALKING ABOUT THIS...

BRRREEUUUUHHH

BRRREUU UHH

BBREUU....HH....HHH

SO MUCH FOR YOUR NONVIOLENT HOLDUP. WE JUST SMOKED A GOAT...

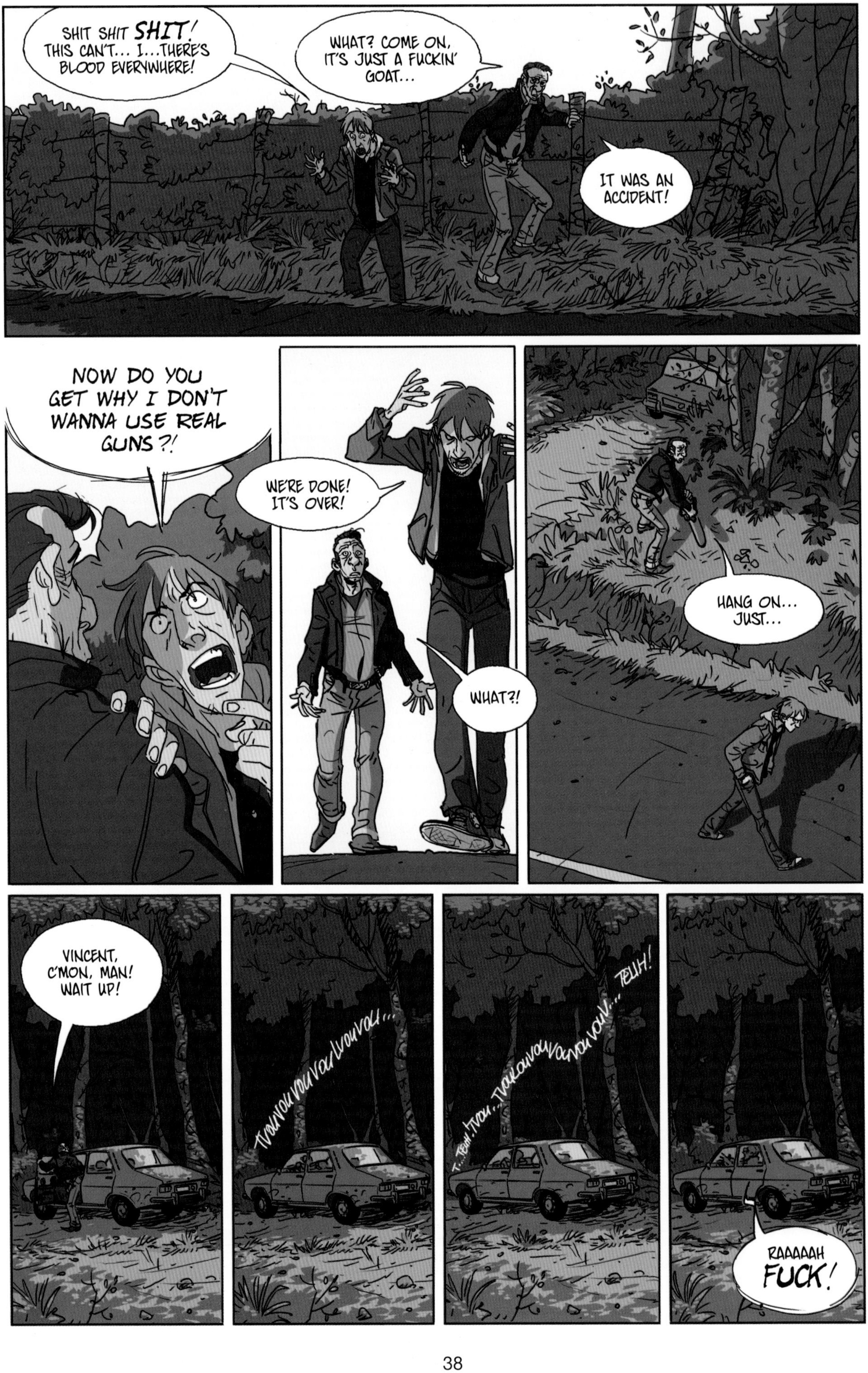
SHIT SHIT SHIT! THIS CAN'T… I…THERE'S BLOOD EVERYWHERE!
WHAT? COME ON, IT'S JUST A FUCKIN' GOAT…
IT WAS AN ACCIDENT!
NOW DO YOU GET WHY I DON'T WANNA USE REAL GUNS?!
WE'RE DONE! IT'S OVER!
WHAT?!
HANG ON… JUST…
VINCENT, C'MON, MAN! WAIT UP!
RAAAAAH FUCK!

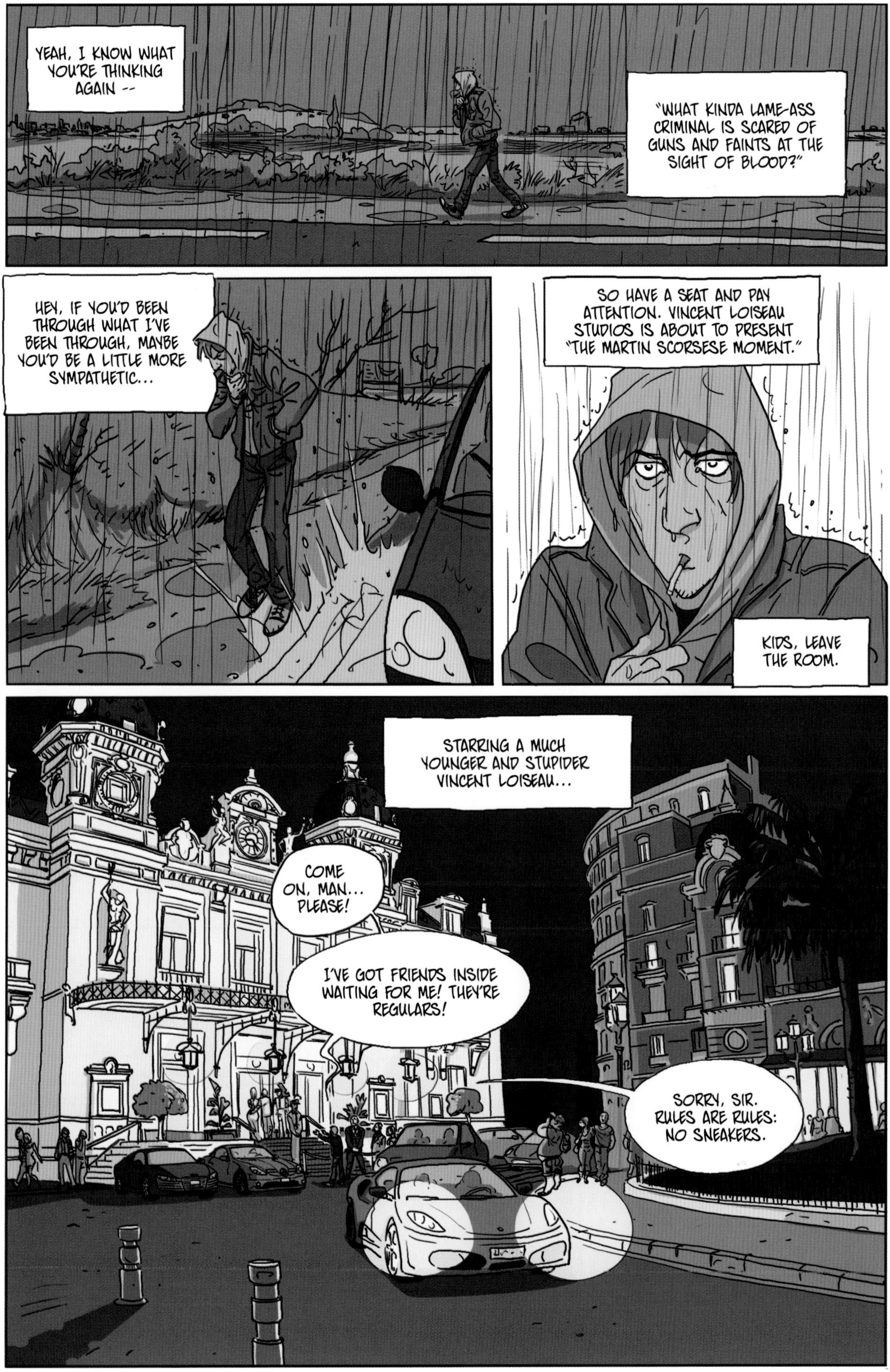
YEAH, I KNOW WHAT YOU'RE THINKING AGAIN --
"WHAT KINDA LAME-ASS CRIMINAL IS SCARED OF GUNS AND FAINTS AT THE SIGHT OF BLOOD?"
HEY, IF YOU'D BEEN THROUGH WHAT I'VE BEEN THROUGH, MAYBE YOU'D BE A LITTLE MORE SYMPATHETIC...
SO HAVE A SEAT AND PAY ATTENTION. VINCENT LOISEAU STUDIOS IS ABOUT TO PRESENT "THE MARTIN SCORSESE MOMENT."
KIDS, LEAVE THE ROOM.
STARRING A MUCH YOUNGER AND STUPIDER VINCENT LOISEAU...
COME ON, MAN... PLEASE!
I'VE GOT FRIENDS INSIDE WAITING FOR ME! THEY'RE REGULARS!
SORRY, SIR. RULES ARE RULES: NO SNEAKERS.

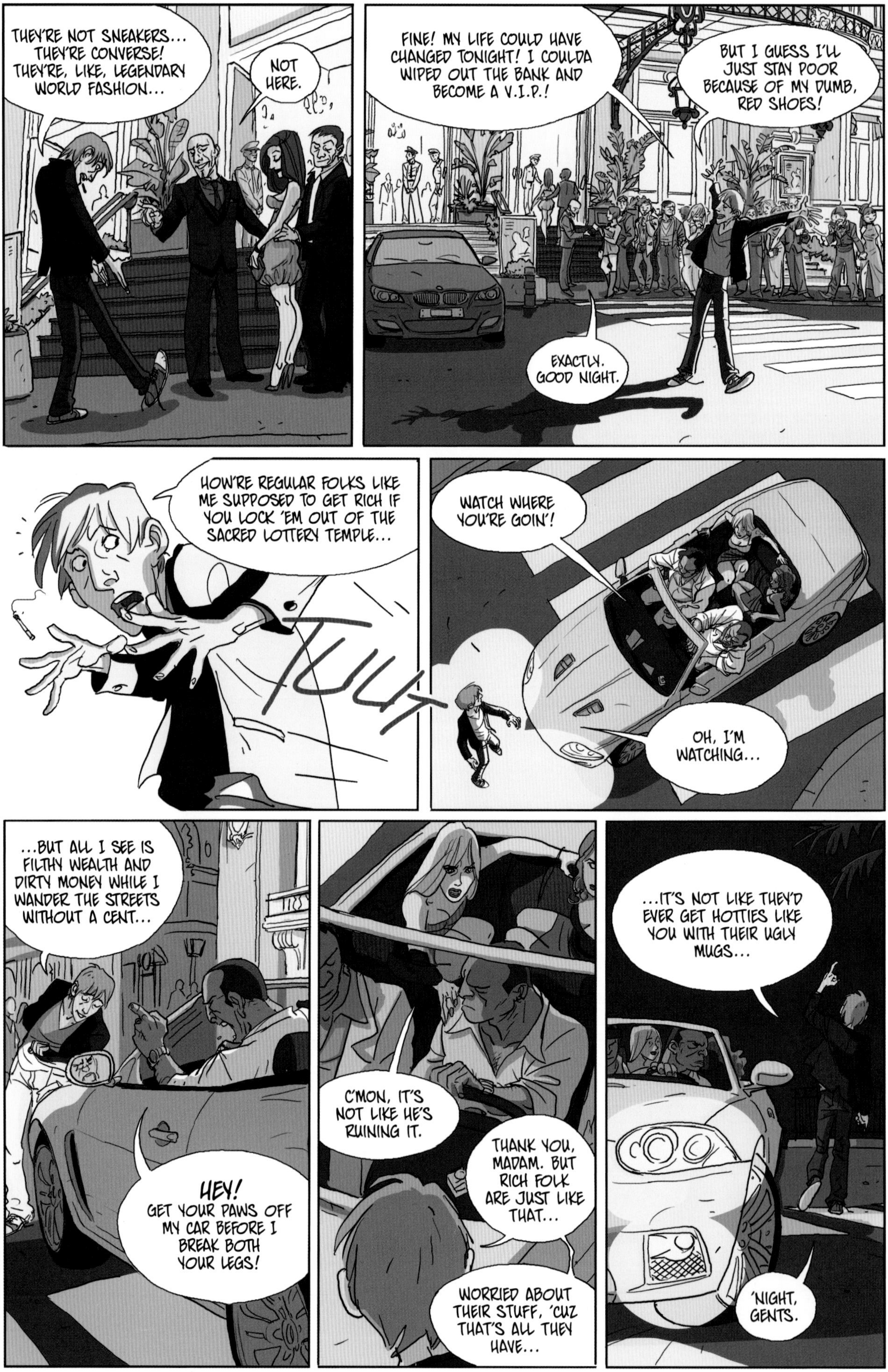

THEY'RE NOT SNEAKERS... THEY'RE CONVERSE! THEY'RE, LIKE, LEGENDARY WORLD FASHION...
NOT HERE.
FINE! MY LIFE COULD HAVE CHANGED TONIGHT! I COULDA WIPED OUT THE BANK AND BECOME A V.I.P.!
BUT I GUESS I'LL JUST STAY POOR BECAUSE OF MY DUMB, RED SHOES!
EXACTLY. GOOD NIGHT.
HOW'RE REGULAR FOLKS LIKE ME SUPPOSED TO GET RICH IF YOU LOCK 'EM OUT OF THE SACRED LOTTERY TEMPLE...
TUUT
WATCH WHERE YOU'RE GOIN'!
OH, I'M WATCHING...
...BUT ALL I SEE IS FILTHY WEALTH AND DIRTY MONEY WHILE I WANDER THE STREETS WITHOUT A CENT...
HEY! GET YOUR PAWS OFF MY CAR BEFORE I BREAK BOTH YOUR LEGS!
C'MON, IT'S NOT LIKE HE'S RUINING IT.
THANK YOU, MADAM. BUT RICH FOLK ARE JUST LIKE THAT...
WORRIED ABOUT THEIR STUFF, 'CUZ THAT'S ALL THEY HAVE...
...IT'S NOT LIKE THEY'D EVER GET HOTTIES LIKE YOU WITH THEIR UGLY MUGS...
'NIGHT, GENTS.

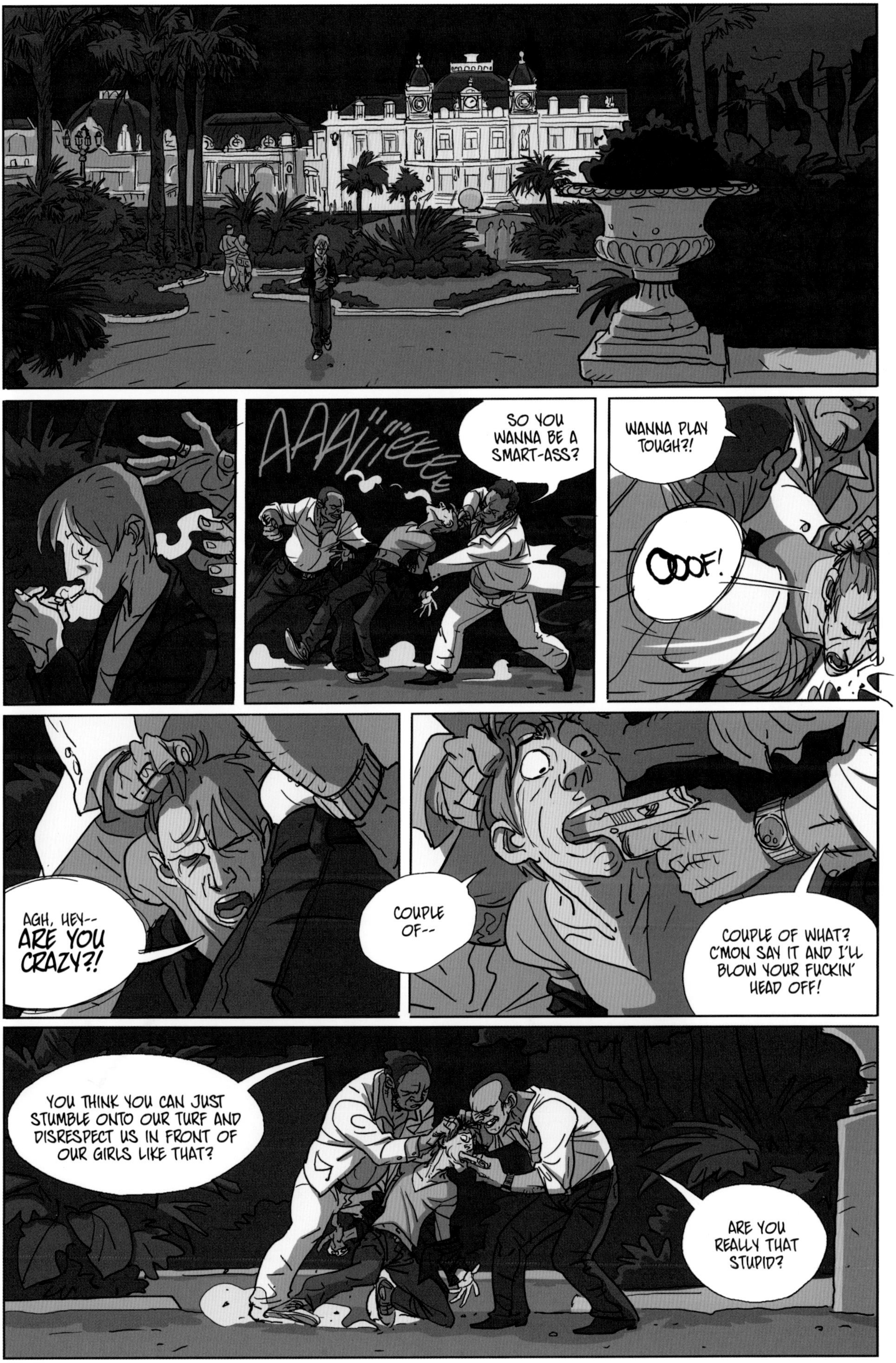
AAAIiieeeee
SO YOU WANNA BE A SMART-ASS?
WANNA PLAY TOUGH?!
OOOF!
AGH, HEY-- ARE YOU CRAZY?!
COUPLE OF--
COUPLE OF WHAT? C'MON SAY IT AND I'LL BLOW YOUR FUCKIN' HEAD OFF!
YOU THINK YOU CAN JUST STUMBLE ONTO OUR TURF AND DISRESPECT US IN FRONT OF OUR GIRLS LIKE THAT?
ARE YOU REALLY THAT STUPID?

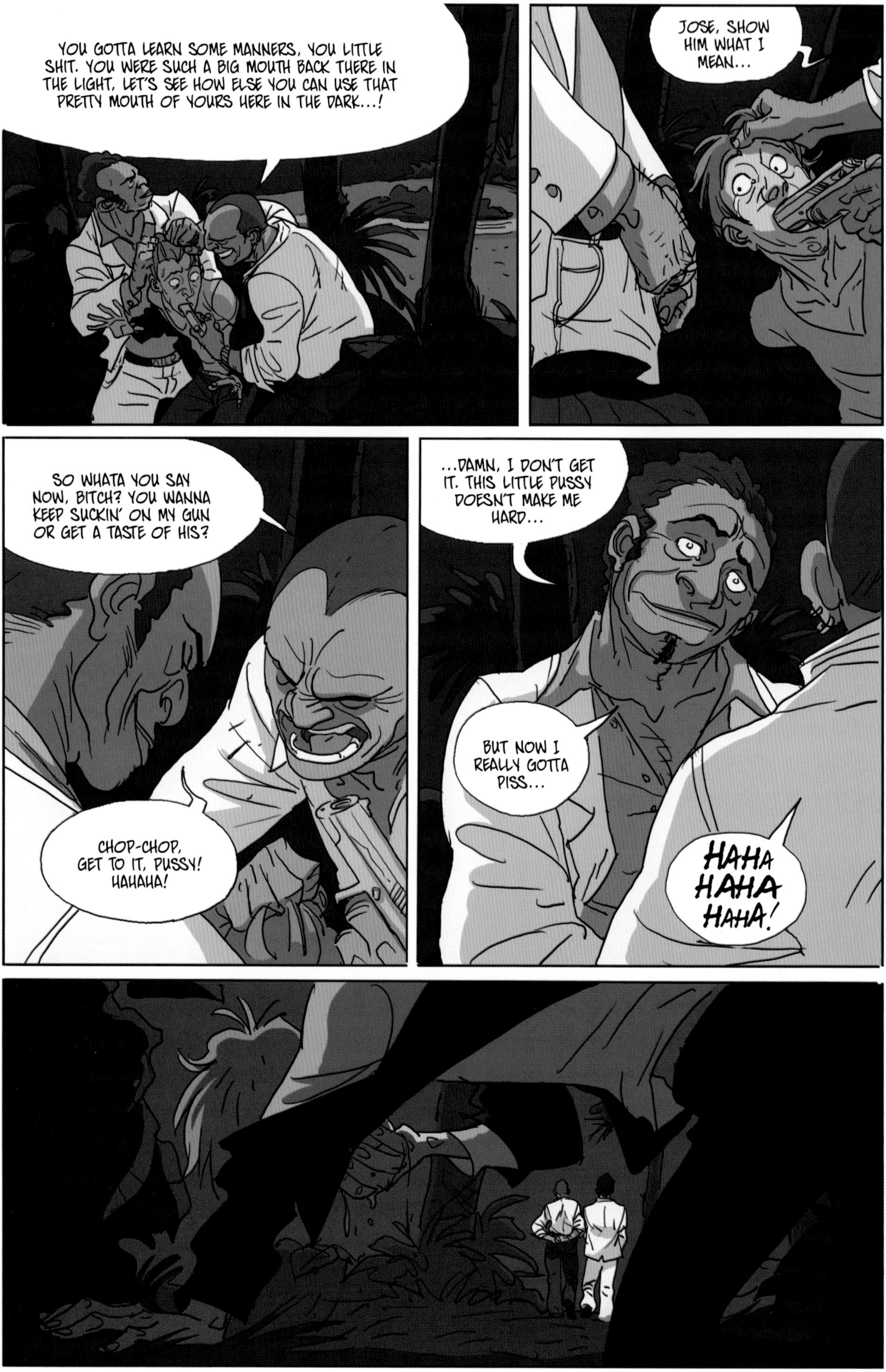
YOU GOTTA LEARN SOME MANNERS, YOU LITTLE SHIT. YOU WERE SUCH A BIG MOUTH BACK THERE IN THE LIGHT, LET'S SEE HOW ELSE YOU CAN USE THAT PRETTY MOUTH OF YOURS HERE IN THE DARK...!
JOSE, SHOW HIM WHAT I MEAN...
SO WHATA YOU SAY NOW, BITCH? YOU WANNA KEEP SUCKIN' ON MY GUN OR GET A TASTE OF HIS?
CHOP-CHOP, GET TO IT, PUSSY! HAHAHA!
...DAMN, I DON'T GET IT. THIS LITTLE PUSSY DOESN'T MAKE ME HARD...
BUT NOW I REALLY GOTTA PISS...
HAHA HAHA HAHA!

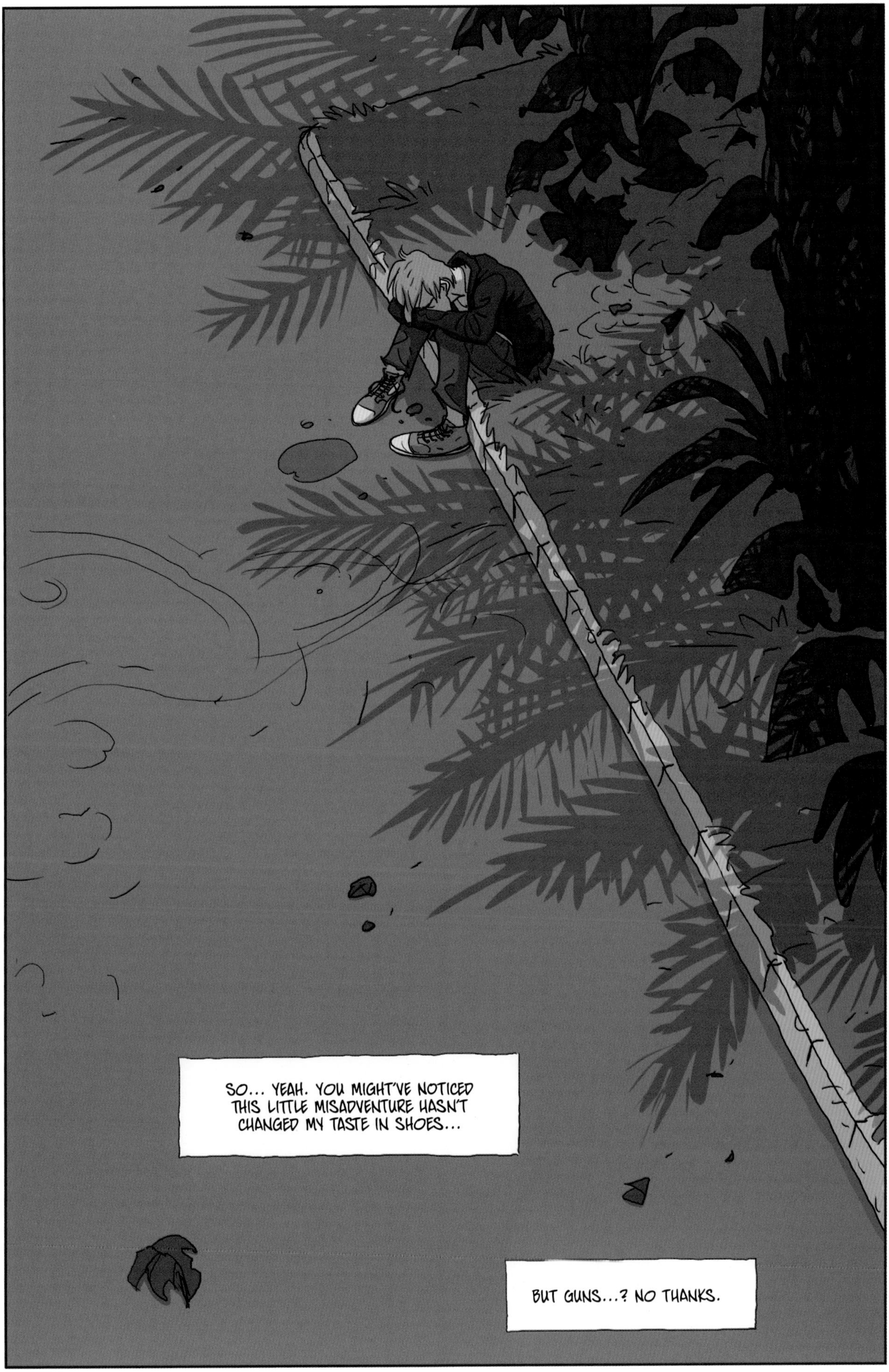
SO... YEAH. YOU MIGHT'VE NOTICED THIS LITTLE MISADVENTURE HASN'T CHANGED MY TASTE IN SHOES...
BUT GUNS...? NO THANKS.

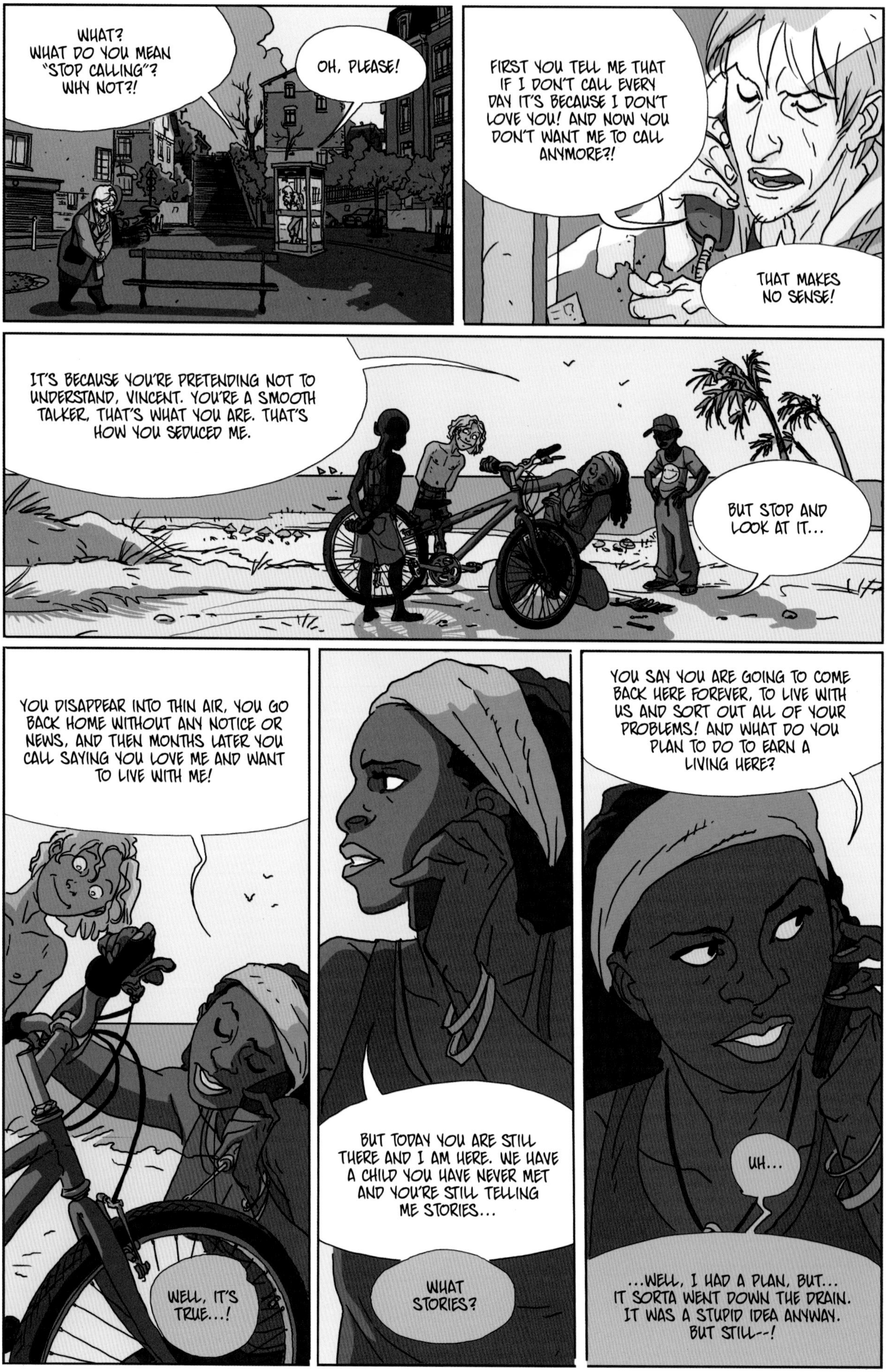
WHAT? WHAT DO YOU MEAN "STOP CALLING"? WHY NOT?!
OH, PLEASE!
FIRST YOU TELL ME THAT IF I DON'T CALL EVERY DAY IT'S BECAUSE I DON'T LOVE YOU! AND NOW YOU DON'T WANT ME TO CALL ANYMORE?!
THAT MAKES NO SENSE!
IT'S BECAUSE YOU'RE PRETENDING NOT TO UNDERSTAND, VINCENT. YOU'RE A SMOOTH TALKER, THAT'S WHAT YOU ARE. THAT'S HOW YOU SEDUCED ME.
BUT STOP AND LOOK AT IT...
YOU DISAPPEAR INTO THIN AIR, YOU GO BACK HOME WITHOUT ANY NOTICE OR NEWS, AND THEN MONTHS LATER YOU CALL SAYING YOU LOVE ME AND WANT TO LIVE WITH ME!
WELL, IT'S TRUE...!
BUT TODAY YOU ARE STILL THERE AND I AM HERE. WE HAVE A CHILD YOU HAVE NEVER MET AND YOU'RE STILL TELLING ME STORIES...
WHAT STORIES?
YOU SAY YOU ARE GOING TO COME BACK HERE FOREVER, TO LIVE WITH US AND SORT OUT ALL OF YOUR PROBLEMS! AND WHAT DO YOU PLAN TO DO TO EARN A LIVING HERE?
UH...
...WELL, I HAD A PLAN, BUT... IT SORTA WENT DOWN THE DRAIN. IT WAS A STUPID IDEA ANYWAY. BUT STILL--!

THAT'S IT, VINCENT! I ALREADY HAVE A CHILD TO TAKE CARE OF! I DON'T WANT ANOTHER ONE!

IN TWO WEEKS, IT WILL BE YOUR SON'S BIRTHDAY. UNTIL THEN, I DON'T WANT YOU TO CALL. BE HERE WITH US ON THAT DAY OR LEAVE US ALONE...

"...FOREVER."

SHE'S NOT ALWAYS GENTLE, RANA. BUT SHE HAS GOOD REASONS TO TREAT ME LIKE DIRT.

OKAY, HERE WE GO.

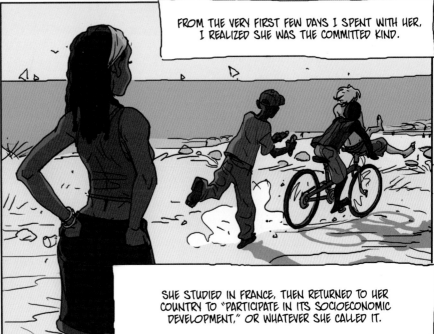

FROM THE VERY FIRST FEW DAYS I SPENT WITH HER, I REALIZED SHE WAS THE COMMITTED KIND.

SHE STUDIED IN FRANCE, THEN RETURNED TO HER COUNTRY TO "PARTICIPATE IN ITS SOCIOECONOMIC DEVELOPMENT," OR WHATEVER SHE CALLED IT.

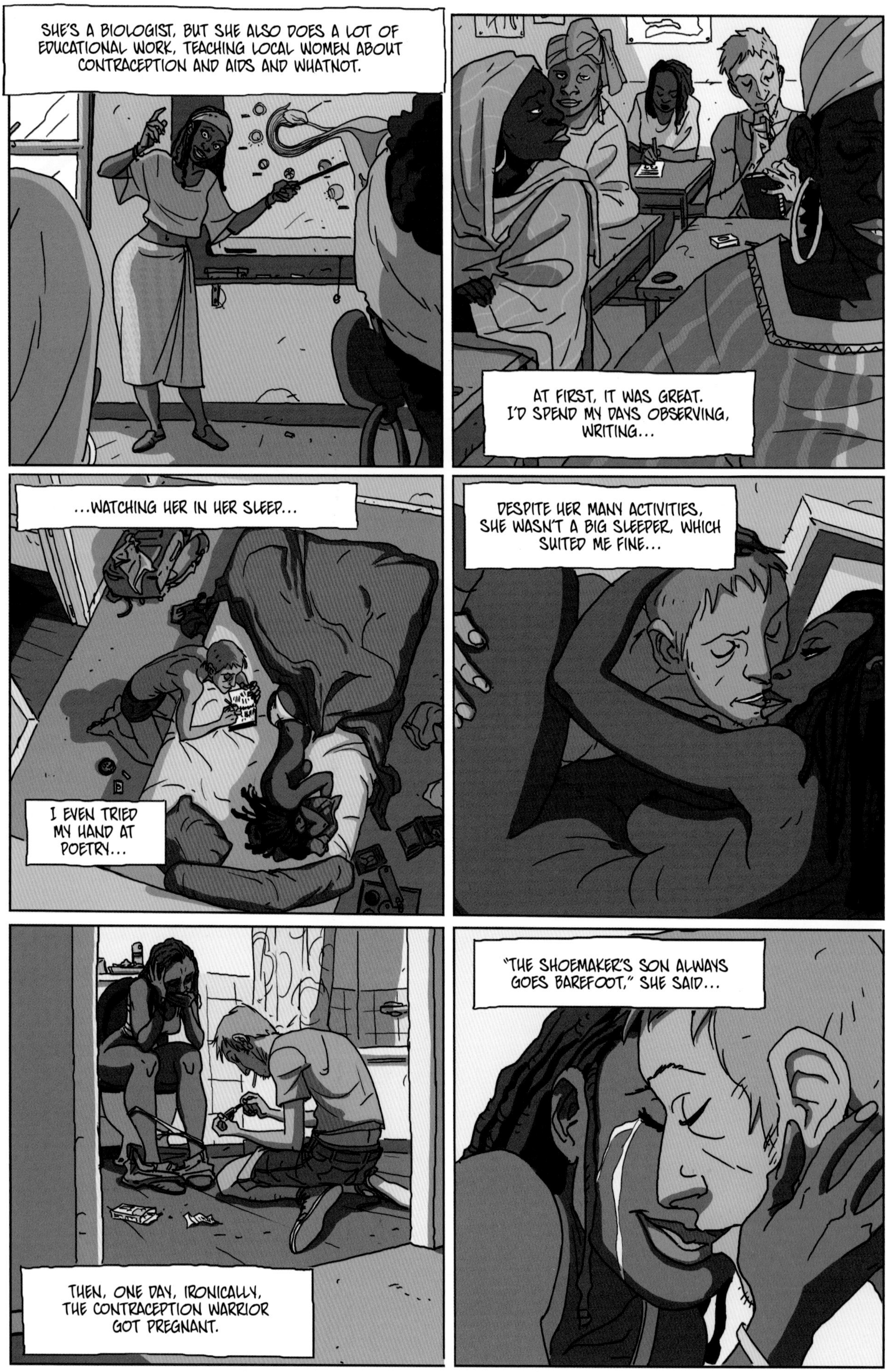
SHE'S A BIOLOGIST, BUT SHE ALSO DOES A LOT OF EDUCATIONAL WORK, TEACHING LOCAL WOMEN ABOUT CONTRACEPTION AND AIDS AND WHATNOT.
AT FIRST, IT WAS GREAT. I'D SPEND MY DAYS OBSERVING, WRITING...
...WATCHING HER IN HER SLEEP...
I EVEN TRIED MY HAND AT POETRY...
DESPITE HER MANY ACTIVITIES, SHE WASN'T A BIG SLEEPER, WHICH SUITED ME FINE...
THEN, ONE DAY, IRONICALLY, THE CONTRACEPTION WARRIOR GOT PREGNANT.
"THE SHOEMAKER'S SON ALWAYS GOES BAREFOOT," SHE SAID...

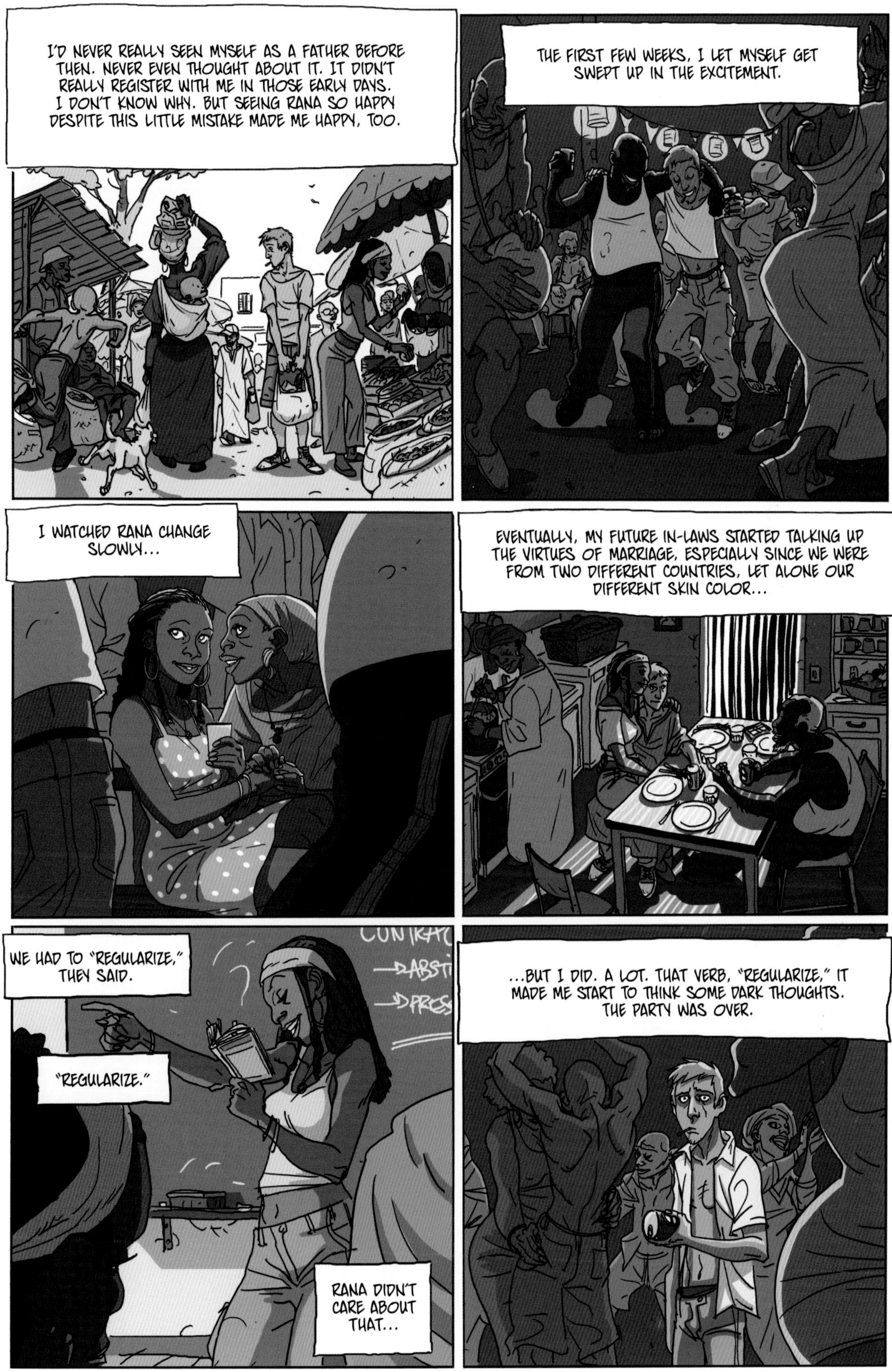
I'D NEVER REALLY SEEN MYSELF AS A FATHER BEFORE THEN. NEVER EVEN THOUGHT ABOUT IT. IT DIDN'T REALLY REGISTER WITH ME IN THOSE EARLY DAYS. I DON'T KNOW WHY. BUT SEEING RANA SO HAPPY DESPITE THIS LITTLE MISTAKE MADE ME HAPPY, TOO.
THE FIRST FEW WEEKS, I LET MYSELF GET SWEPT UP IN THE EXCITEMENT.
I WATCHED RANA CHANGE SLOWLY...
EVENTUALLY, MY FUTURE IN-LAWS STARTED TALKING UP THE VIRTUES OF MARRIAGE, ESPECIALLY SINCE WE WERE FROM TWO DIFFERENT COUNTRIES, LET ALONE OUR DIFFERENT SKIN COLOR...
WE HAD TO "REGULARIZE," THEY SAID.
"REGULARIZE."
RANA DIDN'T CARE ABOUT THAT...
...BUT I DID. A LOT. THAT VERB, "REGULARIZE," IT MADE ME START TO THINK SOME DARK THOUGHTS. THE PARTY WAS OVER.

ALL OF A SUDDEN, I WAS OVERWHELMED BY MY FAMILY'S HISTORY, OBSESSED BY MY GRANDMOTHER... I'D WAKE UP AT NIGHT TO THE SOUND OF MY FATHER SLURPING HIS SOUP...

RIGHT THEN AND THERE, EVERYTHING BECAME CLEAR AND CRUEL: NONE OF THIS AFRICAN ADVENTURE WAS MY OWN DOING. I WAS JUST A SUBCONSCIOUS EXTENSION OF THE FAMILY STORY. A STUPID, PENITENT KID TRYING TO REDEEM HIS FAMILY'S FAULTS.

I WAS SLEEPING WITH OUSMANE'S CORPSE...

I WAS TRYING TO "REGULARIZE."

A COUPLE DAYS AFTER THAT REALIZATION, I CAME DOWN WITH A REALLY BAD FEVER. RANA STAYED BY MY SIDE THE WHOLE TIME.

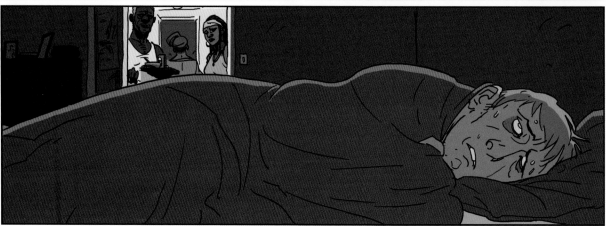

48

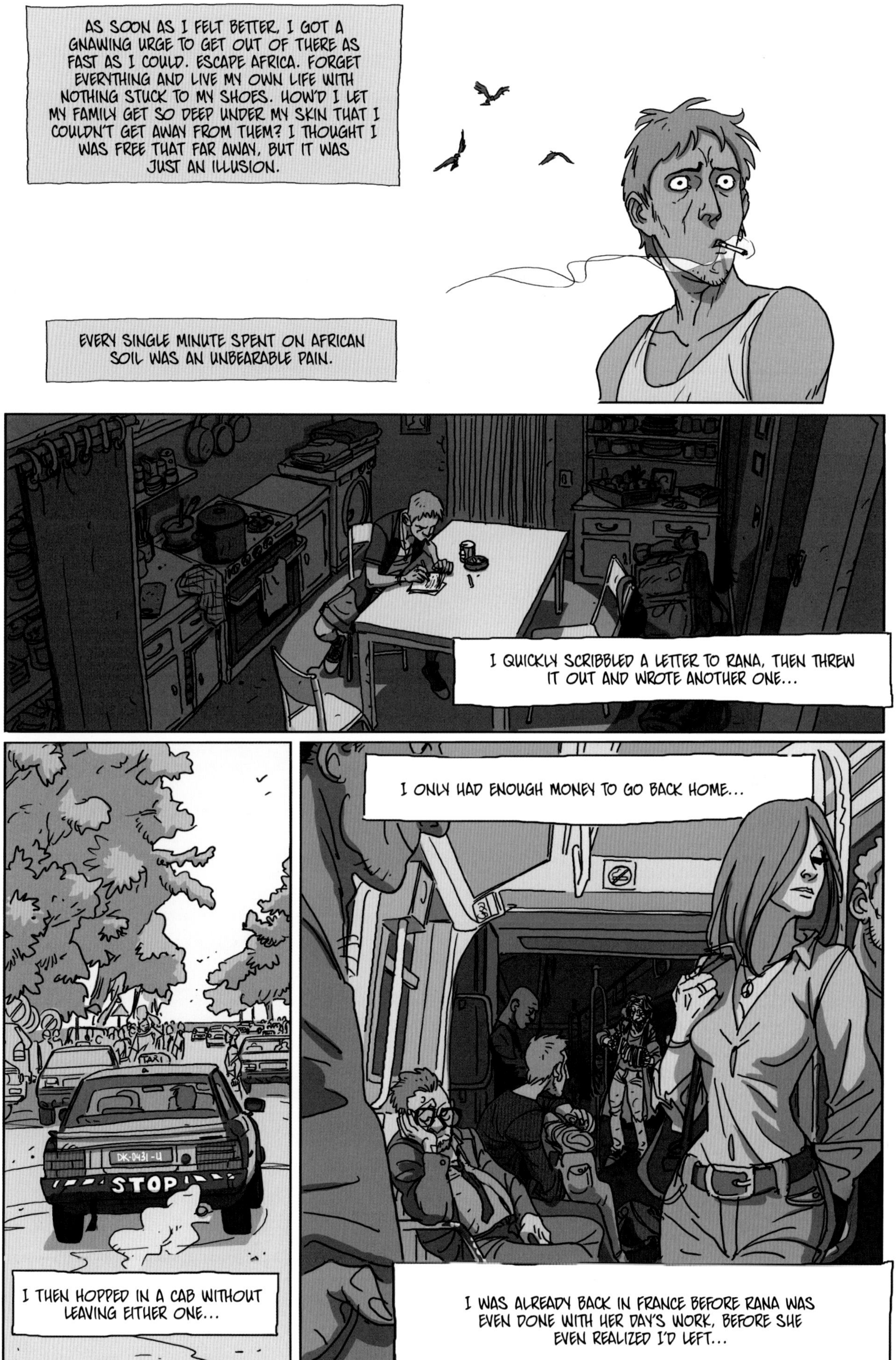
AS SOON AS I FELT BETTER, I GOT A GNAWING URGE TO GET OUT OF THERE AS FAST AS I COULD. ESCAPE AFRICA. FORGET EVERYTHING AND LIVE MY OWN LIFE WITH NOTHING STUCK TO MY SHOES. HOW'D I LET MY FAMILY GET SO DEEP UNDER MY SKIN THAT I COULDN'T GET AWAY FROM THEM? I THOUGHT I WAS FREE THAT FAR AWAY, BUT IT WAS JUST AN ILLUSION.
EVERY SINGLE MINUTE SPENT ON AFRICAN SOIL WAS AN UNBEARABLE PAIN.
I QUICKLY SCRIBBLED A LETTER TO RANA, THEN THREW IT OUT AND WROTE ANOTHER ONE...
TAXI
DK-0431-U
STOP
I THEN HOPPED IN A CAB WITHOUT LEAVING EITHER ONE...
I ONLY HAD ENOUGH MONEY TO GO BACK HOME...
I WAS ALREADY BACK IN FRANCE BEFORE RANA WAS EVEN DONE WITH HER DAY'S WORK, BEFORE SHE EVEN REALIZED I'D LEFT...

I COULDN'T AFFORD AN APARTMENT AND COULDN'T STAND THE THOUGHT OF GOING BACK TO MY PARENTS' HOUSE. I WANDERED BETWEEN HOSTELS, CAFES, AND CRASHING AT SOME OLD FRIENDS' PLACES. I'D HEAL MY SPIRITUAL FLU WITH MASSIVE DOSES OF WHATEVER SUBSTANCES WERE AVAILABLE AT THE TIME...

AND LET ME TELL YOU, THAT COVERED A LOT OF STUFF...

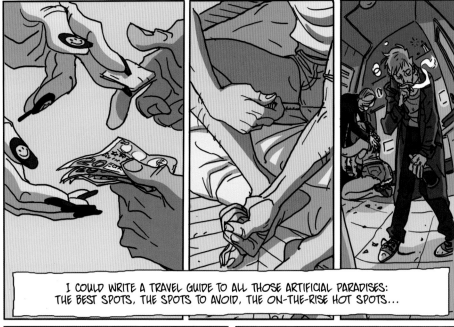

I COULD WRITE A TRAVEL GUIDE TO ALL THOSE ARTIFICIAL PARADISES: THE BEST SPOTS, THE SPOTS TO AVOID, THE ON-THE-RISE HOT SPOTS...

THEN, ONE DAY, I TOOK A FAMILY-SIZED DOSE TO END IT ALL...

...INSIDE A SQUAT WITH MY ZIPPER DOWN AND MY SOCKS FULL OF HOLES...

...REAL CLASSY.

50

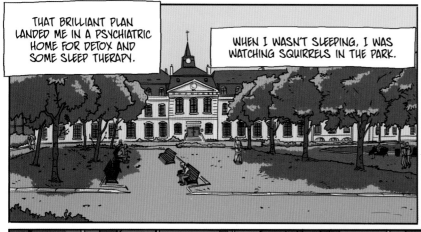

THAT BRILLIANT PLAN LANDED ME IN A PSYCHIATRIC HOME FOR DETOX AND SOME SLEEP THERAPY.

WHEN I WASN'T SLEEPING, I WAS WATCHING SQUIRRELS IN THE PARK.

OR MAKING OUT WITH SOME OTHER PATIENT IN A DESPERATE NEED FOR AFFECTION. I FOUND THEIR EMOTIONAL FRAGILITY COMFORTING.

I'D ALSO TAKE EVERY OPPORTUNITY I COULD TO HAVE LONG, BABBLING, NARCISSISTIC MONOLOGUES WITH THE MOST HARDCORE PATIENTS...

...WHO FRANKLY WEREN'T MUCH DIFFERENT FROM THE DOCTORS, THE WAY THEY DRESSED AND ACTED...

IN FACT, THIS ONE GUY, SALVATORE, WAS A HUGE HELP IN MY OWN PROGRESS...

YEAH, YOU TALK BIG AND BRAG A LOT, BUT THE FACT IS, YOU SAW HER ROUND BELLY AND CRAPPED YOUR PANTS...

I CRAPPED MY PANTS.

I OWE SALVATORE FOR THAT ONE.

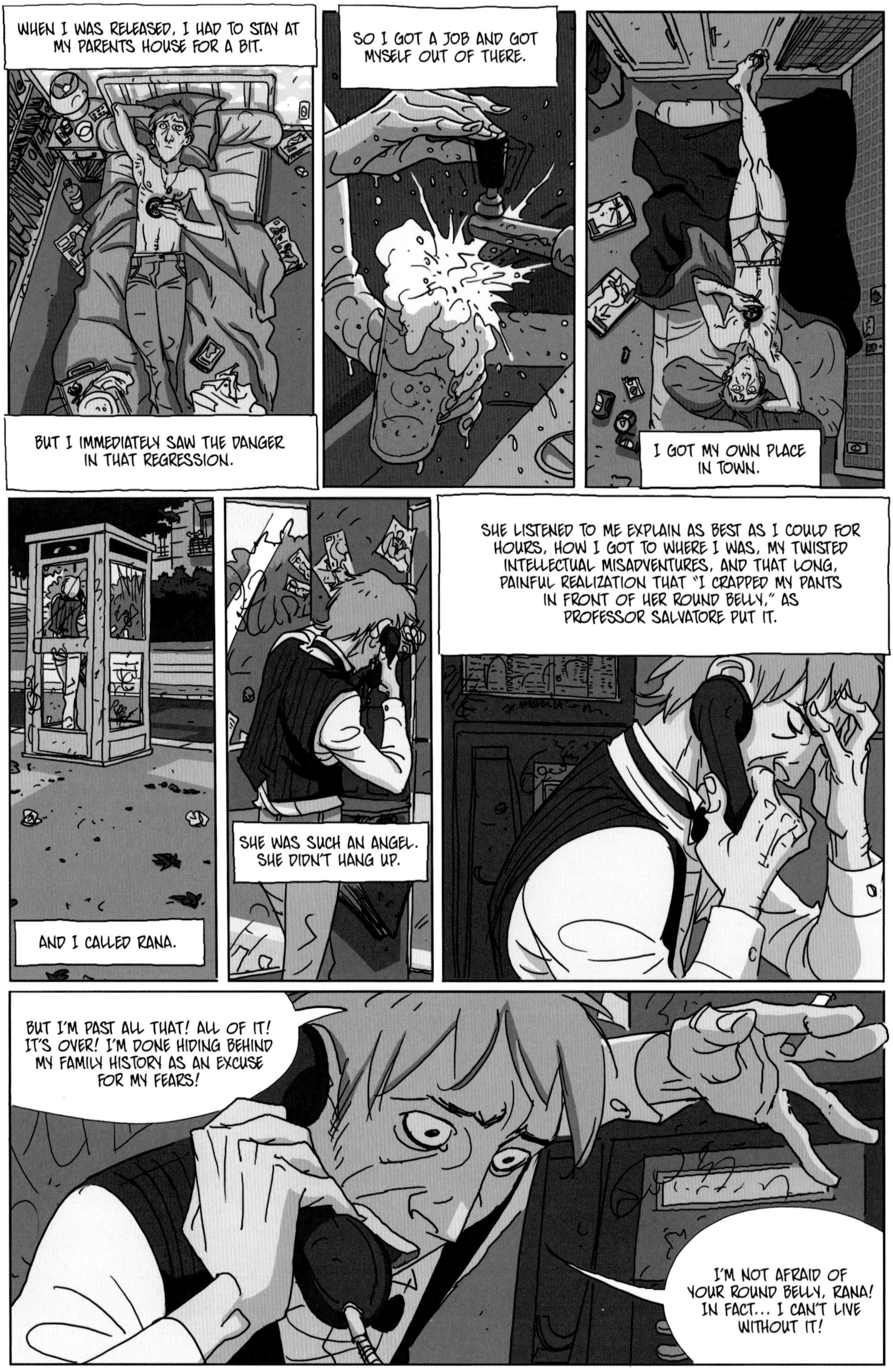
WHEN I WAS RELEASED, I HAD TO STAY AT MY PARENTS HOUSE FOR A BIT.
BUT I IMMEDIATELY SAW THE DANGER IN THAT REGRESSION.
SO I GOT A JOB AND GOT MYSELF OUT OF THERE.
I GOT MY OWN PLACE IN TOWN.
AND I CALLED RANA.
SHE WAS SUCH AN ANGEL. SHE DIDN'T HANG UP.
SHE LISTENED TO ME EXPLAIN AS BEST AS I COULD FOR HOURS, HOW I GOT TO WHERE I WAS, MY TWISTED INTELLECTUAL MISADVENTURES, AND THAT LONG, PAINFUL REALIZATION THAT "I CRAPPED MY PANTS IN FRONT OF HER ROUND BELLY," AS PROFESSOR SALVATORE PUT IT.
BUT I'M PAST ALL THAT! ALL OF IT! IT'S OVER! I'M DONE HIDING BEHIND MY FAMILY HISTORY AS AN EXCUSE FOR MY FEARS!
I'M NOT AFRAID OF YOUR ROUND BELLY, RANA! IN FACT... I CAN'T LIVE WITHOUT IT!

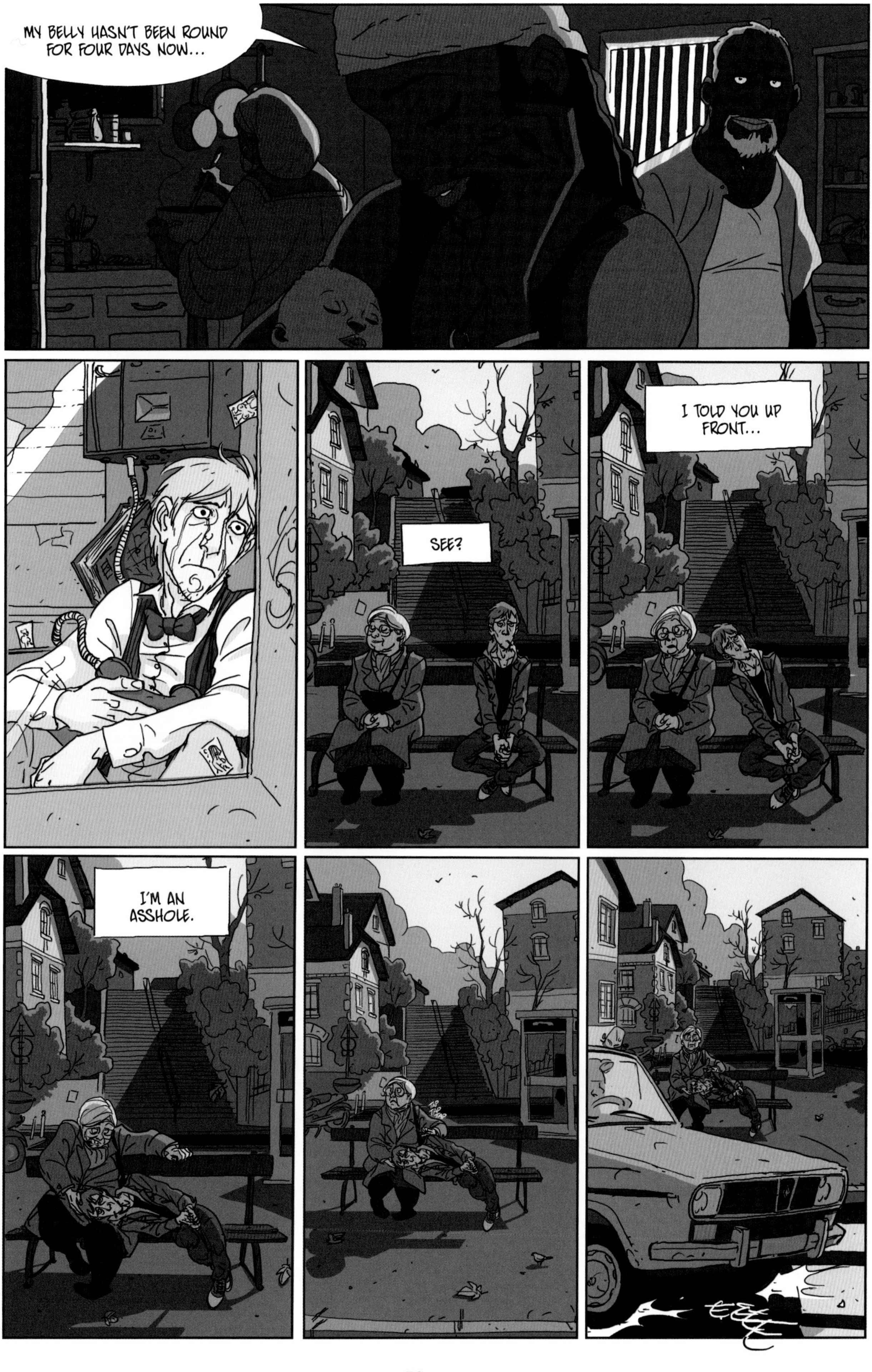
MY BELLY HASN'T BEEN ROUND FOR FOUR DAYS NOW...
SEE?
I TOLD YOU UP FRONT...
I'M AN ASSHOLE.

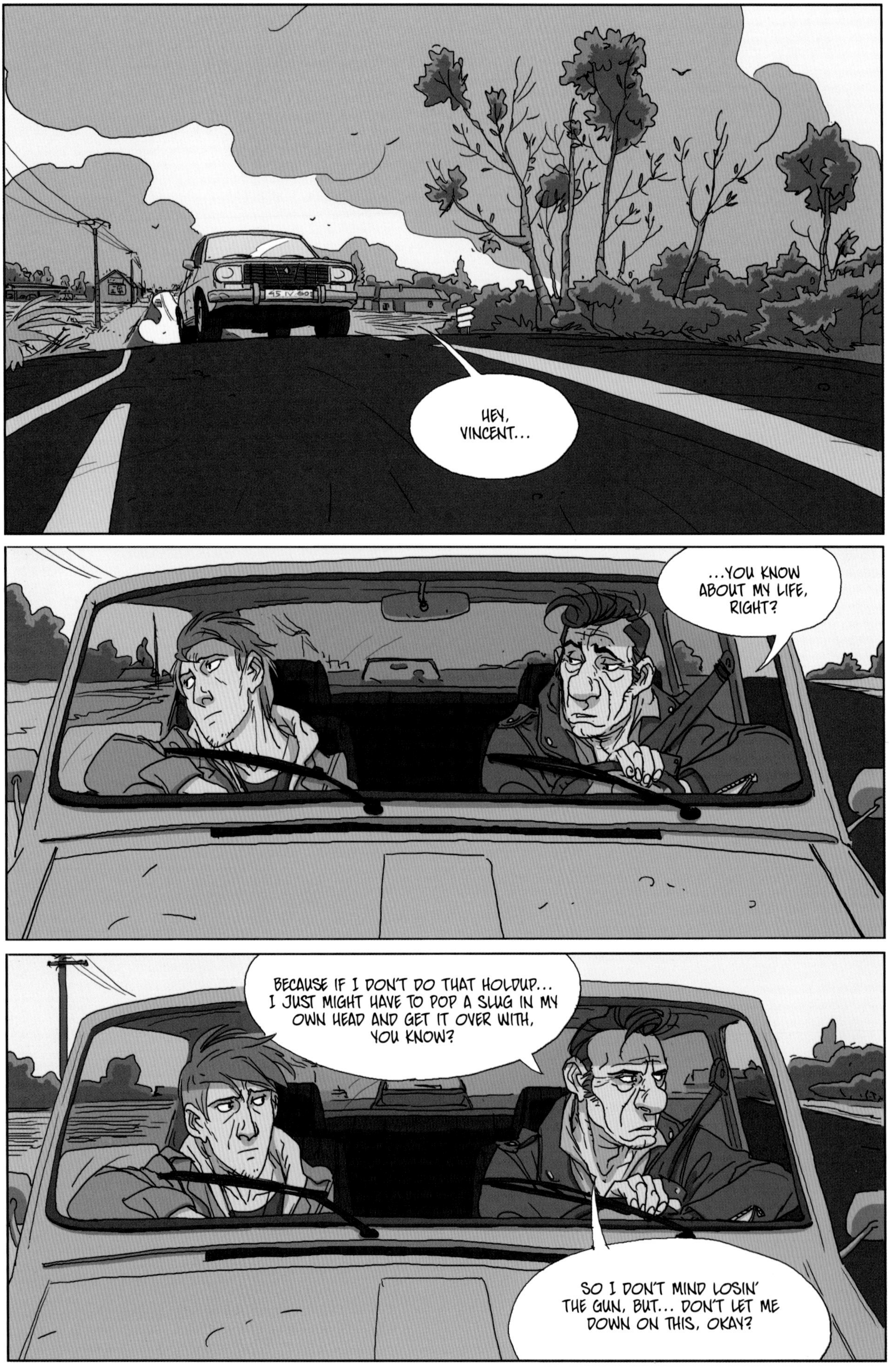
HEY, VINCENT...
...YOU KNOW ABOUT MY LIFE, RIGHT?
BECAUSE IF I DON'T DO THAT HOLDUP... I JUST MIGHT HAVE TO POP A SLUG IN MY OWN HEAD AND GET IT OVER WITH, YOU KNOW?
SO I DON'T MIND LOSIN' THE GUN, BUT... DON'T LET ME DOWN ON THIS, OKAY?

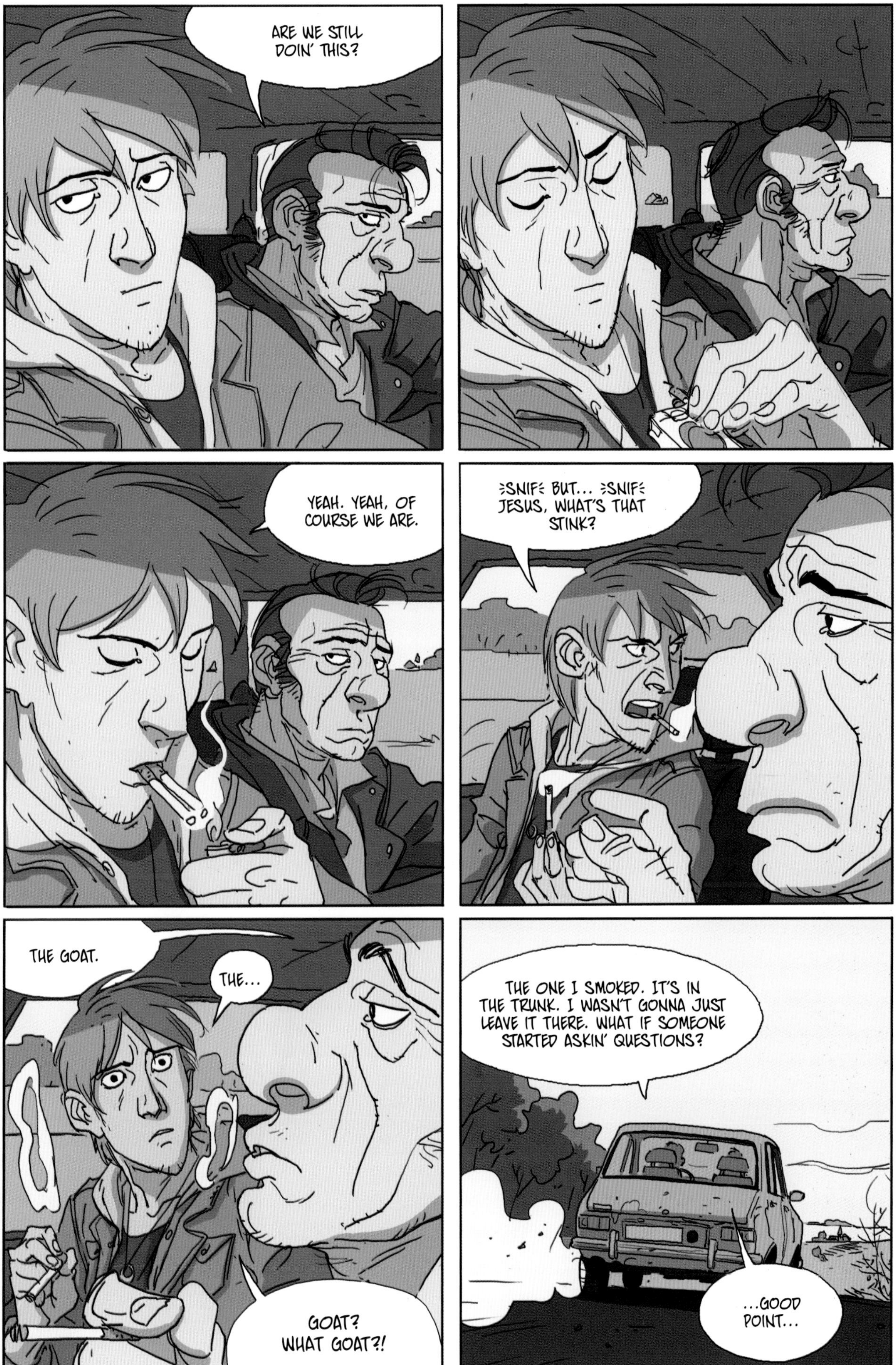
ARE WE STILL DOIN' THIS?
YEAH. YEAH, OF COURSE WE ARE.
≶SNIF≶ BUT... ≶SNIF≶ JESUS, WHAT'S THAT STINK?
THE GOAT.
THE...
GOAT? WHAT GOAT?!
THE ONE I SMOKED. IT'S IN THE TRUNK. I WASN'T GONNA JUST LEAVE IT THERE. WHAT IF SOMEONE STARTED ASKIN' QUESTIONS?
...GOOD POINT...

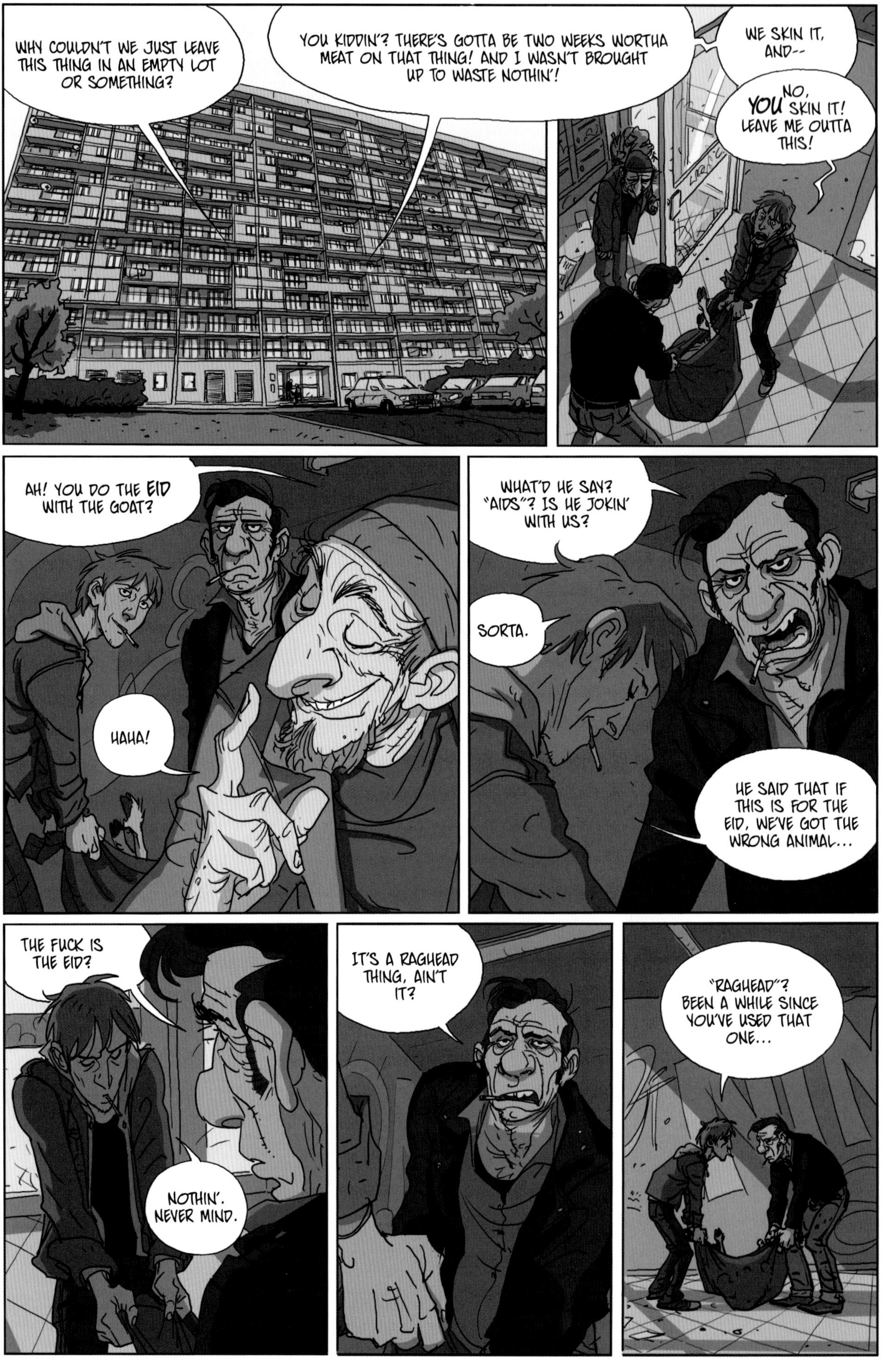
WHY COULDN'T WE JUST LEAVE THIS THING IN AN EMPTY LOT OR SOMETHING?
YOU KIDDIN'? THERE'S GOTTA BE TWO WEEKS WORTHA MEAT ON THAT THING! AND I WASN'T BROUGHT UP TO WASTE NOTHIN'!
WE SKIN IT, AND--
NO, YOU SKIN IT! LEAVE ME OUTTA THIS!
AH! YOU DO THE EID WITH THE GOAT?
HAHA!
WHAT'D HE SAY? "AIDS"? IS HE JOKIN' WITH US?
SORTA.
HE SAID THAT IF THIS IS FOR THE EID, WE'VE GOT THE WRONG ANIMAL...
THE FUCK IS THE EID?
NOTHIN'. NEVER MIND.
IT'S A RAGHEAD THING, AIN'T IT?
"RAGHEAD"? BEEN A WHILE SINCE YOU'VE USED THAT ONE...

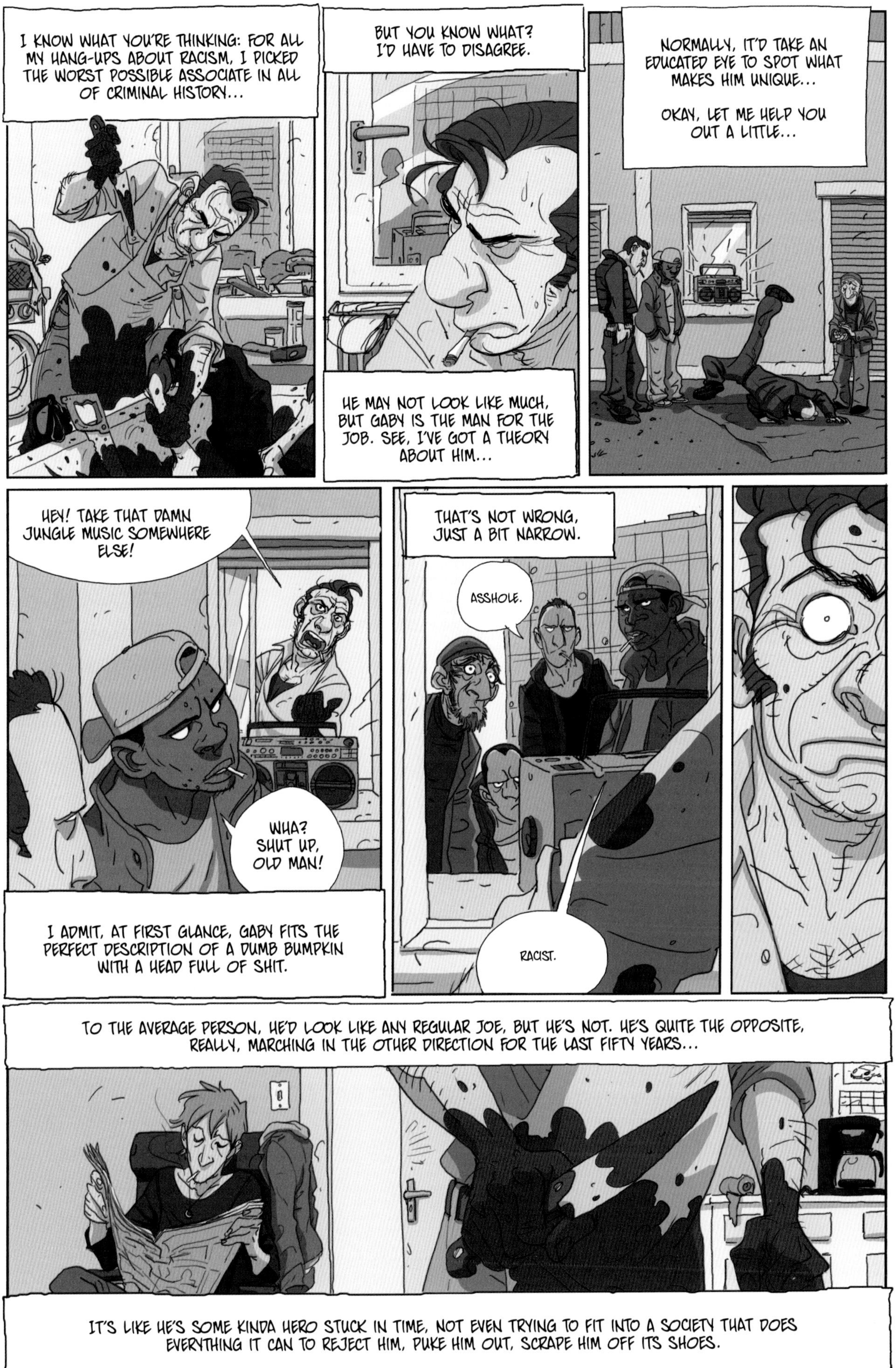
I KNOW WHAT YOU'RE THINKING: FOR ALL MY HANG-UPS ABOUT RACISM, I PICKED THE WORST POSSIBLE ASSOCIATE IN ALL OF CRIMINAL HISTORY...
BUT YOU KNOW WHAT? I'D HAVE TO DISAGREE.
HE MAY NOT LOOK LIKE MUCH, BUT GABY IS THE MAN FOR THE JOB. SEE, I'VE GOT A THEORY ABOUT HIM...
NORMALLY, IT'D TAKE AN EDUCATED EYE TO SPOT WHAT MAKES HIM UNIQUE...
OKAY, LET ME HELP YOU OUT A LITTLE...
HEY! TAKE THAT DAMN JUNGLE MUSIC SOMEWHERE ELSE!
WHA? SHUT UP, OLD MAN!
I ADMIT, AT FIRST GLANCE, GABY FITS THE PERFECT DESCRIPTION OF A DUMB BUMPKIN WITH A HEAD FULL OF SHIT.
THAT'S NOT WRONG, JUST A BIT NARROW.
ASSHOLE.
RACIST.
TO THE AVERAGE PERSON, HE'D LOOK LIKE ANY REGULAR JOE, BUT HE'S NOT. HE'S QUITE THE OPPOSITE, REALLY, MARCHING IN THE OTHER DIRECTION FOR THE LAST FIFTY YEARS...
IT'S LIKE HE'S SOME KINDA HERO STUCK IN TIME, NOT EVEN TRYING TO FIT INTO A SOCIETY THAT DOES EVERYTHING IT CAN TO REJECT HIM, PUKE HIM OUT, SCRAPE HIM OFF ITS SHOES.

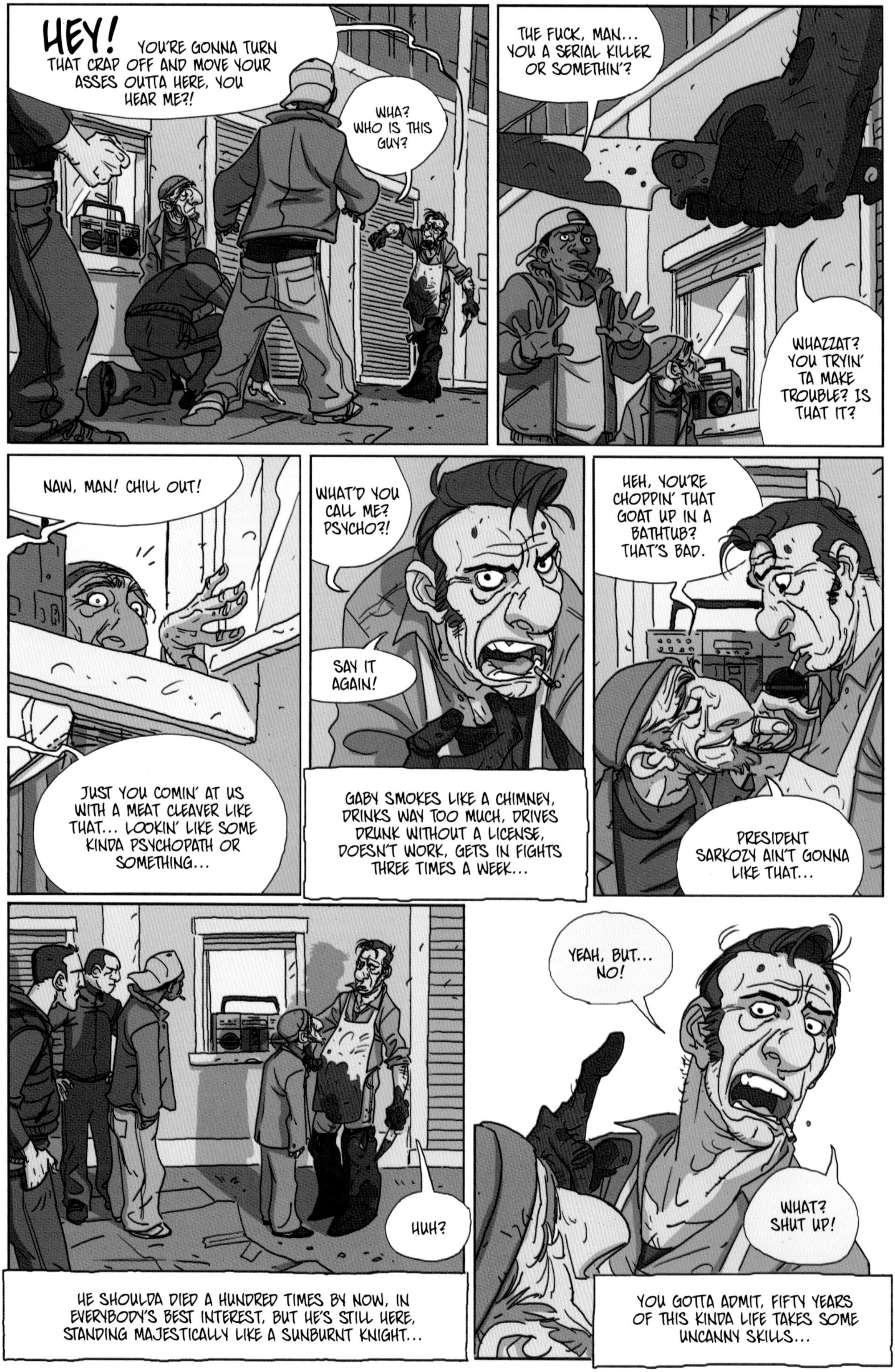
HEY! YOU'RE GONNA TURN THAT CRAP OFF AND MOVE YOUR ASSES OUTTA HERE, YOU HEAR ME?!
WHA? WHO IS THIS GUY?
THE FUCK, MAN... YOU A SERIAL KILLER OR SOMETHIN'?
WHAZZAT? YOU TRYIN' TA MAKE TROUBLE? IS THAT IT?
NAW, MAN! CHILL OUT!
JUST YOU COMIN' AT US WITH A MEAT CLEAVER LIKE THAT... LOOKIN' LIKE SOME KINDA PSYCHOPATH OR SOMETHING...
WHAT'D YOU CALL ME? PSYCHO?!
SAY IT AGAIN!
GABY SMOKES LIKE A CHIMNEY, DRINKS WAY TOO MUCH, DRIVES DRUNK WITHOUT A LICENSE, DOESN'T WORK, GETS IN FIGHTS THREE TIMES A WEEK...
HEH, YOU'RE CHOPPIN' THAT GOAT UP IN A BATHTUB? THAT'S BAD.
PRESIDENT SARKOZY AIN'T GONNA LIKE THAT...
HUH?
HE SHOULDA DIED A HUNDRED TIMES BY NOW, IN EVERYBODY'S BEST INTEREST, BUT HE'S STILL HERE, STANDING MAJESTICALLY LIKE A SUNBURNT KNIGHT...
YEAH, BUT... NO!
WHAT? SHUT UP!
YOU GOTTA ADMIT, FIFTY YEARS OF THIS KINDA LIFE TAKES SOME UNCANNY SKILLS...

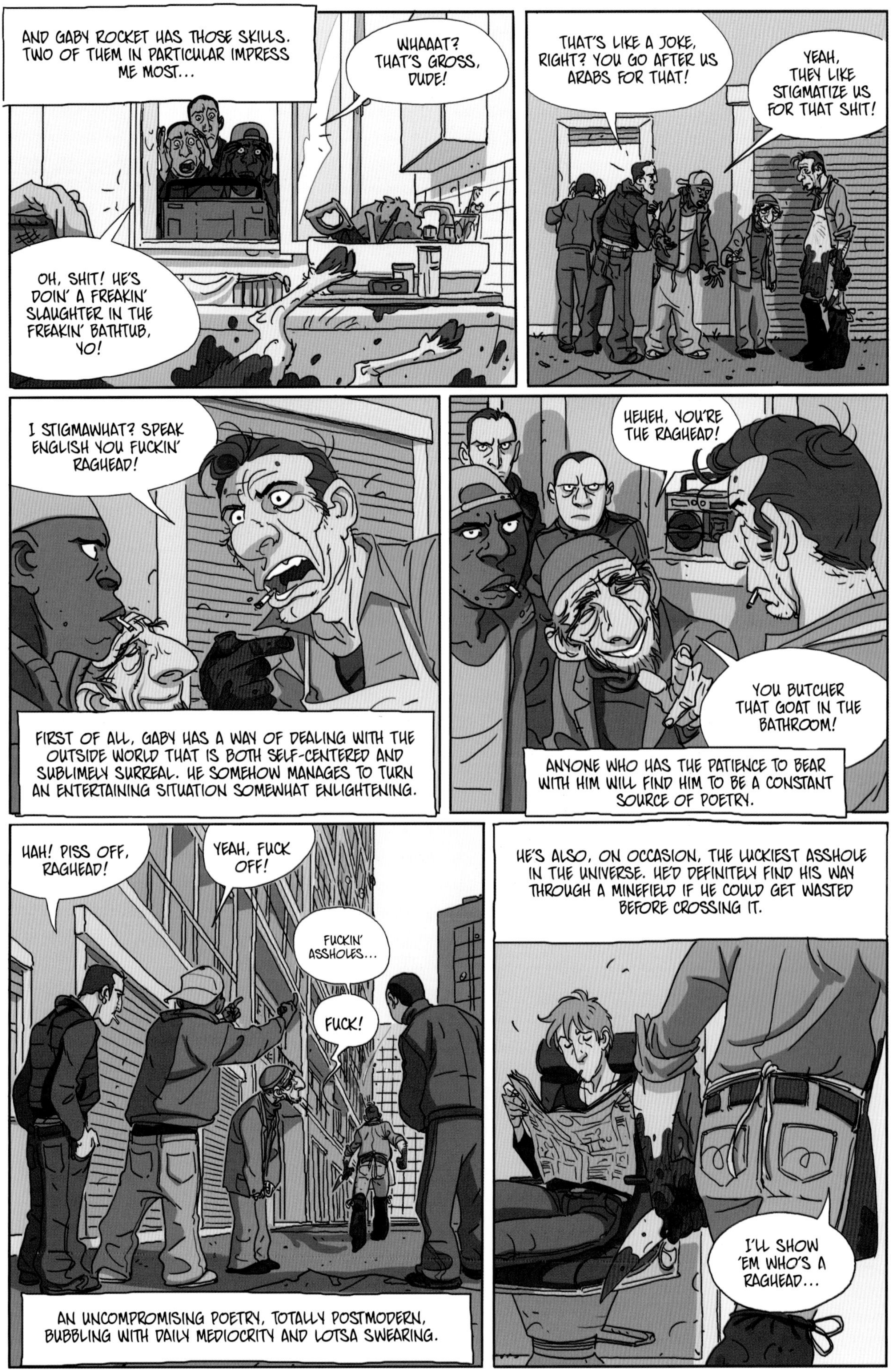
AND GABY ROCKET HAS THOSE SKILLS. TWO OF THEM IN PARTICULAR IMPRESS ME MOST...
WHAAAT? THAT'S GROSS, DUDE!
OH, SHIT! HE'S DOIN' A FREAKIN' SLAUGHTER IN THE FREAKIN' BATHTUB, YO!
THAT'S LIKE A JOKE, RIGHT? YOU GO AFTER US ARABS FOR THAT!
YEAH, THEY LIKE STIGMATIZE US FOR THAT SHIT!
I STIGMAWHAT? SPEAK ENGLISH YOU FUCKIN' RAGHEAD!
FIRST OF ALL, GABY HAS A WAY OF DEALING WITH THE OUTSIDE WORLD THAT IS BOTH SELF-CENTERED AND SUBLIMELY SURREAL. HE SOMEHOW MANAGES TO TURN AN ENTERTAINING SITUATION SOMEWHAT ENLIGHTENING.
HEHEH, YOU'RE THE RAGHEAD!
YOU BUTCHER THAT GOAT IN THE BATHROOM!
ANYONE WHO HAS THE PATIENCE TO BEAR WITH HIM WILL FIND HIM TO BE A CONSTANT SOURCE OF POETRY.
HAH! PISS OFF, RAGHEAD!
YEAH, FUCK OFF!
FUCKIN' ASSHOLES...
FUCK!
AN UNCOMPROMISING POETRY, TOTALLY POSTMODERN, BUBBLING WITH DAILY MEDIOCRITY AND LOTSA SWEARING.
HE'S ALSO, ON OCCASION, THE LUCKIEST ASSHOLE IN THE UNIVERSE. HE'D DEFINITELY FIND HIS WAY THROUGH A MINEFIELD IF HE COULD GET WASTED BEFORE CROSSING IT.
I'LL SHOW 'EM WHO'S A RAGHEAD...

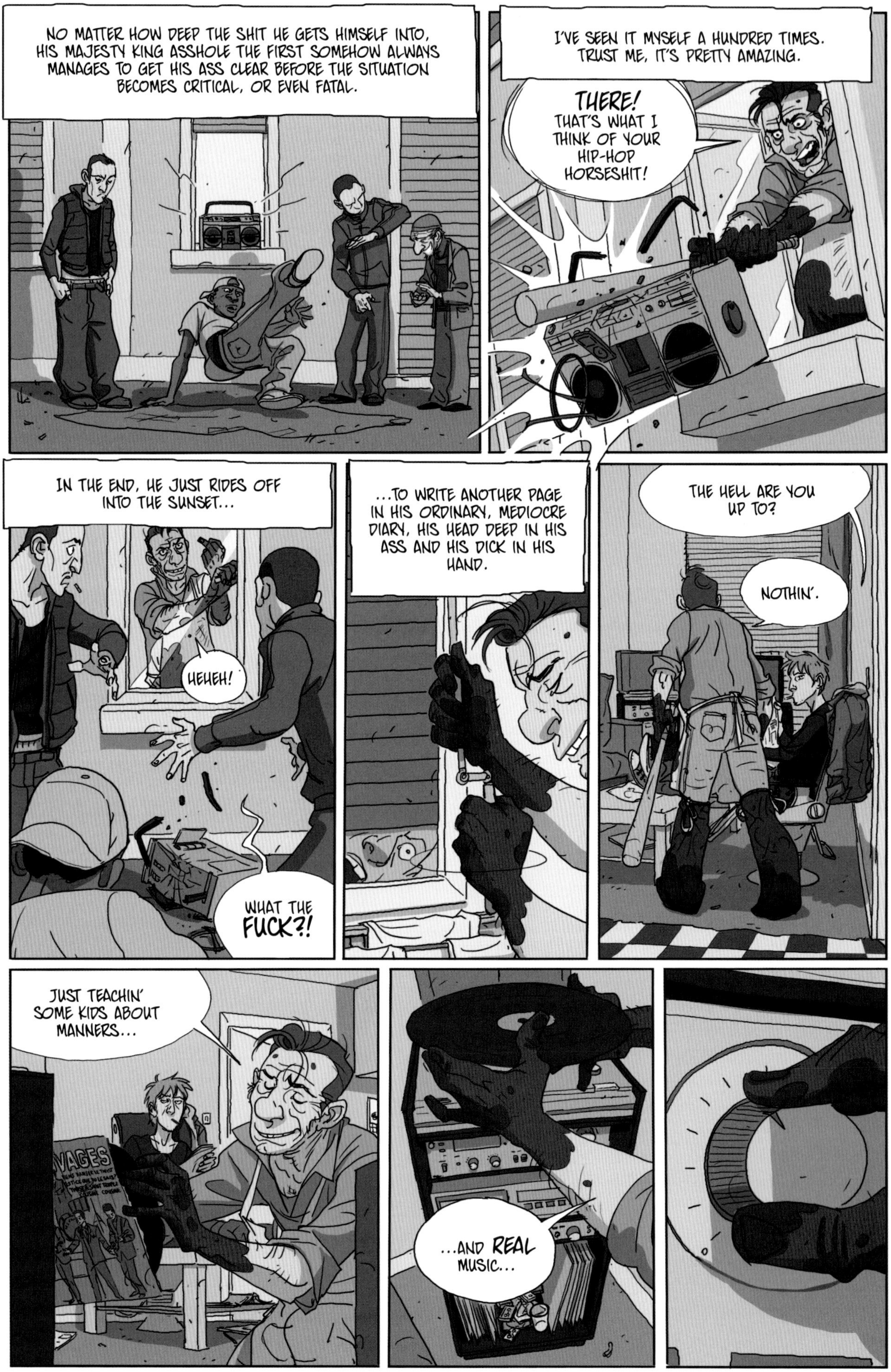
NO MATTER HOW DEEP THE SHIT HE GETS HIMSELF INTO, HIS MAJESTY KING ASSHOLE THE FIRST SOMEHOW ALWAYS MANAGES TO GET HIS ASS CLEAR BEFORE THE SITUATION BECOMES CRITICAL, OR EVEN FATAL.
I'VE SEEN IT MYSELF A HUNDRED TIMES. TRUST ME, IT'S PRETTY AMAZING.
THERE! THAT'S WHAT I THINK OF YOUR HIP-HOP HORSESHIT!
IN THE END, HE JUST RIDES OFF INTO THE SUNSET...
HEHEH!
WHAT THE FUCK?!
...TO WRITE ANOTHER PAGE IN HIS ORDINARY, MEDIOCRE DIARY, HIS HEAD DEEP IN HIS ASS AND HIS DICK IN HIS HAND.
THE HELL ARE YOU UP TO?
NOTHIN'.
JUST TEACHIN' SOME KIDS ABOUT MANNERS...
...AND REAL MUSIC...

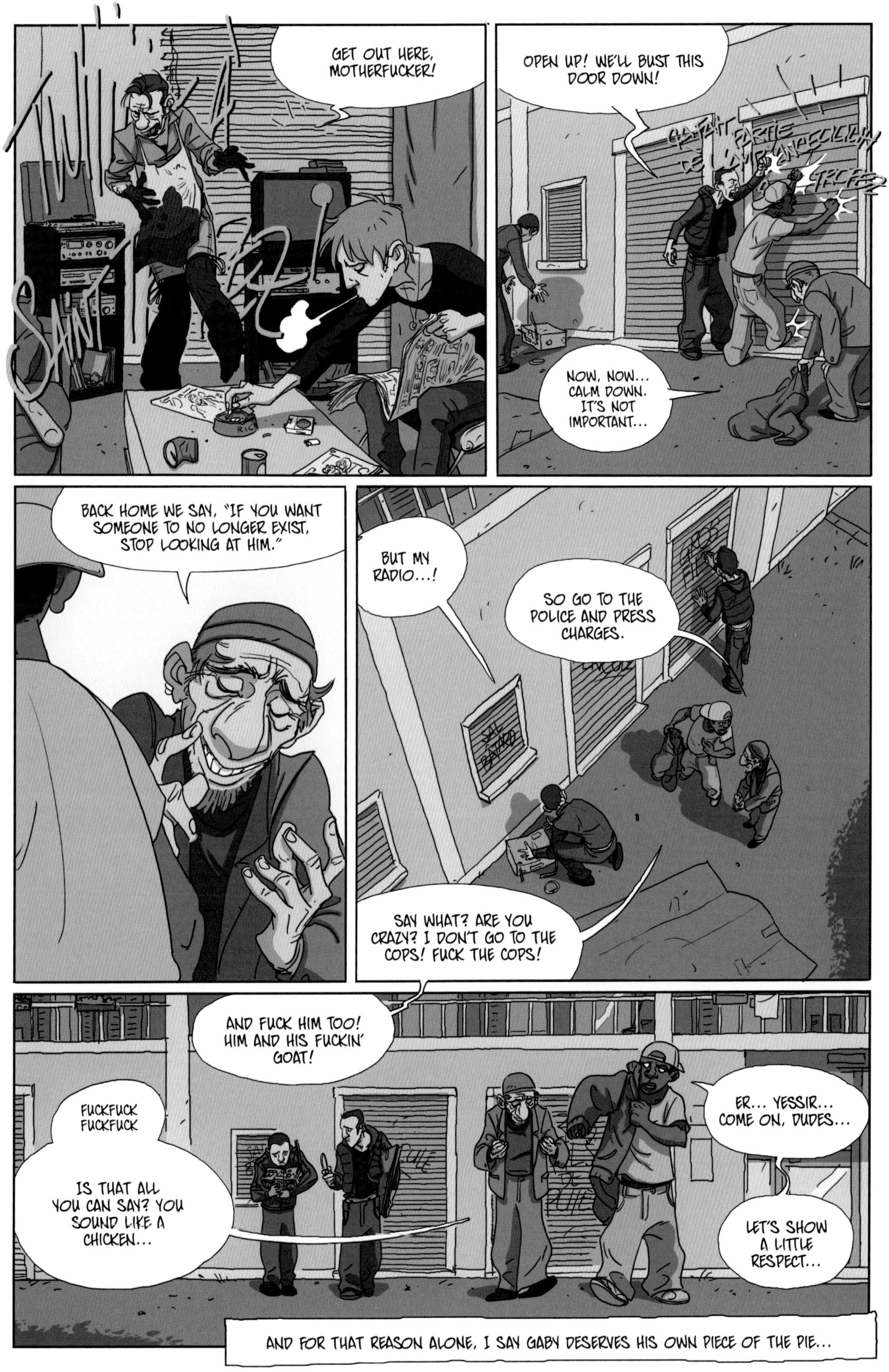
GET OUT HERE, MOTHERFUCKER!
TWIIIIIIIIII
SAINT-TROPEZ!
OPEN UP! WE'LL BUST THIS DOOR DOWN!
NOW, NOW... CALM DOWN. IT'S NOT IMPORTANT...
BACK HOME WE SAY, "IF YOU WANT SOMEONE TO NO LONGER EXIST, STOP LOOKING AT HIM."
BUT MY RADIO...!
SO GO TO THE POLICE AND PRESS CHARGES.
SAY WHAT? ARE YOU CRAZY? I DON'T GO TO THE COPS! FUCK THE COPS!
AND FUCK HIM TOO! HIM AND HIS FUCKIN' GOAT!
FUCKFUCK FUCKFUCK
IS THAT ALL YOU CAN SAY? YOU SOUND LIKE A CHICKEN...
ER... YESSIR... COME ON, DUDES...
LET'S SHOW A LITTLE RESPECT...
AND FOR THAT REASON ALONE, I SAY GABY DESERVES HIS OWN PIECE OF THE PIE...

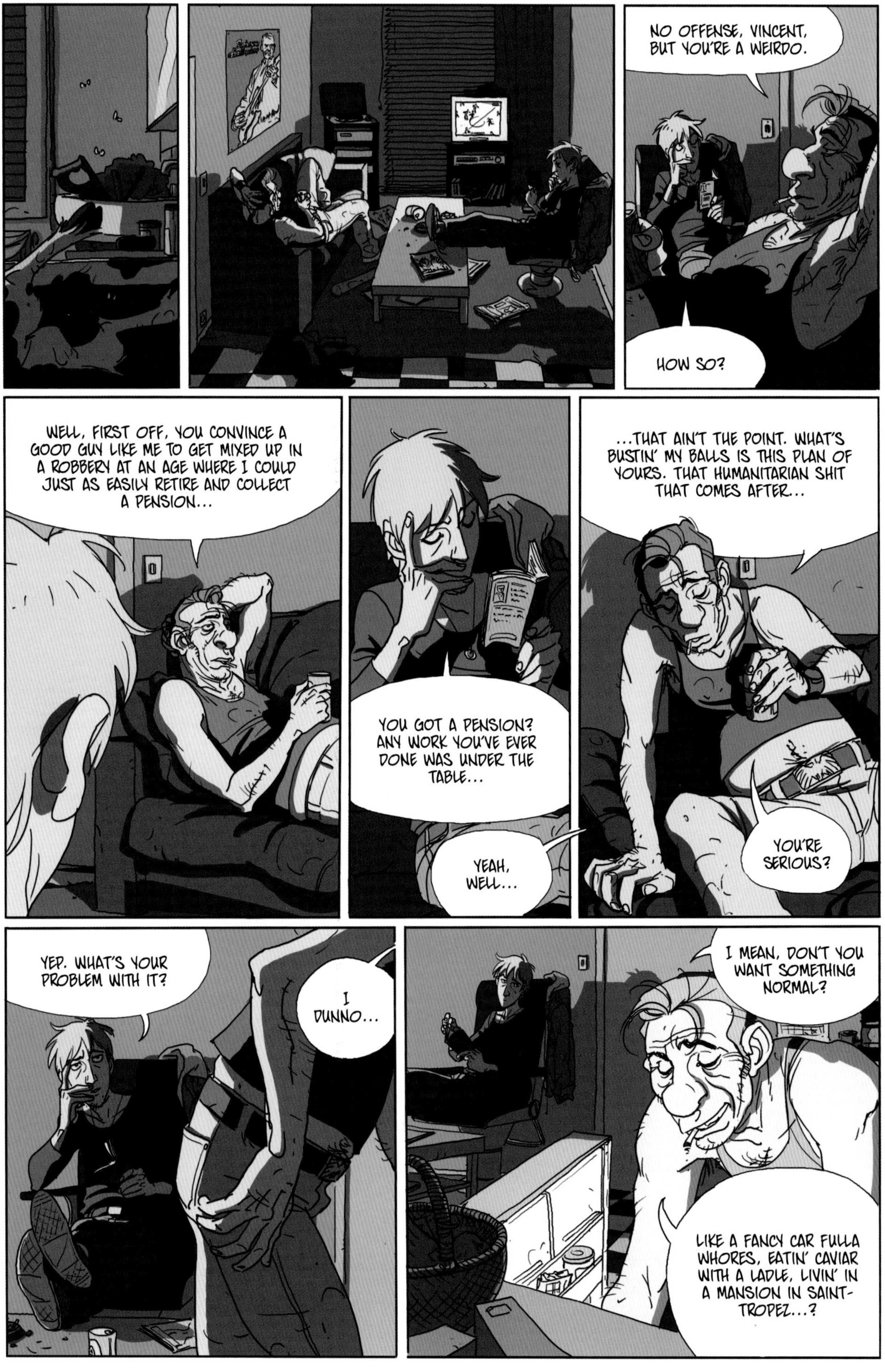
NO OFFENSE, VINCENT, BUT YOU'RE A WEIRDO.
HOW SO?
WELL, FIRST OFF, YOU CONVINCE A GOOD GUY LIKE ME TO GET MIXED UP IN A ROBBERY AT AN AGE WHERE I COULD JUST AS EASILY RETIRE AND COLLECT A PENSION...
YOU GOT A PENSION? ANY WORK YOU'VE EVER DONE WAS UNDER THE TABLE...
YEAH, WELL...
...THAT AIN'T THE POINT. WHAT'S BUSTIN' MY BALLS IS THIS PLAN OF YOURS. THAT HUMANITARIAN SHIT THAT COMES AFTER...
YOU'RE SERIOUS?
YEP. WHAT'S YOUR PROBLEM WITH IT?
I DUNNO...
I MEAN, DON'T YOU WANT SOMETHING NORMAL?
LIKE A FANCY CAR FULLA WHORES, EATIN' CAVIAR WITH A LADLE, LIVIN' IN A MANSION IN SAINT-TROPEZ...?

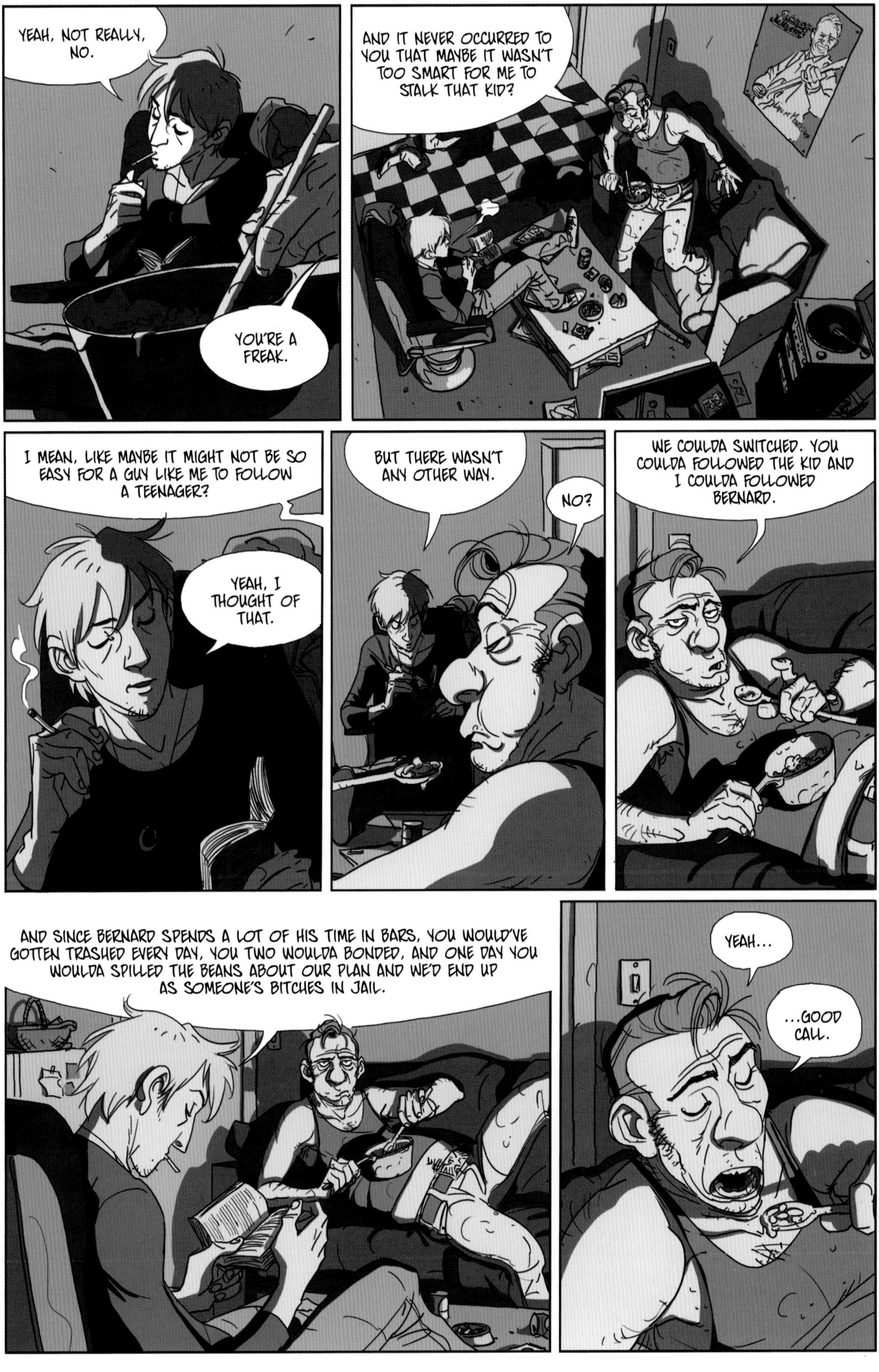
YEAH, NOT REALLY, NO.
YOU'RE A FREAK.
AND IT NEVER OCCURRED TO YOU THAT MAYBE IT WASN'T TOO SMART FOR ME TO STALK THAT KID?
I MEAN, LIKE MAYBE IT MIGHT NOT BE SO EASY FOR A GUY LIKE ME TO FOLLOW A TEENAGER?
YEAH, I THOUGHT OF THAT.
BUT THERE WASN'T ANY OTHER WAY.
NO?
WE COULDA SWITCHED. YOU COULDA FOLLOWED THE KID AND I COULDA FOLLOWED BERNARD.
AND SINCE BERNARD SPENDS A LOT OF HIS TIME IN BARS, YOU WOULD'VE GOTTEN TRASHED EVERY DAY, YOU TWO WOULDA BONDED, AND ONE DAY YOU WOULDA SPILLED THE BEANS ABOUT OUR PLAN AND WE'D END UP AS SOMEONE'S BITCHES IN JAIL.
YEAH...
...GOOD CALL.

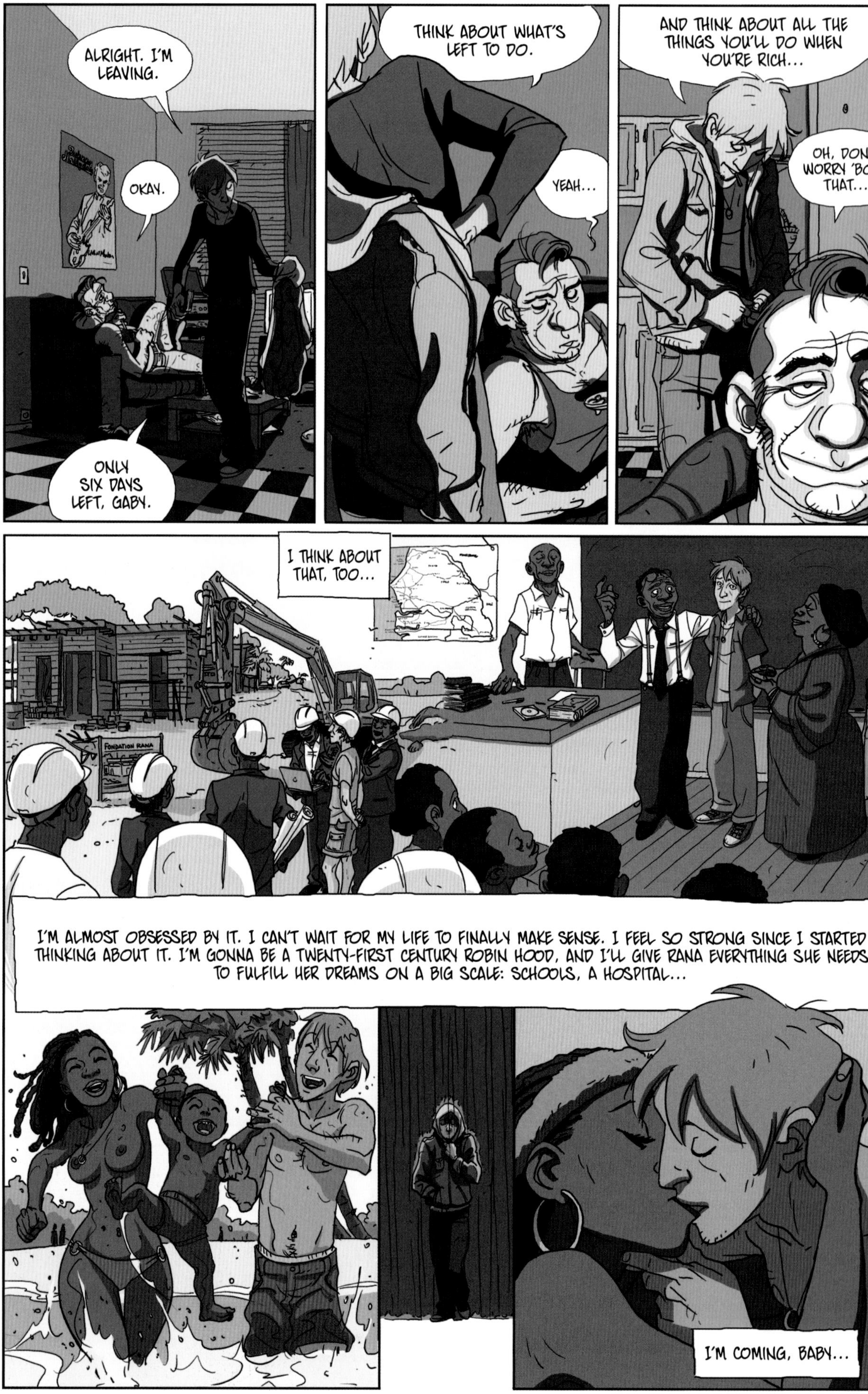
ALRIGHT. I'M LEAVING.
OKAY.
ONLY SIX DAYS LEFT, GABY.
THINK ABOUT WHAT'S LEFT TO DO.
YEAH...
AND THINK ABOUT ALL THE THINGS YOU'LL DO WHEN YOU'RE RICH...
OH, DON'T WORRY 'BOUT THAT...
I THINK ABOUT THAT, TOO...
FONDATION RANA
I'M ALMOST OBSESSED BY IT. I CAN'T WAIT FOR MY LIFE TO FINALLY MAKE SENSE. I FEEL SO STRONG SINCE I STARTED THINKING ABOUT IT. I'M GONNA BE A TWENTY-FIRST CENTURY ROBIN HOOD, AND I'LL GIVE RANA EVERYTHING SHE NEEDS TO FULFILL HER DREAMS ON A BIG SCALE: SCHOOLS, A HOSPITAL...
I'M COMING, BABY...

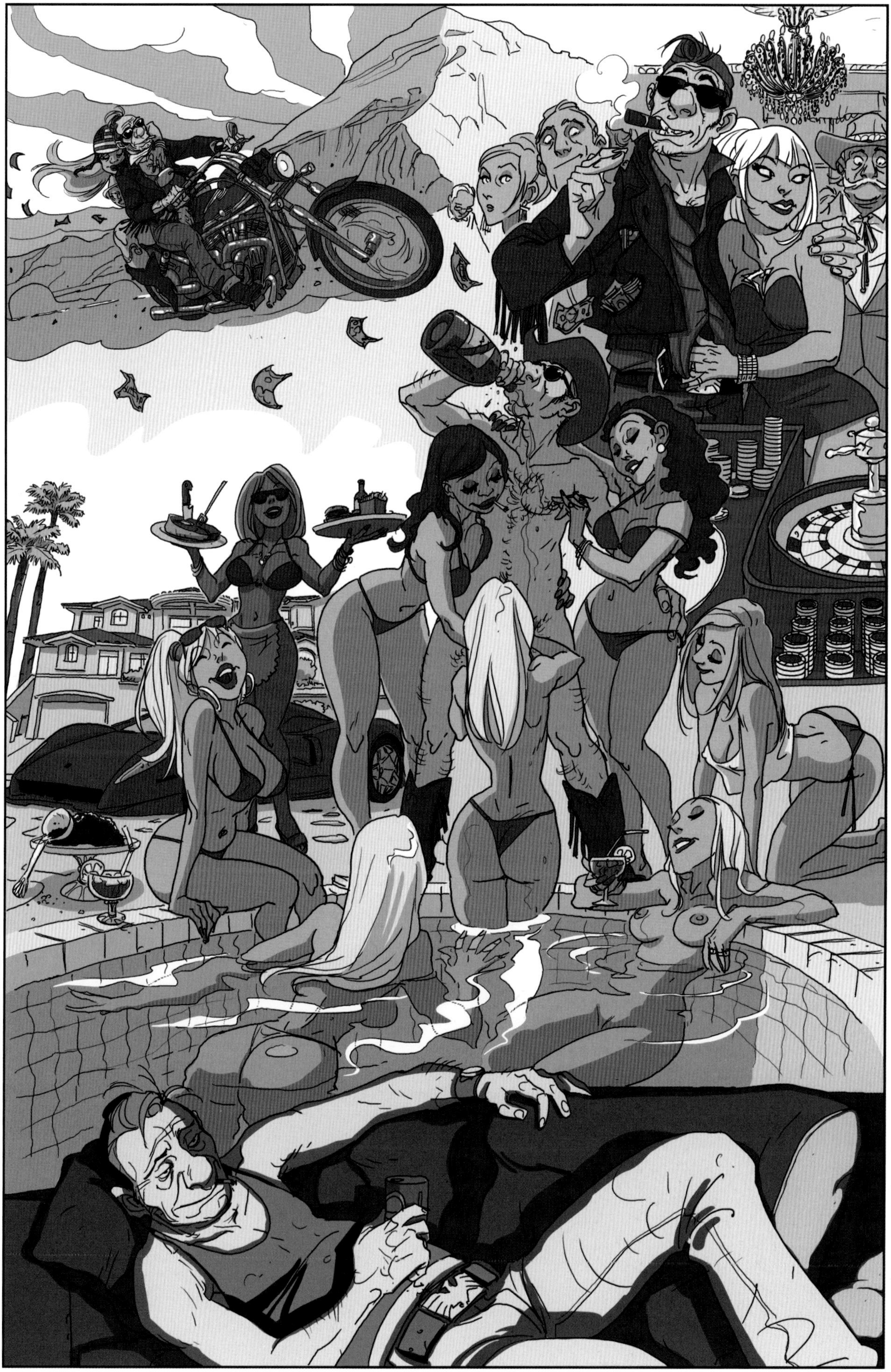

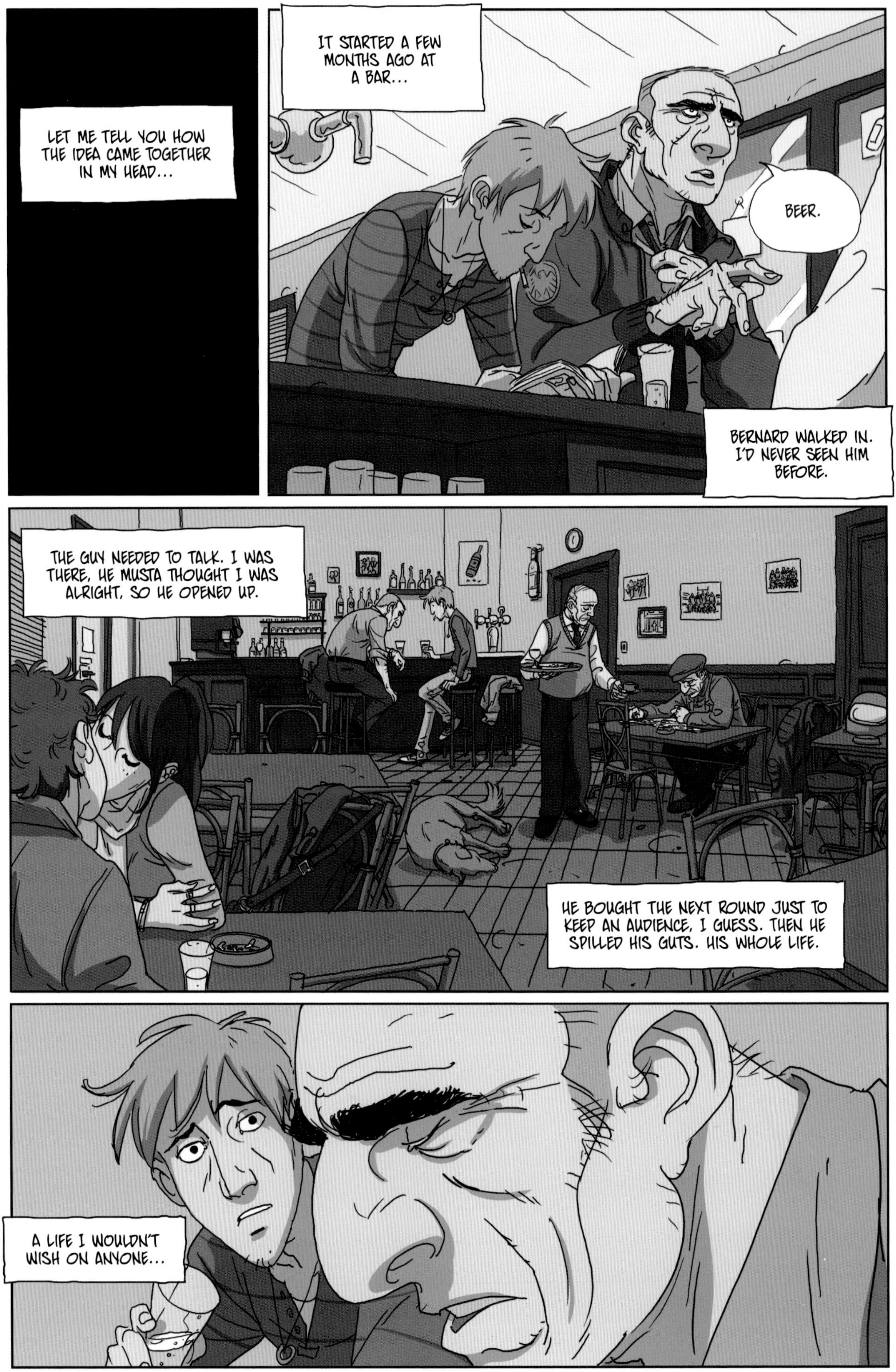

LET ME TELL YOU HOW THE IDEA CAME TOGETHER IN MY HEAD...
IT STARTED A FEW MONTHS AGO AT A BAR...
BEER.
BERNARD WALKED IN. I'D NEVER SEEN HIM BEFORE.
THE GUY NEEDED TO TALK. I WAS THERE, HE MUSTA THOUGHT I WAS ALRIGHT, SO HE OPENED UP.
HE BOUGHT THE NEXT ROUND JUST TO KEEP AN AUDIENCE, I GUESS. THEN HE SPILLED HIS GUTS. HIS WHOLE LIFE.
A LIFE I WOULDN'T WISH ON ANYONE...

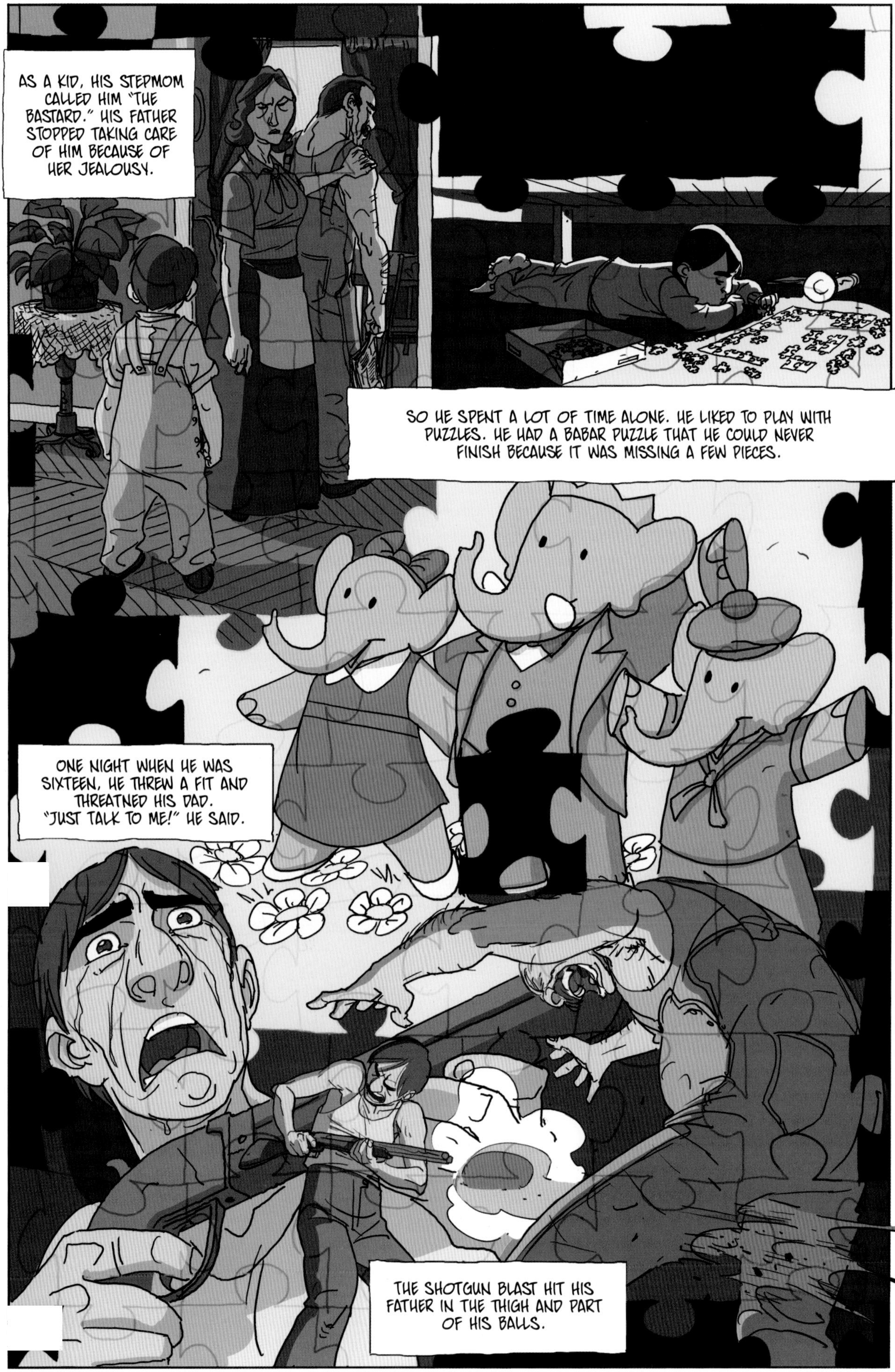
AS A KID, HIS STEPMOM CALLED HIM "THE BASTARD." HIS FATHER STOPPED TAKING CARE OF HIM BECAUSE OF HER JEALOUSY.
SO HE SPENT A LOT OF TIME ALONE. HE LIKED TO PLAY WITH PUZZLES. HE HAD A BABAR PUZZLE THAT HE COULD NEVER FINISH BECAUSE IT WAS MISSING A FEW PIECES.
ONE NIGHT WHEN HE WAS SIXTEEN, HE THREW A FIT AND THREATNED HIS DAD. "JUST TALK TO ME!" HE SAID.
THE SHOTGUN BLAST HIT HIS FATHER IN THE THIGH AND PART OF HIS BALLS.

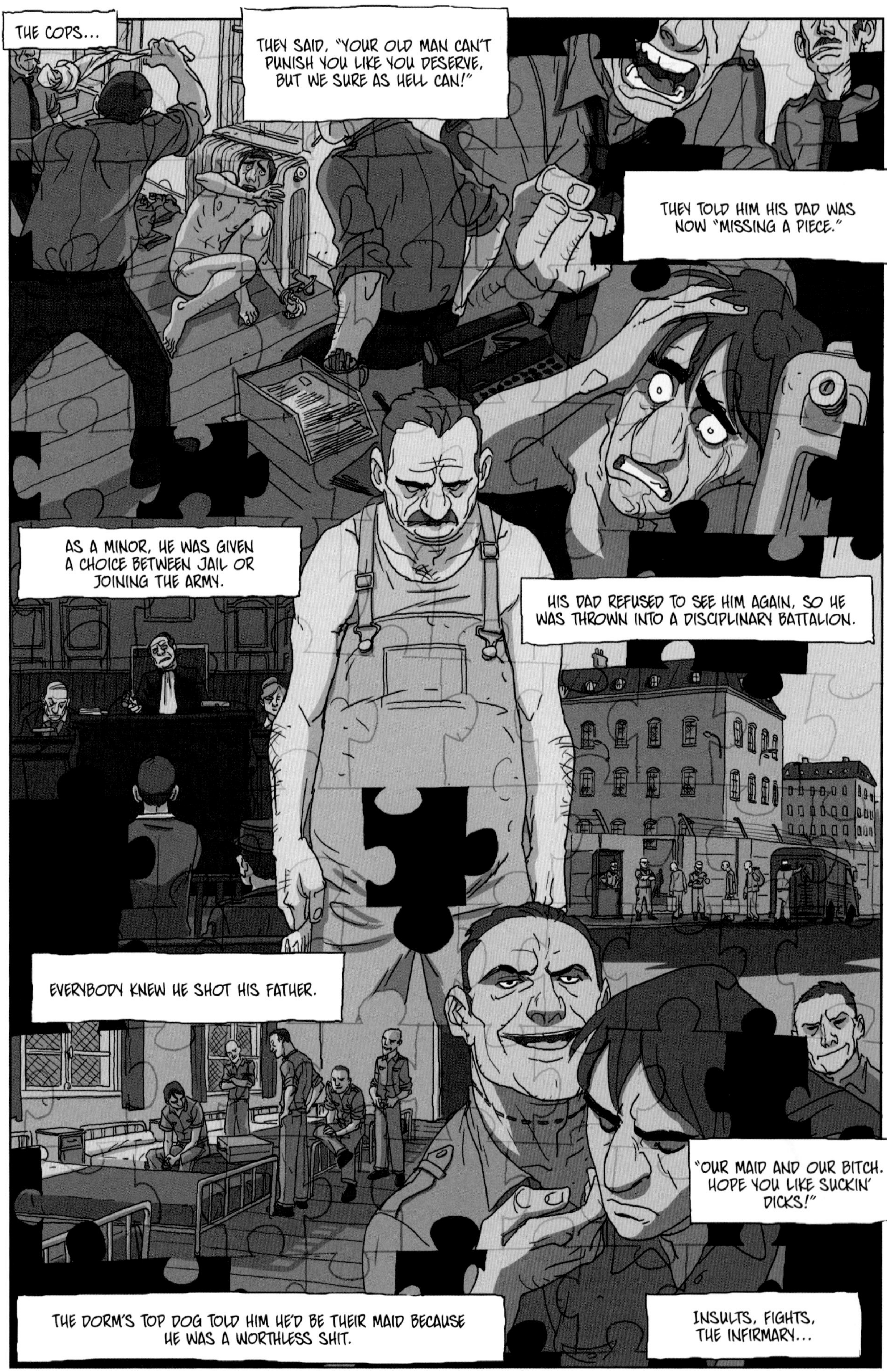
THE COPS...
THEY SAID, "YOUR OLD MAN CAN'T PUNISH YOU LIKE YOU DESERVE, BUT WE SURE AS HELL CAN!"
THEY TOLD HIM HIS DAD WAS NOW "MISSING A PIECE."
AS A MINOR, HE WAS GIVEN A CHOICE BETWEEN JAIL OR JOINING THE ARMY.
HIS DAD REFUSED TO SEE HIM AGAIN, SO HE WAS THROWN INTO A DISCIPLINARY BATTALION.
EVERYBODY KNEW HE SHOT HIS FATHER.
"OUR MAID AND OUR BITCH. HOPE YOU LIKE SUCKIN' DICKS!"
THE DORM'S TOP DOG TOLD HIM HE'D BE THEIR MAID BECAUSE HE WAS A WORTHLESS SHIT.
INSULTS, FIGHTS, THE INFIRMARY...

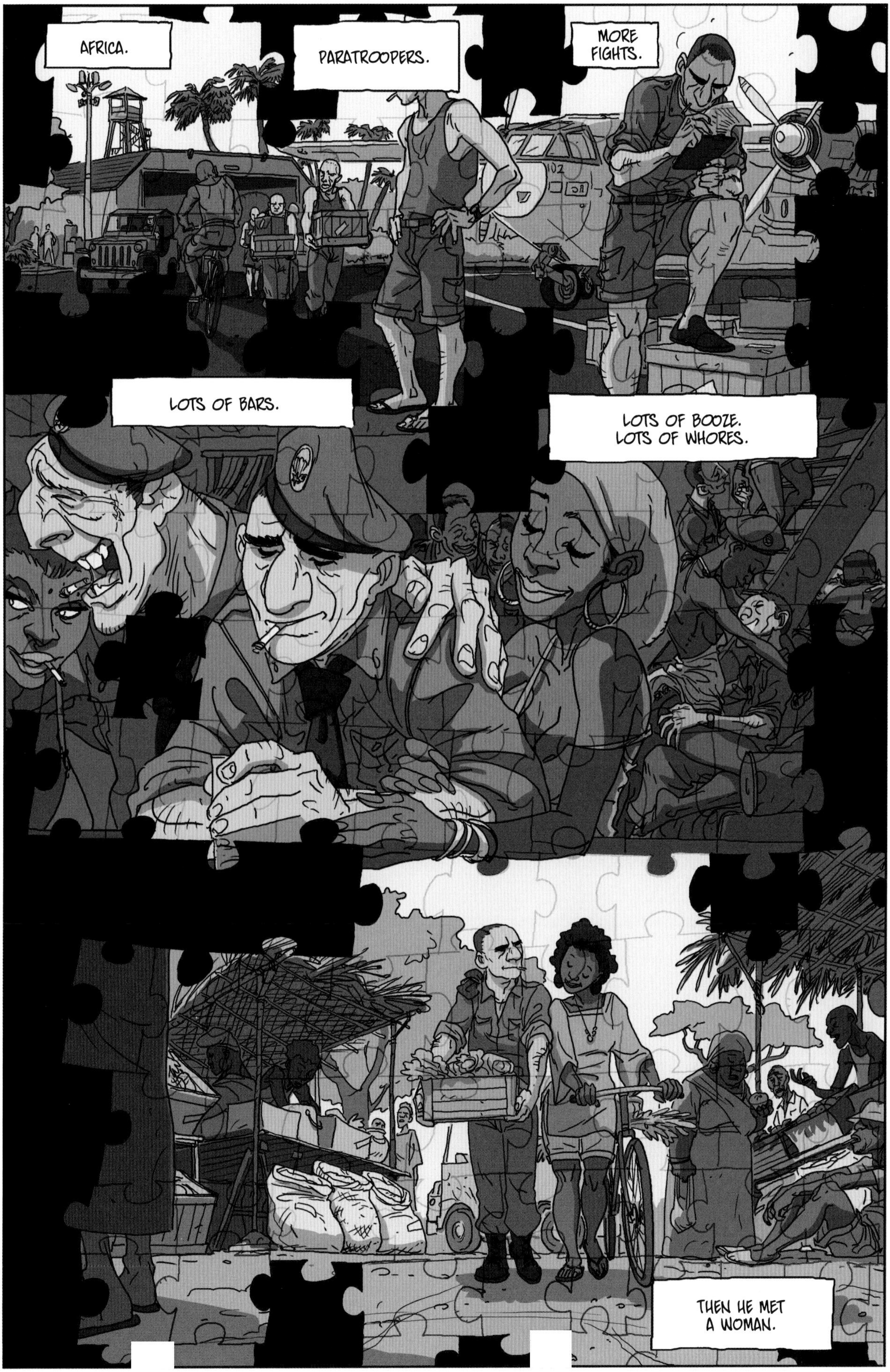
AFRICA.
PARATROOPERS.
MORE FIGHTS.
LOTS OF BARS.
LOTS OF BOOZE. LOTS OF WHORES.
THEN HE MET A WOMAN.

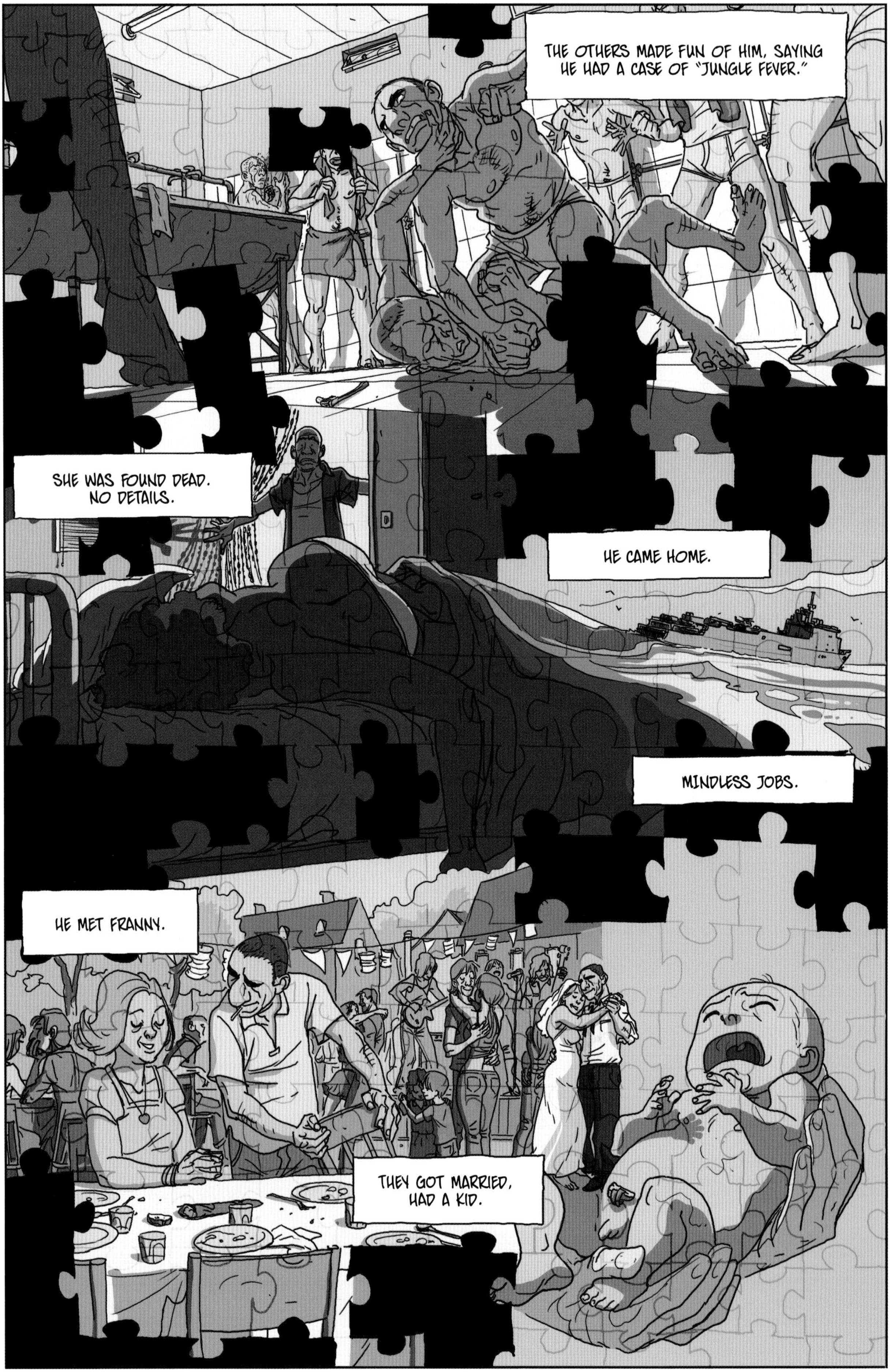
THE OTHERS MADE FUN OF HIM, SAYING HE HAD A CASE OF "JUNGLE FEVER."
SHE WAS FOUND DEAD. NO DETAILS.
HE CAME HOME.
MINDLESS JOBS.
HE MET FRANNY.
THEY GOT MARRIED, HAD A KID.

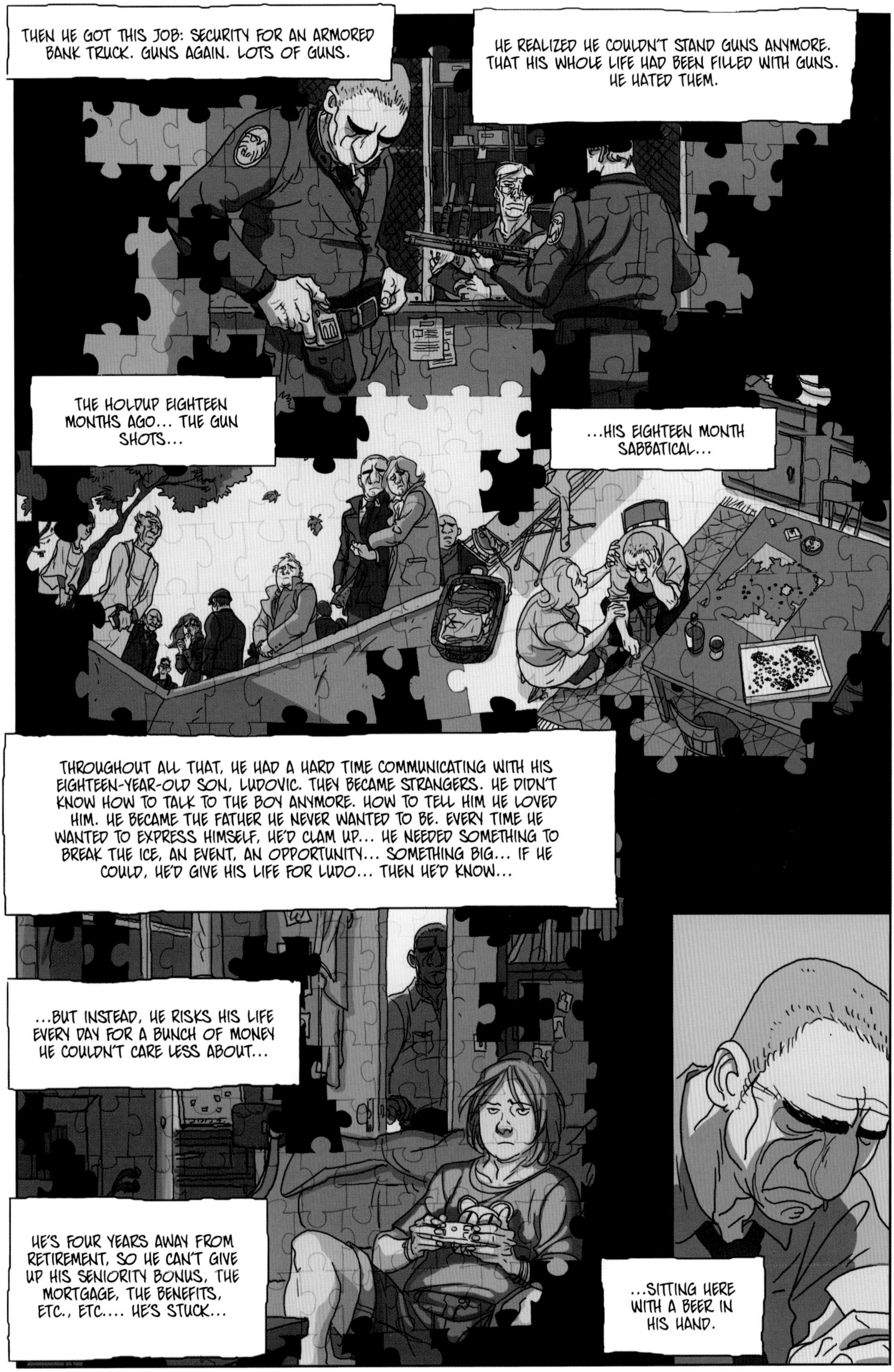
THEN HE GOT THIS JOB: SECURITY FOR AN ARMORED BANK TRUCK. GUNS AGAIN. LOTS OF GUNS.
HE REALIZED HE COULDN'T STAND GUNS ANYMORE. THAT HIS WHOLE LIFE HAD BEEN FILLED WITH GUNS. HE HATED THEM.
THE HOLDUP EIGHTEEN MONTHS AGO... THE GUN SHOTS...
...HIS EIGHTEEN MONTH SABBATICAL...
THROUGHOUT ALL THAT, HE HAD A HARD TIME COMMUNICATING WITH HIS EIGHTEEN-YEAR-OLD SON, LUDOVIC. THEY BECAME STRANGERS. HE DIDN'T KNOW HOW TO TALK TO THE BOY ANYMORE. HOW TO TELL HIM HE LOVED HIM. HE BECAME THE FATHER HE NEVER WANTED TO BE. EVERY TIME HE WANTED TO EXPRESS HIMSELF, HE'D CLAM UP... HE NEEDED SOMETHING TO BREAK THE ICE, AN EVENT, AN OPPORTUNITY... SOMETHING BIG... IF HE COULD, HE'D GIVE HIS LIFE FOR LUDO... THEN HE'D KNOW...
...BUT INSTEAD, HE RISKS HIS LIFE EVERY DAY FOR A BUNCH OF MONEY HE COULDN'T CARE LESS ABOUT...
HE'S FOUR YEARS AWAY FROM RETIREMENT, SO HE CAN'T GIVE UP HIS SENIORITY BONUS, THE MORTGAGE, THE BENEFITS, ETC., ETC.... HE'S STUCK...
...SITTING HERE WITH A BEER IN HIS HAND.

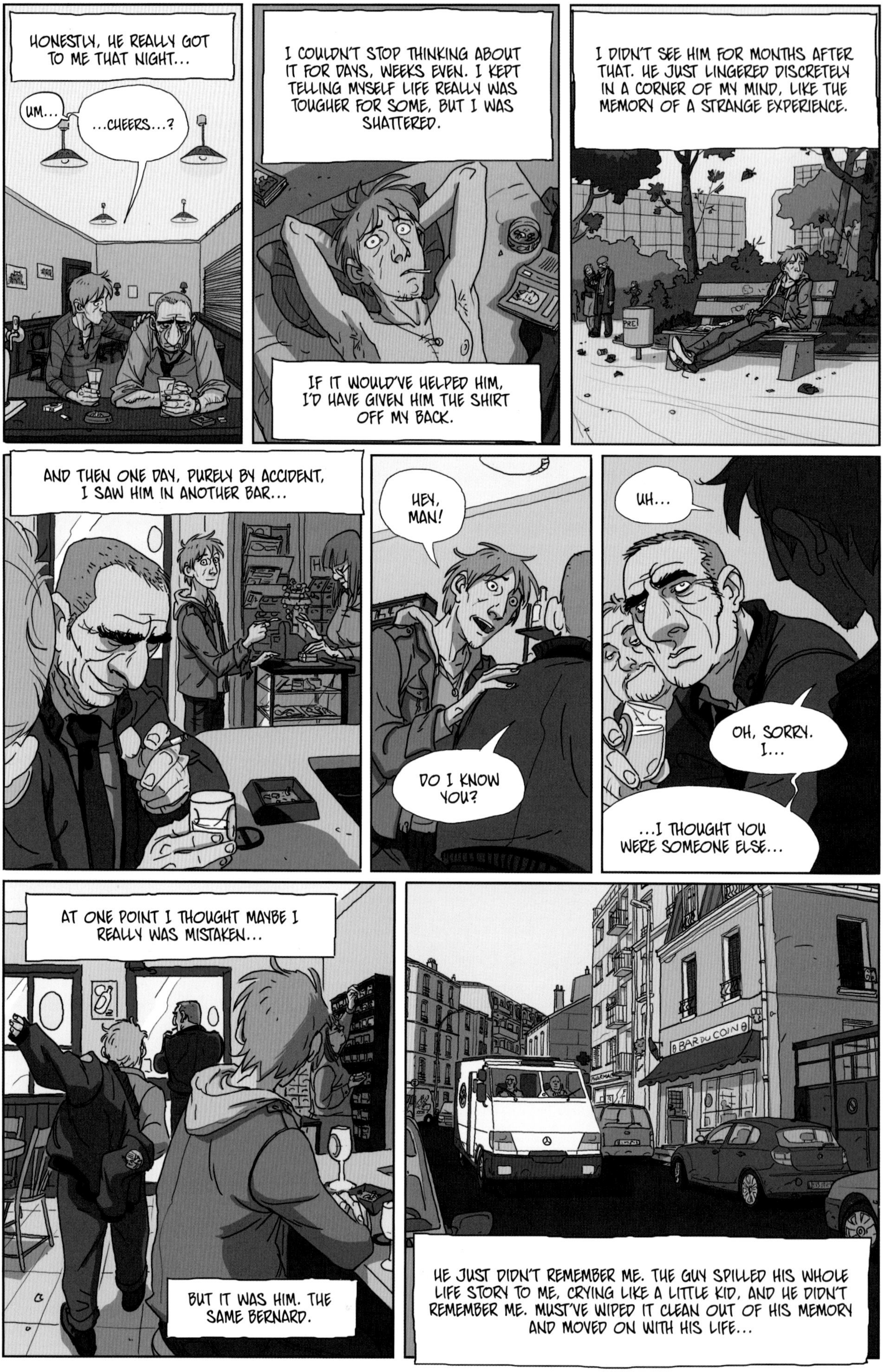
HONESTLY, HE REALLY GOT TO ME THAT NIGHT...
UM...
...CHEERS...?
I COULDN'T STOP THINKING ABOUT IT FOR DAYS, WEEKS EVEN. I KEPT TELLING MYSELF LIFE REALLY WAS TOUGHER FOR SOME, BUT I WAS SHATTERED.
IF IT WOULD'VE HELPED HIM, I'D HAVE GIVEN HIM THE SHIRT OFF MY BACK.
I DIDN'T SEE HIM FOR MONTHS AFTER THAT. HE JUST LINGERED DISCRETELY IN A CORNER OF MY MIND, LIKE THE MEMORY OF A STRANGE EXPERIENCE.
AND THEN ONE DAY, PURELY BY ACCIDENT, I SAW HIM IN ANOTHER BAR...
HEY, MAN!
DO I KNOW YOU?
UH...
OH, SORRY. I...
...I THOUGHT YOU WERE SOMEONE ELSE...
AT ONE POINT I THOUGHT MAYBE I REALLY WAS MISTAKEN...
BUT IT WAS HIM. THE SAME BERNARD.
BAR DU COIN
HE JUST DIDN'T REMEMBER ME. THE GUY SPILLED HIS WHOLE LIFE STORY TO ME, CRYING LIKE A LITTLE KID, AND HE DIDN'T REMEMBER ME. MUST'VE WIPED IT CLEAN OUT OF HIS MEMORY AND MOVED ON WITH HIS LIFE...

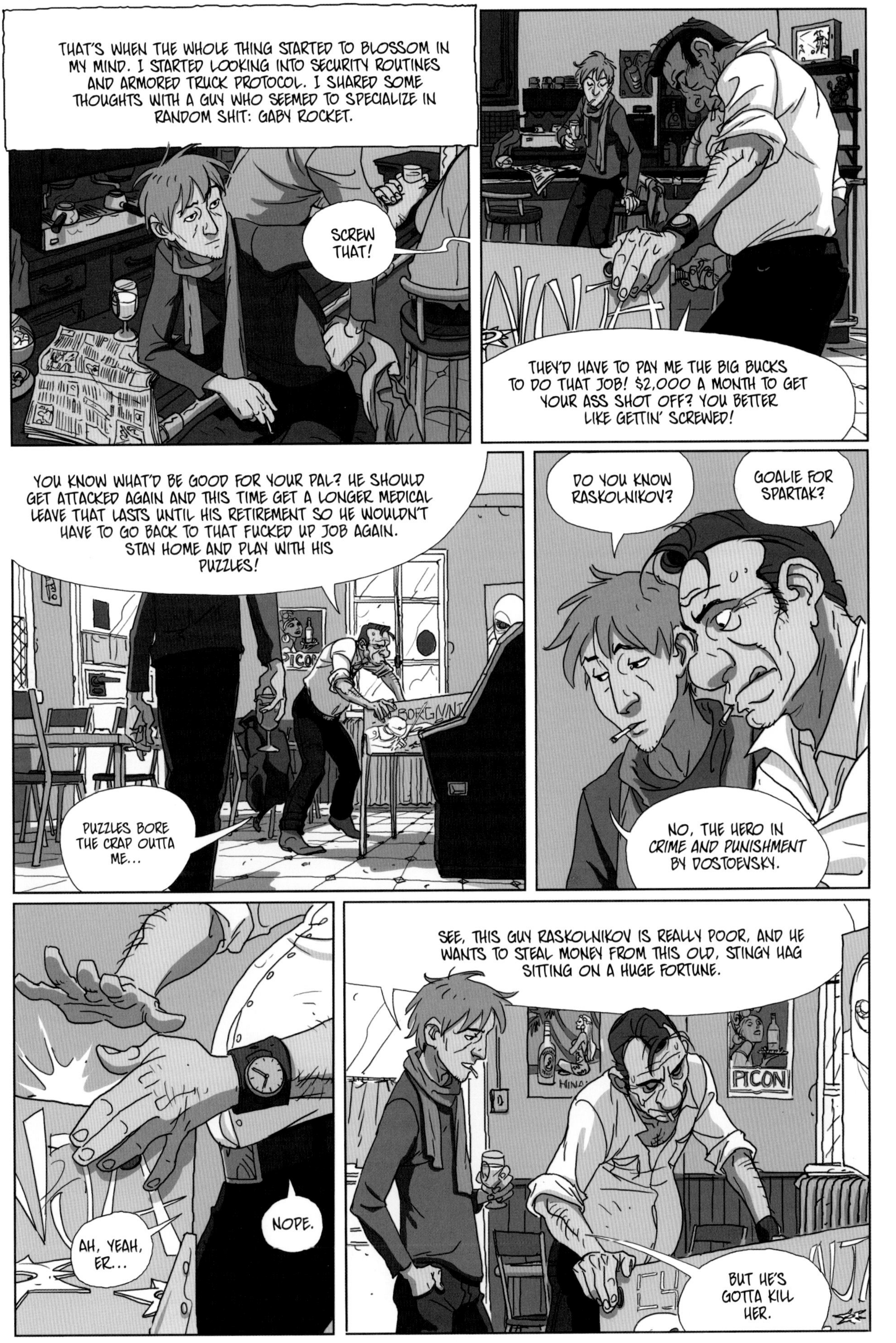
THAT'S WHEN THE WHOLE THING STARTED TO BLOSSOM IN MY MIND. I STARTED LOOKING INTO SECURITY ROUTINES AND ARMORED TRUCK PROTOCOL. I SHARED SOME THOUGHTS WITH A GUY WHO SEEMED TO SPECIALIZE IN RANDOM SHIT: GABY ROCKET.
SCREW THAT!
THEY'D HAVE TO PAY ME THE BIG BUCKS TO DO THAT JOB! $2,000 A MONTH TO GET YOUR ASS SHOT OFF? YOU BETTER LIKE GETTIN' SCREWED!
YOU KNOW WHAT'D BE GOOD FOR YOUR PAL? HE SHOULD GET ATTACKED AGAIN AND THIS TIME GET A LONGER MEDICAL LEAVE THAT LASTS UNTIL HIS RETIREMENT SO HE WOULDN'T HAVE TO GO BACK TO THAT FUCKED UP JOB AGAIN. STAY HOME AND PLAY WITH HIS PUZZLES!
PICON
PUZZLES BORE THE CRAP OUTTA ME...
DO YOU KNOW RASKOLNIKOV?
GOALIE FOR SPARTAK?
NO, THE HERO IN CRIME AND PUNISHMENT BY DOSTOEVSKY.
AH, YEAH, ER...
NOPE.
SEE, THIS GUY RASKOLNIKOV IS REALLY POOR, AND HE WANTS TO STEAL MONEY FROM THIS OLD, STINGY HAG SITTING ON A HUGE FORTUNE.
PICON
BUT HE'S GOTTA KILL HER.

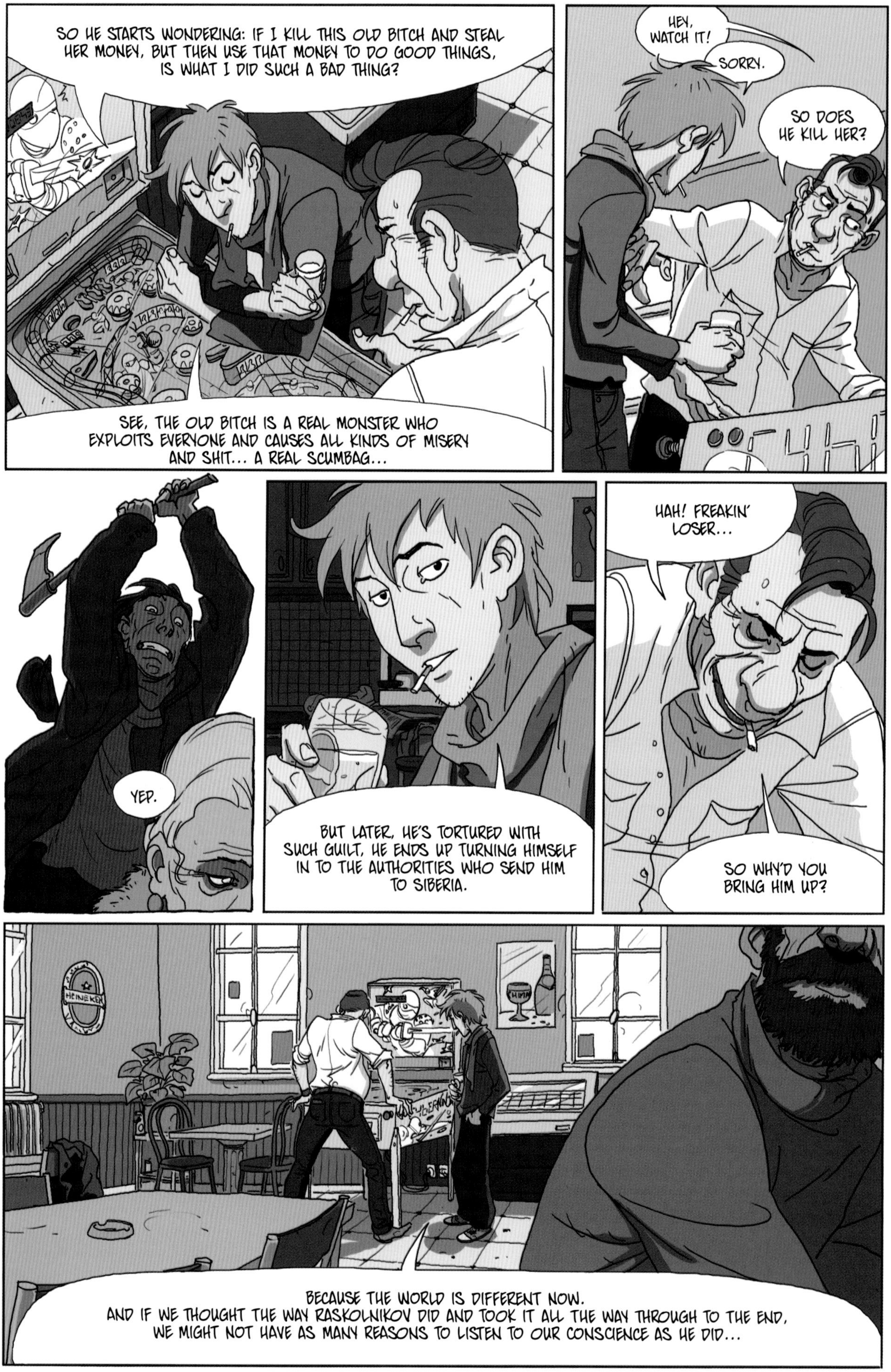
SO HE STARTS WONDERING: IF I KILL THIS OLD BITCH AND STEAL HER MONEY, BUT THEN USE THAT MONEY TO DO GOOD THINGS, IS WHAT I DID SUCH A BAD THING?
SEE, THE OLD BITCH IS A REAL MONSTER WHO EXPLOITS EVERYONE AND CAUSES ALL KINDS OF MISERY AND SHIT... A REAL SCUMBAG...
HEY, WATCH IT!
SORRY.
SO DOES HE KILL HER?
YEP.
BUT LATER, HE'S TORTURED WITH SUCH GUILT, HE ENDS UP TURNING HIMSELF IN TO THE AUTHORITIES WHO SEND HIM TO SIBERIA.
HAH! FREAKIN' LOSER...
SO WHY'D YOU BRING HIM UP?
HEINEKEN
BECAUSE THE WORLD IS DIFFERENT NOW.
AND IF WE THOUGHT THE WAY RASKOLNIKOV DID AND TOOK IT ALL THE WAY THROUGH TO THE END,
WE MIGHT NOT HAVE AS MANY REASONS TO LISTEN TO OUR CONSCIENCE AS HE DID...

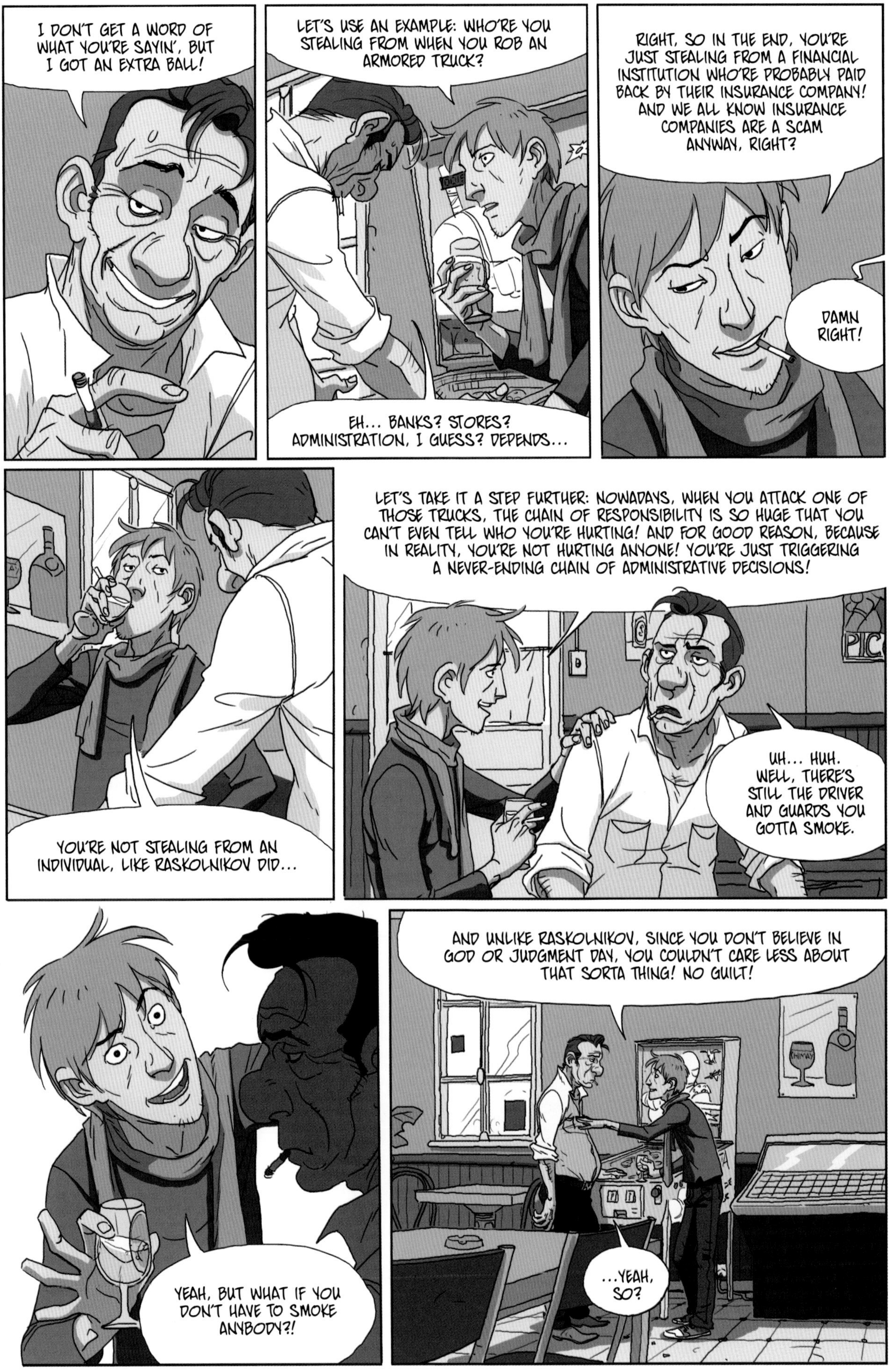
I DON'T GET A WORD OF WHAT YOU'RE SAYIN', BUT I GOT AN EXTRA BALL!
LET'S USE AN EXAMPLE: WHO'RE YOU STEALING FROM WHEN YOU ROB AN ARMORED TRUCK?
EH... BANKS? STORES? ADMINISTRATION, I GUESS? DEPENDS...
RIGHT, SO IN THE END, YOU'RE JUST STEALING FROM A FINANCIAL INSTITUTION WHO'RE PROBABLY PAID BACK BY THEIR INSURANCE COMPANY! AND WE ALL KNOW INSURANCE COMPANIES ARE A SCAM ANYWAY, RIGHT?
DAMN RIGHT!
YOU'RE NOT STEALING FROM AN INDIVIDUAL, LIKE RASKOLNIKOV DID...
LET'S TAKE IT A STEP FURTHER: NOWADAYS, WHEN YOU ATTACK ONE OF THOSE TRUCKS, THE CHAIN OF RESPONSIBILITY IS SO HUGE THAT YOU CAN'T EVEN TELL WHO YOU'RE HURTING! AND FOR GOOD REASON, BECAUSE IN REALITY, YOU'RE NOT HURTING ANYONE! YOU'RE JUST TRIGGERING A NEVER-ENDING CHAIN OF ADMINISTRATIVE DECISIONS!
UH... HUH. WELL, THERE'S STILL THE DRIVER AND GUARDS YOU GOTTA SMOKE.
YEAH, BUT WHAT IF YOU DON'T HAVE TO SMOKE ANYBODY?!
AND UNLIKE RASKOLNIKOV, SINCE YOU DON'T BELIEVE IN GOD OR JUDGMENT DAY, YOU COULDN'T CARE LESS ABOUT THAT SORTA THING! NO GUILT!
...YEAH, SO?

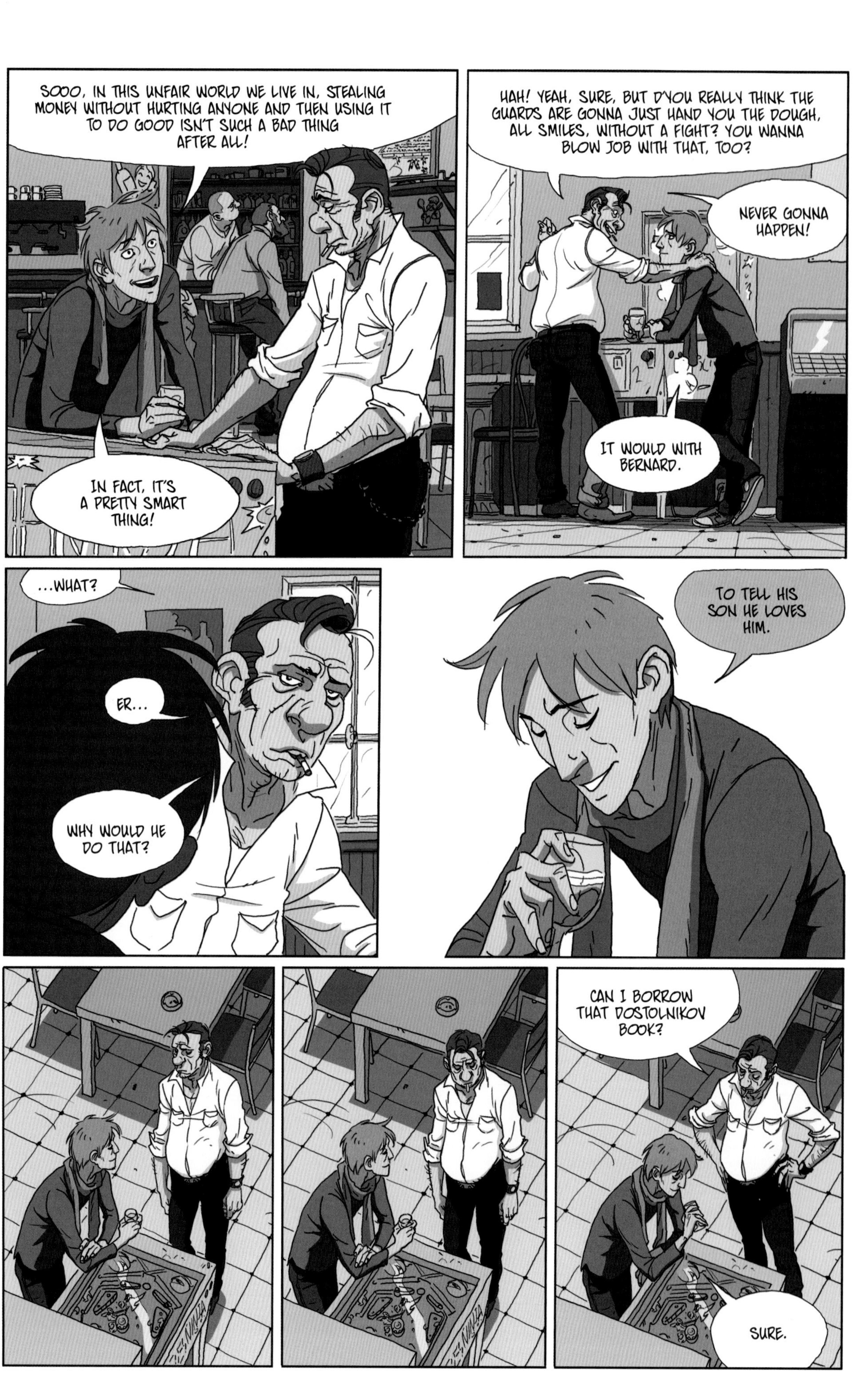
SOOO, IN THIS UNFAIR WORLD WE LIVE IN, STEALING MONEY WITHOUT HURTING ANYONE AND THEN USING IT TO DO GOOD ISN'T SUCH A BAD THING AFTER ALL!
IN FACT, IT'S A PRETTY SMART THING!
HAH! YEAH, SURE, BUT D'YOU REALLY THINK THE GUARDS ARE GONNA JUST HAND YOU THE DOUGH, ALL SMILES, WITHOUT A FIGHT? YOU WANNA BLOW JOB WITH THAT, TOO?
NEVER GONNA HAPPEN!
IT WOULD WITH BERNARD.
...WHAT?
ER...
WHY WOULD HE DO THAT?
TO TELL HIS SON HE LOVES HIM.
CAN I BORROW THAT DOSTOLNIKOV BOOK?
SURE.

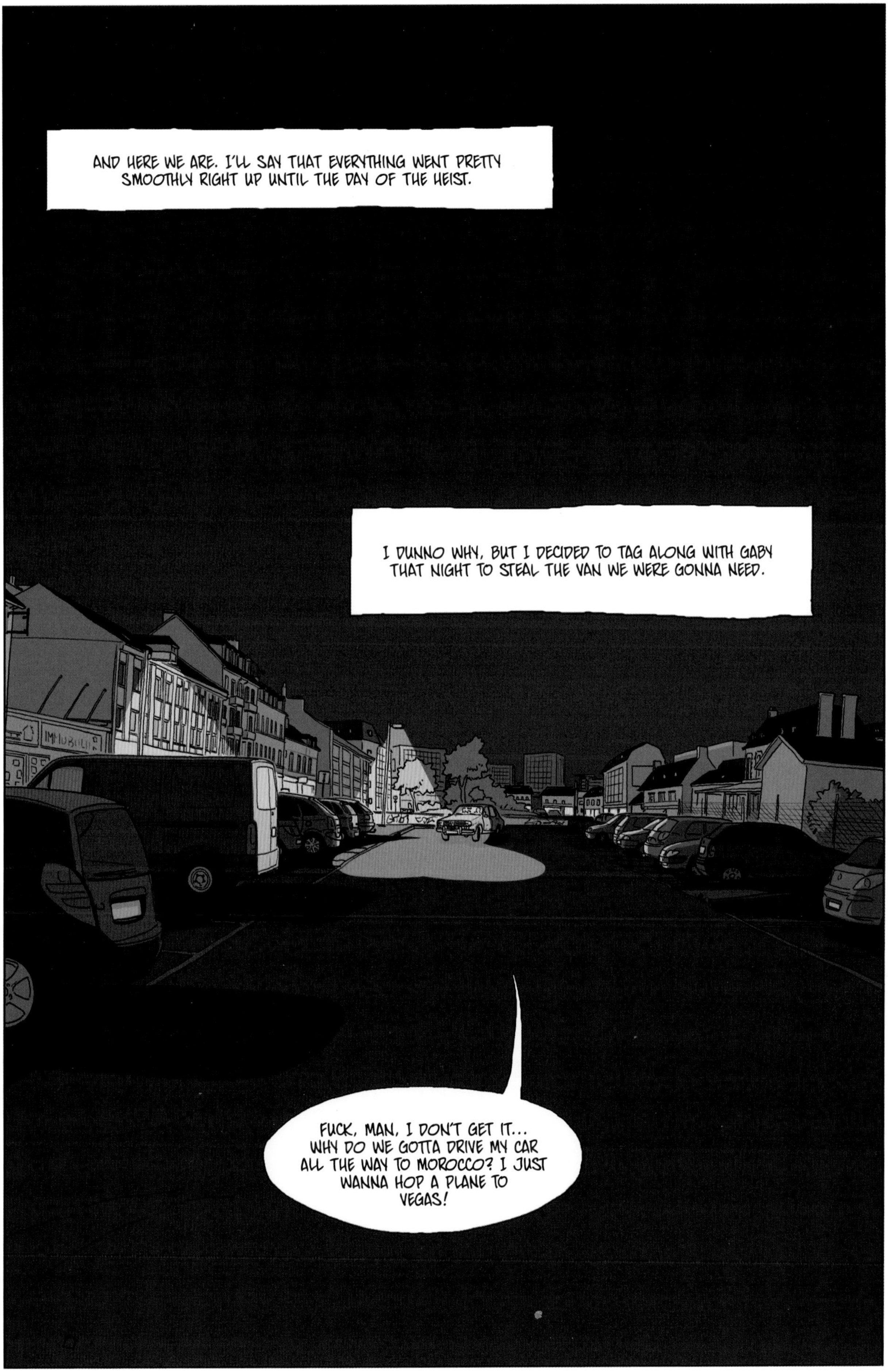
AND HERE WE ARE. I'LL SAY THAT EVERYTHING WENT PRETTY SMOOTHLY RIGHT UP UNTIL THE DAY OF THE HEIST.
I DUNNO WHY, BUT I DECIDED TO TAG ALONG WITH GABY THAT NIGHT TO STEAL THE VAN WE WERE GONNA NEED.
FUCK, MAN, I DON'T GET IT... WHY DO WE GOTTA DRIVE MY CAR ALL THE WAY TO MOROCCO? I JUST WANNA HOP A PLANE TO VEGAS!

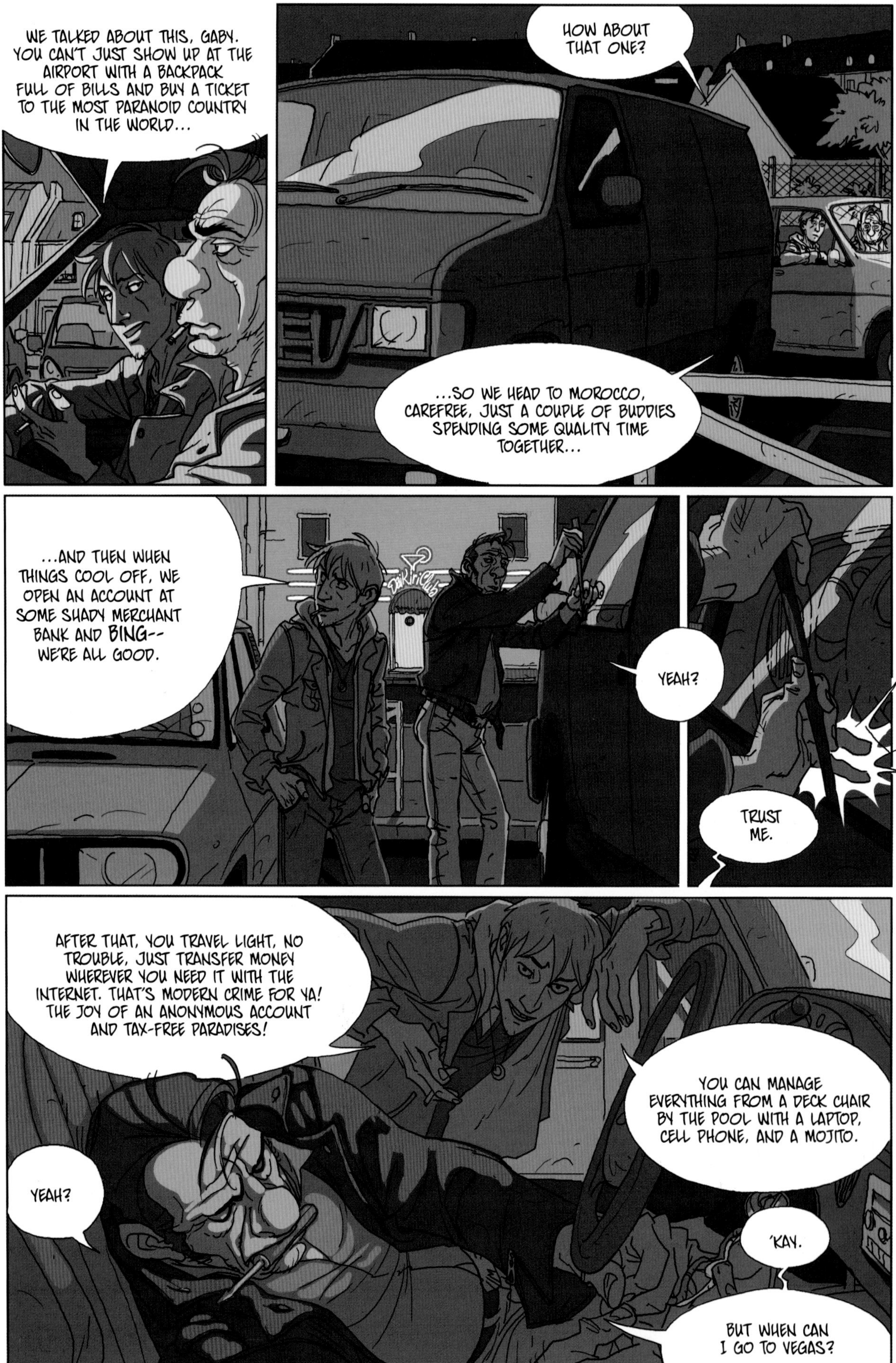
WE TALKED ABOUT THIS, GABY. YOU CAN'T JUST SHOW UP AT THE AIRPORT WITH A BACKPACK FULL OF BILLS AND BUY A TICKET TO THE MOST PARANOID COUNTRY IN THE WORLD...
HOW ABOUT THAT ONE?
...SO WE HEAD TO MOROCCO, CAREFREE, JUST A COUPLE OF BUDDIES SPENDING SOME QUALITY TIME TOGETHER...
...AND THEN WHEN THINGS COOL OFF, WE OPEN AN ACCOUNT AT SOME SHADY MERCHANT BANK AND BING-- WE'RE ALL GOOD.
YEAH?
TRUST ME.
AFTER THAT, YOU TRAVEL LIGHT, NO TROUBLE, JUST TRANSFER MONEY WHEREVER YOU NEED IT WITH THE INTERNET. THAT'S MODERN CRIME FOR YA! THE JOY OF AN ANONYMOUS ACCOUNT AND TAX-FREE PARADISES!
YOU CAN MANAGE EVERYTHING FROM A DECK CHAIR BY THE POOL WITH A LAPTOP, CELL PHONE, AND A MOJITO.
YEAH?
'KAY.
BUT WHEN CAN I GO TO VEGAS?

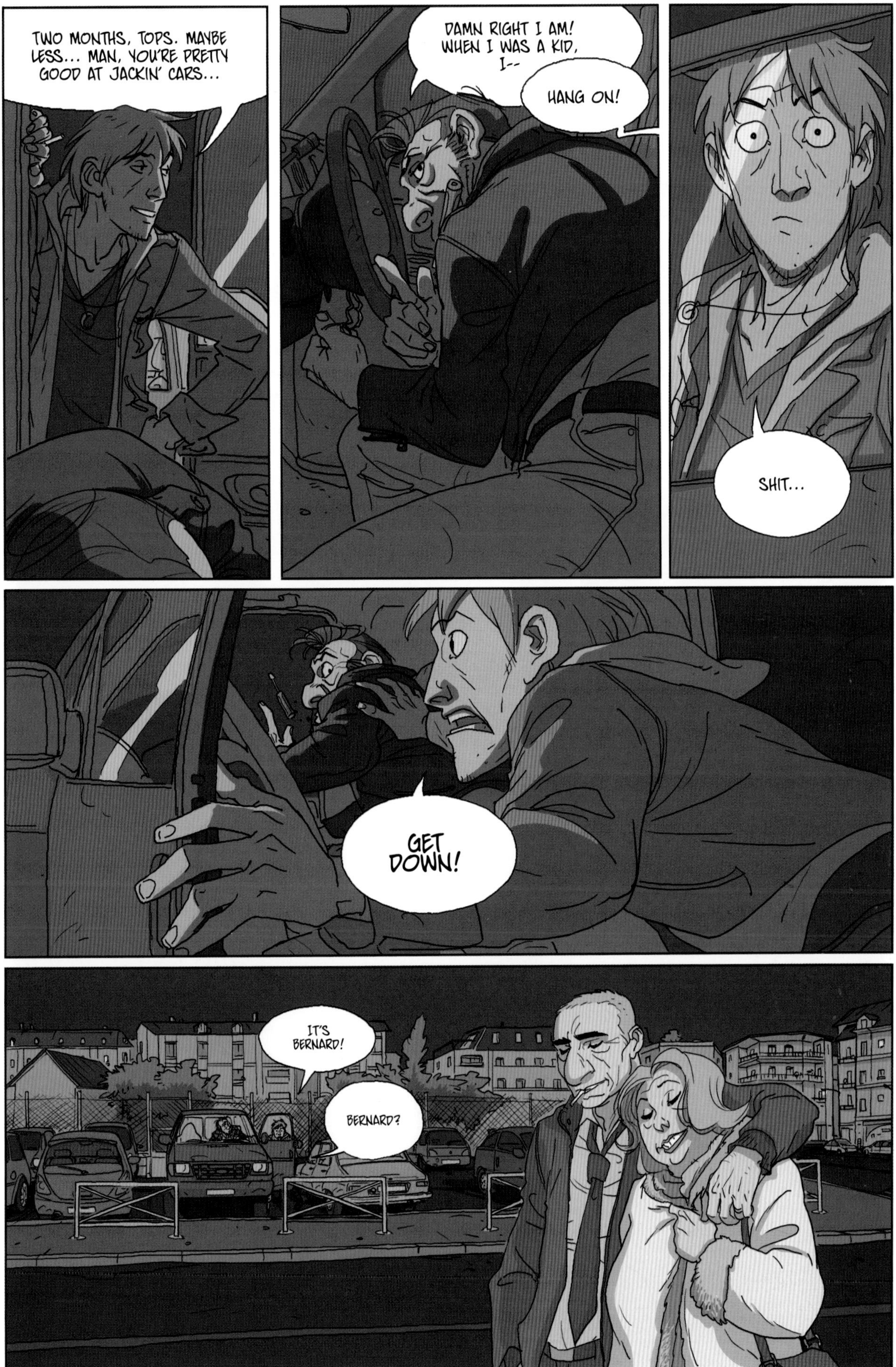
TWO MONTHS, TOPS. MAYBE LESS... MAN, YOU'RE PRETTY GOOD AT JACKIN' CARS...
DAMN RIGHT I AM! WHEN I WAS A KID, I--
HANG ON!
SHIT...
GET DOWN!
IT'S BERNARD!
BERNARD?

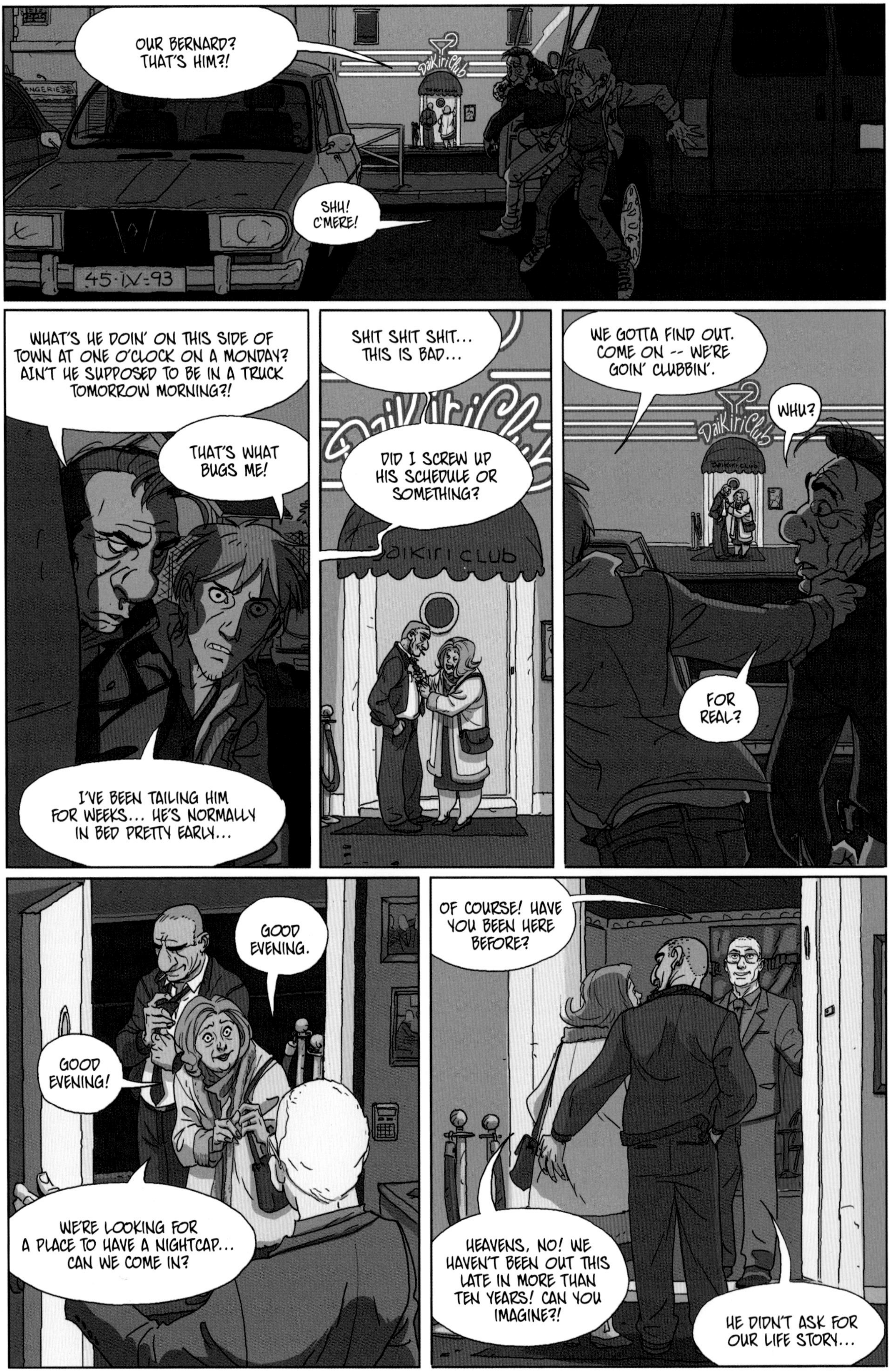
OUR BERNARD? THAT'S HIM?!
SHU! C'MERE!
WHAT'S HE DOIN' ON THIS SIDE OF TOWN AT ONE O'CLOCK ON A MONDAY? AIN'T HE SUPPOSED TO BE IN A TRUCK TOMORROW MORNING?!
THAT'S WHAT BUGS ME!
I'VE BEEN TAILING HIM FOR WEEKS... HE'S NORMALLY IN BED PRETTY EARLY...
SHIT SHIT SHIT... THIS IS BAD...
DID I SCREW UP HIS SCHEDULE OR SOMETHING?
WE GOTTA FIND OUT. COME ON -- WE'RE GOIN' CLUBBIN'.
WHU?
FOR REAL?
GOOD EVENING.
GOOD EVENING!
WE'RE LOOKING FOR A PLACE TO HAVE A NIGHTCAP... CAN WE COME IN?
OF COURSE! HAVE YOU BEEN HERE BEFORE?
HEAVENS, NO! WE HAVEN'T BEEN OUT THIS LATE IN MORE THAN TEN YEARS! CAN YOU IMAGINE?!
HE DIDN'T ASK FOR OUR LIFE STORY...

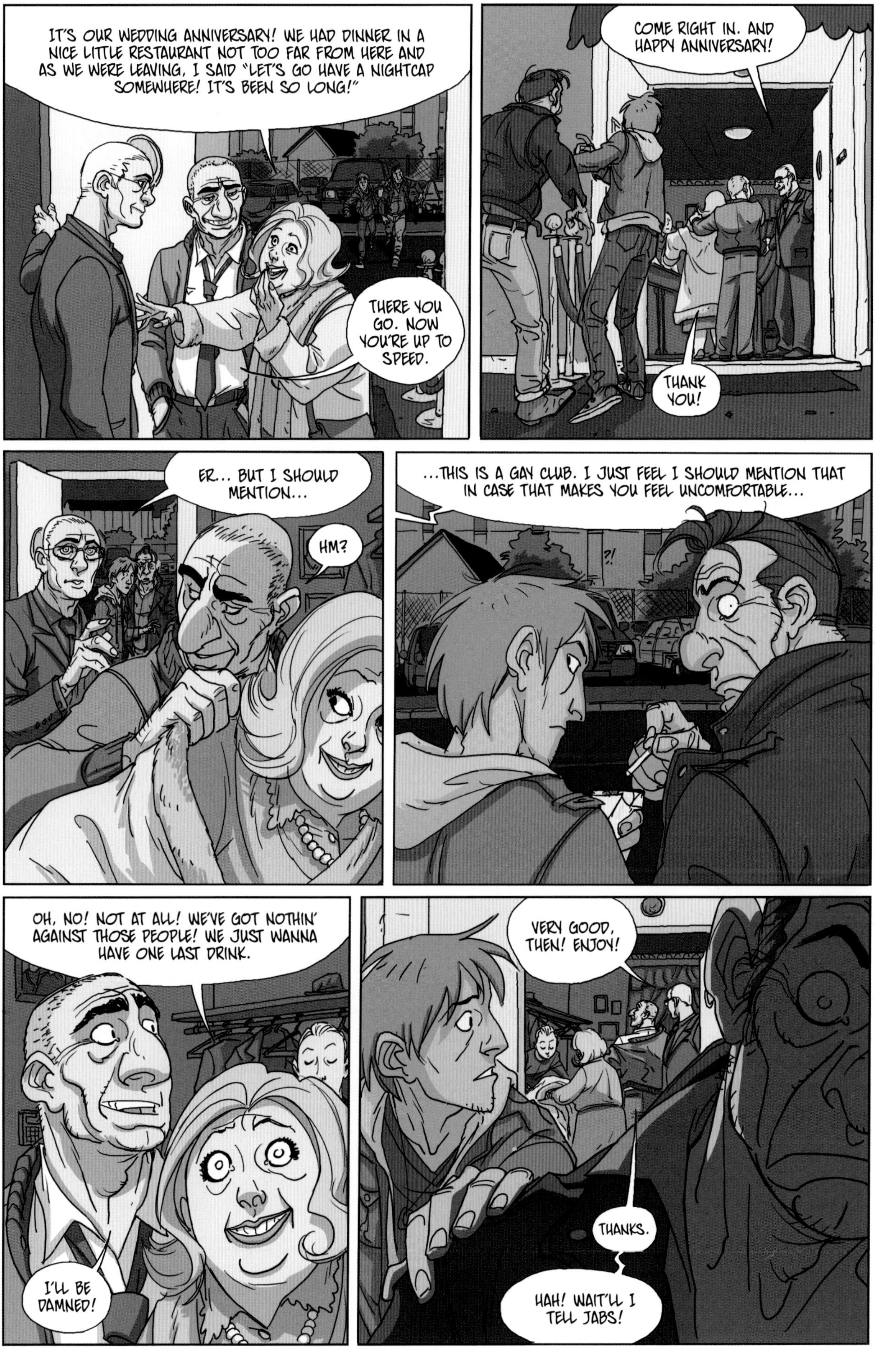
IT'S OUR WEDDING ANNIVERSARY! WE HAD DINNER IN A NICE LITTLE RESTAURANT NOT TOO FAR FROM HERE AND AS WE WERE LEAVING, I SAID "LET'S GO HAVE A NIGHTCAP SOMEWHERE! IT'S BEEN SO LONG!"
THERE YOU GO. NOW YOU'RE UP TO SPEED.
COME RIGHT IN. AND HAPPY ANNIVERSARY!
THANK YOU!
ER... BUT I SHOULD MENTION...
HM?
...THIS IS A GAY CLUB. I JUST FEEL I SHOULD MENTION THAT IN CASE THAT MAKES YOU FEEL UNCOMFORTABLE...
?!
OH, NO! NOT AT ALL! WE'VE GOT NOTHIN' AGAINST THOSE PEOPLE! WE JUST WANNA HAVE ONE LAST DRINK.
I'LL BE DAMNED!
VERY GOOD, THEN! ENJOY!
THANKS.
HAH! WAIT'LL I TELL JABS!

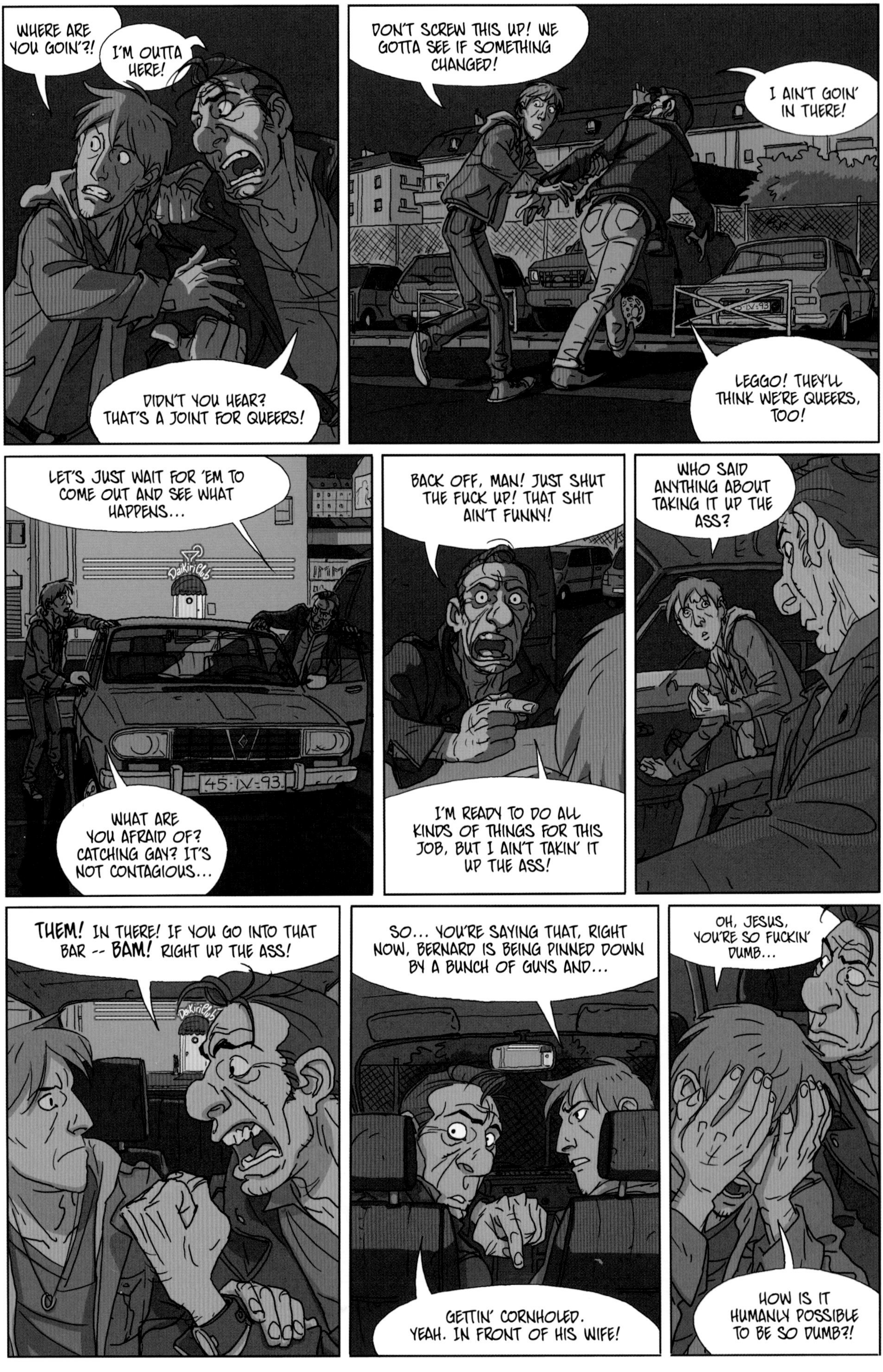
WHERE ARE YOU GOIN'?!
I'M OUTTA HERE!
DIDN'T YOU HEAR? THAT'S A JOINT FOR QUEERS!
DON'T SCREW THIS UP! WE GOTTA SEE IF SOMETHING CHANGED!
I AIN'T GOIN' IN THERE!
LEGGO! THEY'LL THINK WE'RE QUEERS, TOO!
LET'S JUST WAIT FOR 'EM TO COME OUT AND SEE WHAT HAPPENS...
45-IV-93
WHAT ARE YOU AFRAID OF? CATCHING GAY? IT'S NOT CONTAGIOUS...
BACK OFF, MAN! JUST SHUT THE FUCK UP! THAT SHIT AIN'T FUNNY!
I'M READY TO DO ALL KINDS OF THINGS FOR THIS JOB, BUT I AIN'T TAKIN' IT UP THE ASS!
WHO SAID ANYTHING ABOUT TAKING IT UP THE ASS?
THEM! IN THERE! IF YOU GO INTO THAT BAR -- BAM! RIGHT UP THE ASS!
SO... YOU'RE SAYING THAT, RIGHT NOW, BERNARD IS BEING PINNED DOWN BY A BUNCH OF GUYS AND...
GETTIN' CORNHOLED. YEAH. IN FRONT OF HIS WIFE!
OH, JESUS, YOU'RE SO FUCKIN' DUMB...
HOW IS IT HUMANLY POSSIBLE TO BE SO DUMB?!

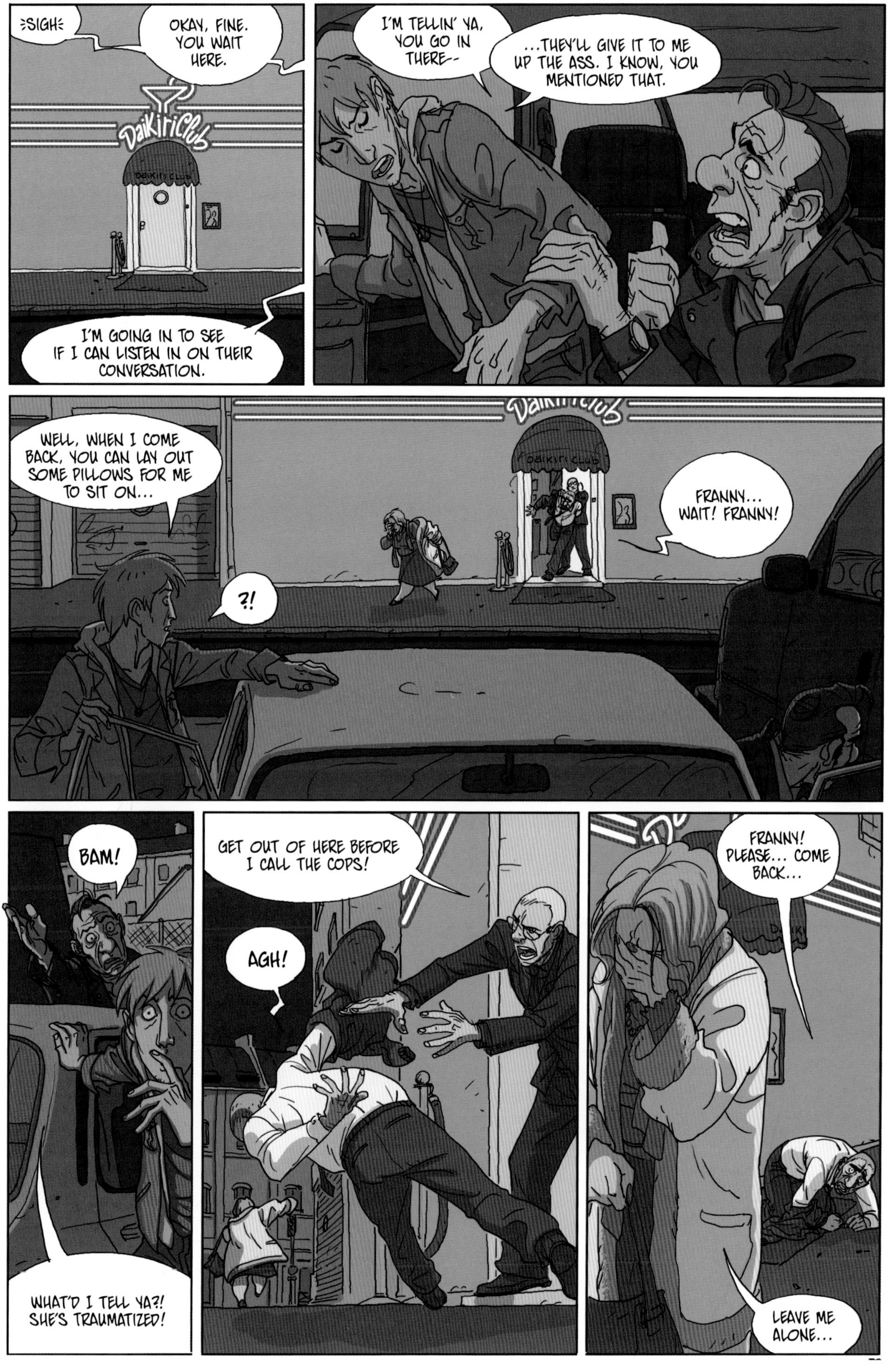

SIGH
OKAY, FINE. YOU WAIT HERE.
I'M GOING IN TO SEE IF I CAN LISTEN IN ON THEIR CONVERSATION.
I'M TELLIN' YA, YOU GO IN THERE--
...THEY'LL GIVE IT TO ME UP THE ASS. I KNOW, YOU MENTIONED THAT.
DaiKiri Club
WELL, WHEN I COME BACK, YOU CAN LAY OUT SOME PILLOWS FOR ME TO SIT ON...
FRANNY... WAIT! FRANNY!
?!
BAM!
WHAT'D I TELL YA?! SHE'S TRAUMATIZED!
GET OUT OF HERE BEFORE I CALL THE COPS!
AGH!
FRANNY! PLEASE... COME BACK...
LEAVE ME ALONE...

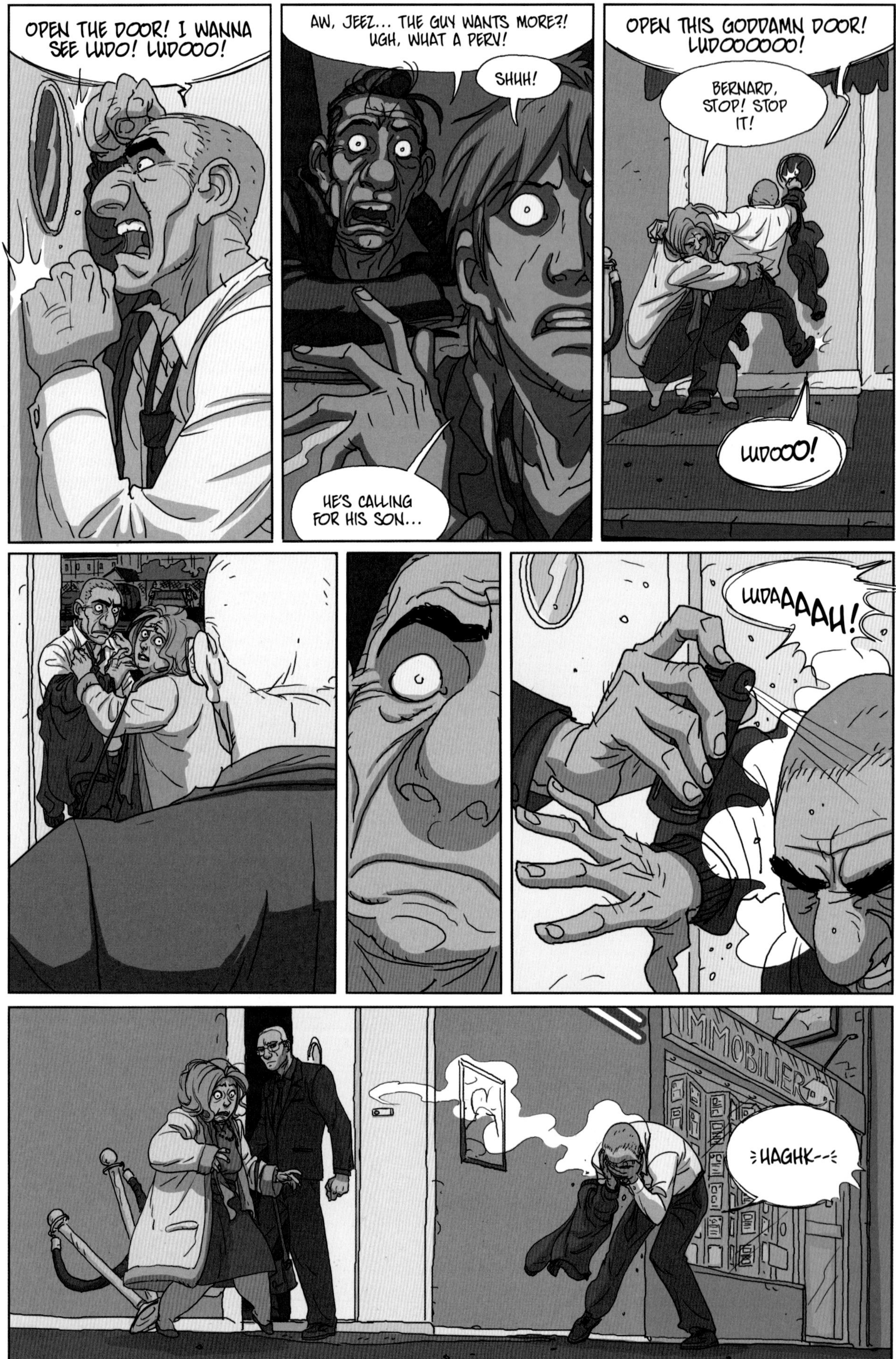
OPEN THE DOOR! I WANNA SEE LUDO! LUDOOO!
AW, JEEZ... THE GUY WANTS MORE?! UGH, WHAT A PERV!
SHHH!
HE'S CALLING FOR HIS SON...
OPEN THIS GODDAMN DOOR! LUDOOOOOO!
BERNARD, STOP! STOP IT!
LUDOOO!
LUDAAAAH!
HAGHK--

BERNARD!

≈RREEUUH≈

≈KOF≈ ≈KOFF≈

HOLY SHIT...

≈HURGH!≈

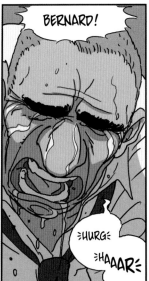

BERNARD!

≈HURG≈ ≈HAAAR≈

HELP! HELP US!

MY HUSBAND IS HAVING A STROKE!

HEEELP!

WHAT'S WRONG WITH HIM?

WHAT'S WRONG IS YOU KILLED HIM WITH THAT STUFF! CALL AN AMBULANCE!

≈RRAAUUGH≈

DON'T WORRY, THAT'LL FIX HIM RIGHT UP. HERE PAL -- OPEN WIDE!

WHY THE HELL'D HE JUMP ON MY BARTENDER LIKE THAT? DOES HE NORMALLY GO AROUND ATTACKING PEOPLE IN PUBLIC? YOU REALLY SHOULD JUST GO...

≈REUGH≈

PLEASE, SIR... THERE'S A KID IN THERE... HIS NAME IS LUDOVIC... HE'S...

...HE'S OUR SON.

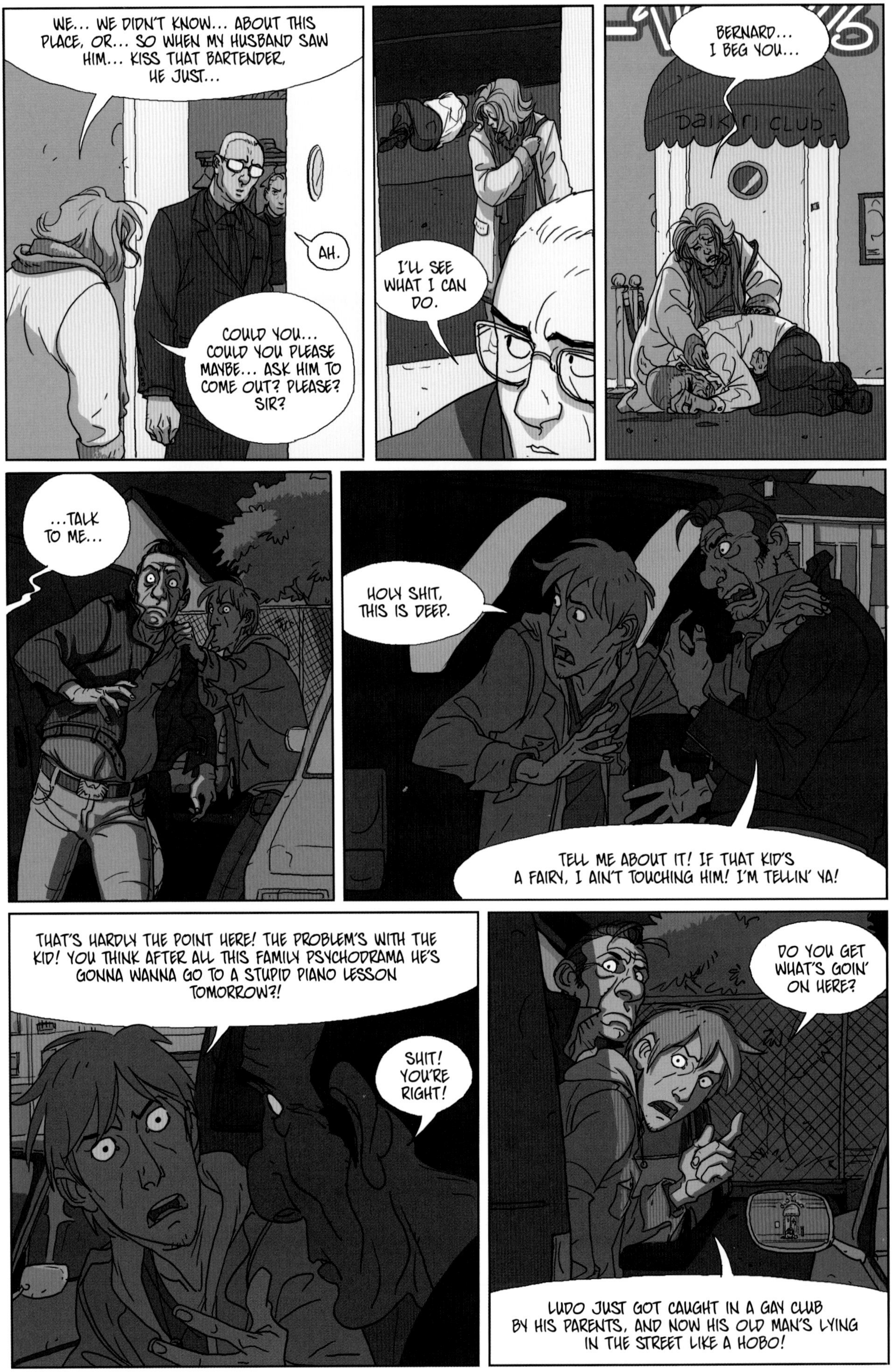
WE... WE DIDN'T KNOW... ABOUT THIS PLACE, OR... SO WHEN MY HUSBAND SAW HIM... KISS THAT BARTENDER, HE JUST...
AH.
COULD YOU... COULD YOU PLEASE MAYBE... ASK HIM TO COME OUT? PLEASE? SIR?
I'LL SEE WHAT I CAN DO.
BERNARD... I BEG YOU...
DAIKIRI CLUB
...TALK TO ME...
HOLY SHIT, THIS IS DEEP.
TELL ME ABOUT IT! IF THAT KID'S A FAIRY, I AIN'T TOUCHING HIM! I'M TELLIN' YA!
THAT'S HARDLY THE POINT HERE! THE PROBLEM'S WITH THE KID! YOU THINK AFTER ALL THIS FAMILY PSYCHODRAMA HE'S GONNA WANNA GO TO A STUPID PIANO LESSON TOMORROW?!
SHIT! YOU'RE RIGHT!
DO YOU GET WHAT'S GOIN' ON HERE?
LUDO JUST GOT CAUGHT IN A GAY CLUB BY HIS PARENTS, AND NOW HIS OLD MAN'S LYING IN THE STREET LIKE A HOBO!

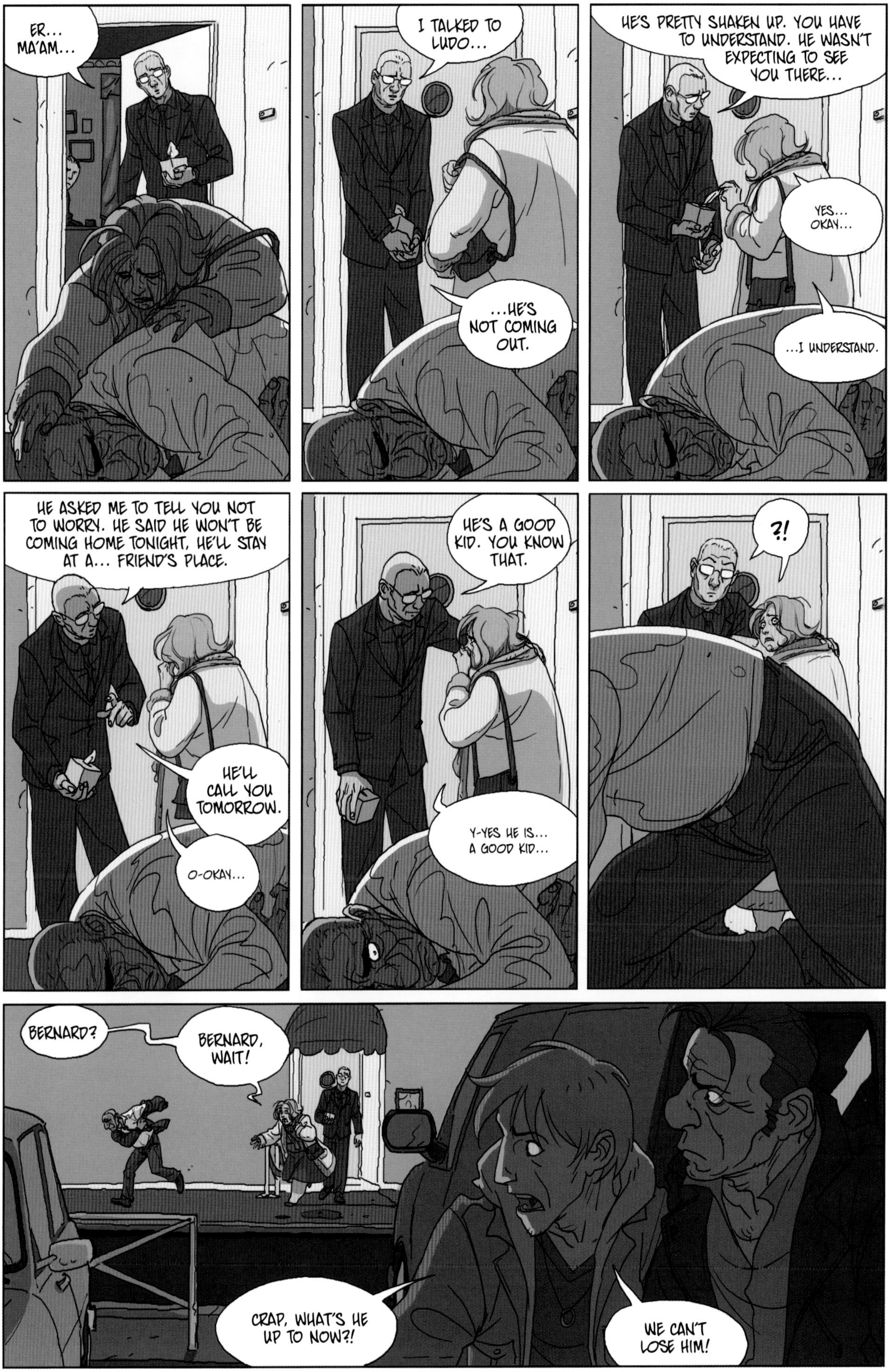

ER... MA'AM...
I TALKED TO LUDO...
...HE'S NOT COMING OUT.
HE'S PRETTY SHAKEN UP. YOU HAVE TO UNDERSTAND. HE WASN'T EXPECTING TO SEE YOU THERE...
YES... OKAY...
...I UNDERSTAND.
HE ASKED ME TO TELL YOU NOT TO WORRY. HE SAID HE WON'T BE COMING HOME TONIGHT, HE'LL STAY AT A... FRIEND'S PLACE.
HE'LL CALL YOU TOMORROW.
O-OKAY...
HE'S A GOOD KID. YOU KNOW THAT.
Y-YES HE IS... A GOOD KID...
?!
BERNARD?
BERNARD, WAIT!
CRAP, WHAT'S HE UP TO NOW?!
WE CAN'T LOSE HIM!

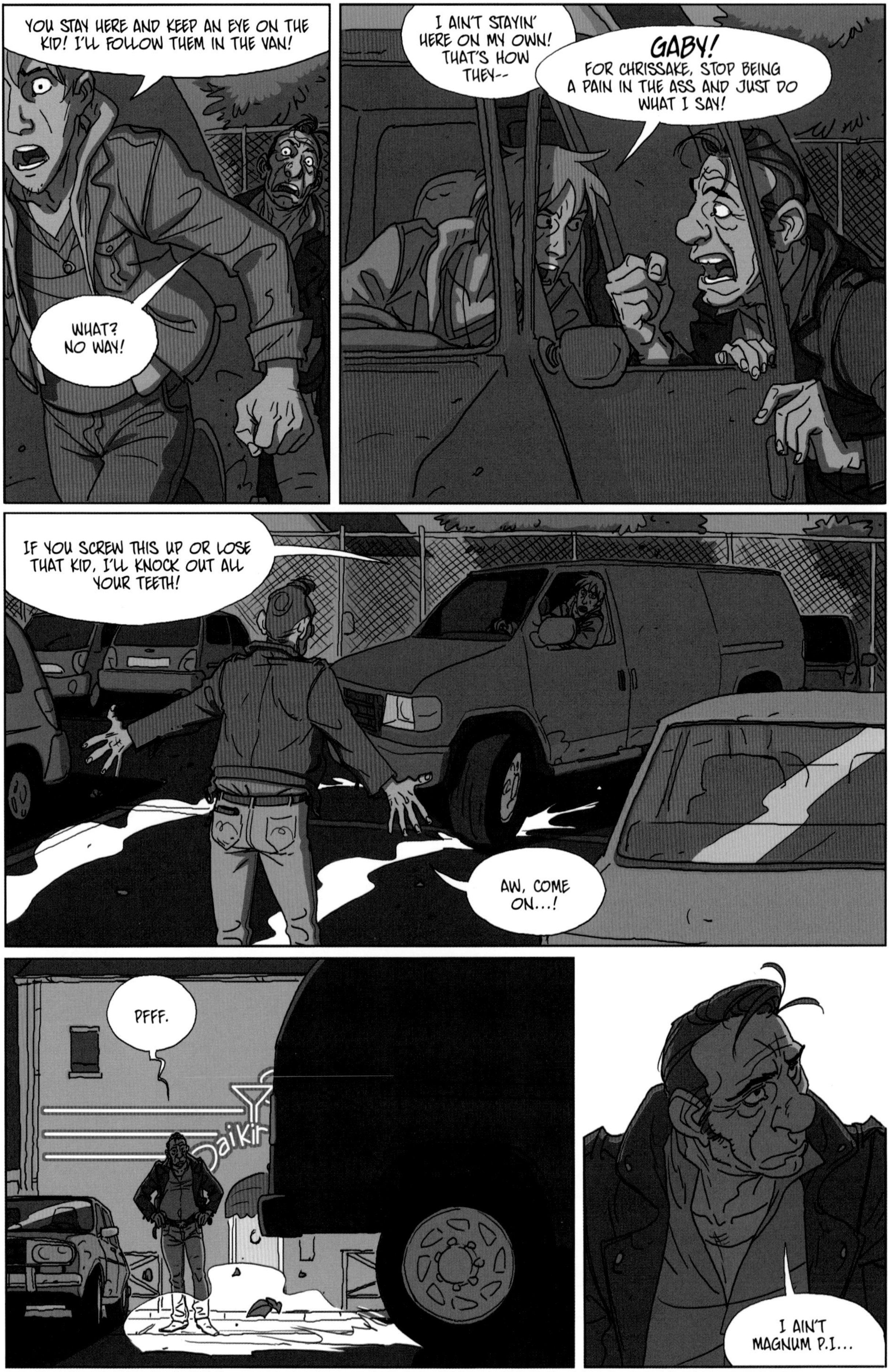
YOU STAY HERE AND KEEP AN EYE ON THE KID! I'LL FOLLOW THEM IN THE VAN!
WHAT? NO WAY!
I AIN'T STAYIN' HERE ON MY OWN! THAT'S HOW THEY--
GABY! FOR CHRISSAKE, STOP BEING A PAIN IN THE ASS AND JUST DO WHAT I SAY!
IF YOU SCREW THIS UP OR LOSE THAT KID, I'LL KNOCK OUT ALL YOUR TEETH!
AW, COME ON...!
PFFF.
I AIN'T MAGNUM P.I...

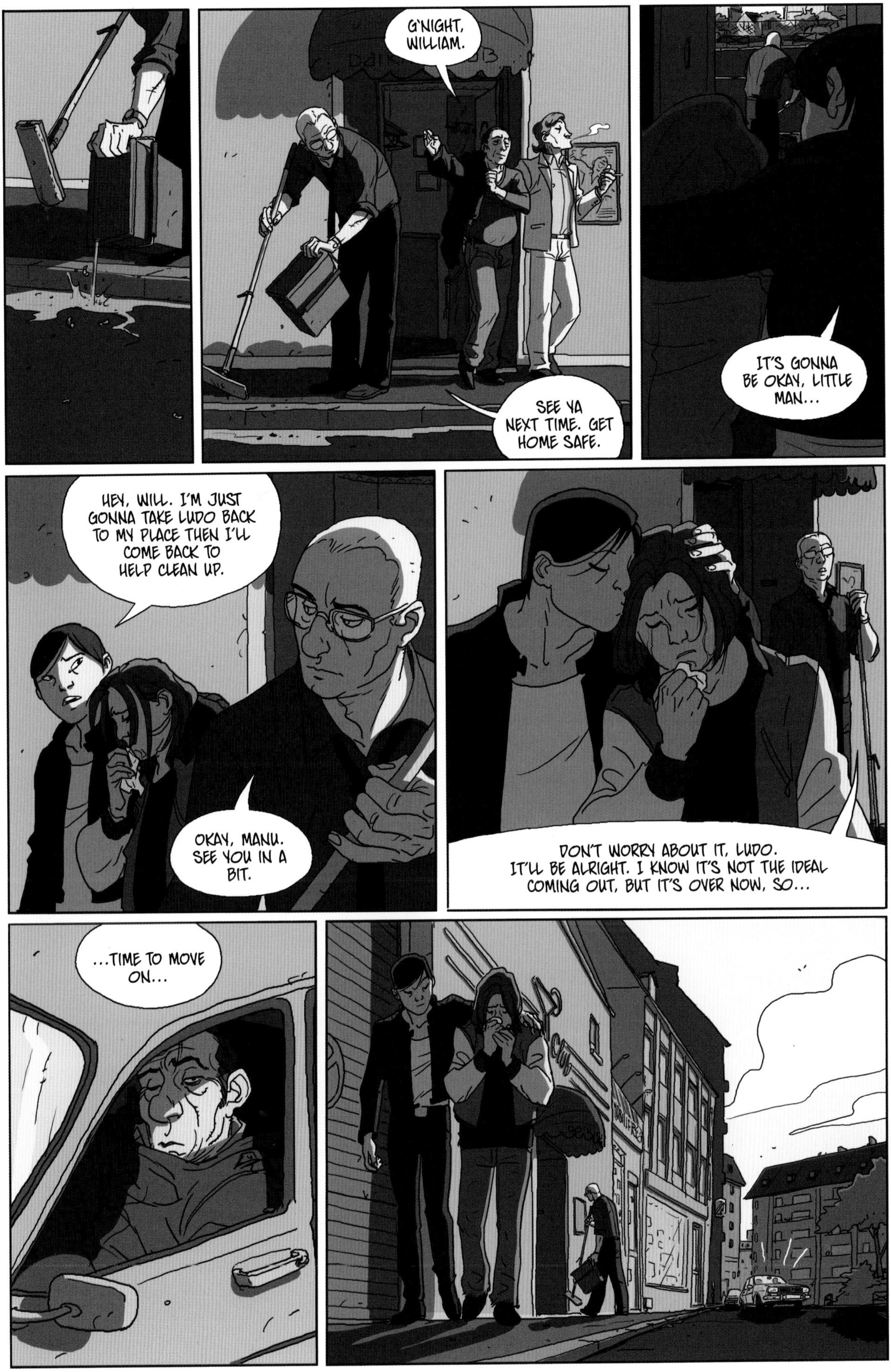
G'NIGHT, WILLIAM.
SEE YA NEXT TIME. GET HOME SAFE.
IT'S GONNA BE OKAY, LITTLE MAN...
HEY, WILL. I'M JUST GONNA TAKE LUDO BACK TO MY PLACE THEN I'LL COME BACK TO HELP CLEAN UP.
OKAY, MANU. SEE YOU IN A BIT.
DON'T WORRY ABOUT IT, LUDO. IT'LL BE ALRIGHT. I KNOW IT'S NOT THE IDEAL COMING OUT, BUT IT'S OVER NOW, SO...
...TIME TO MOVE ON...

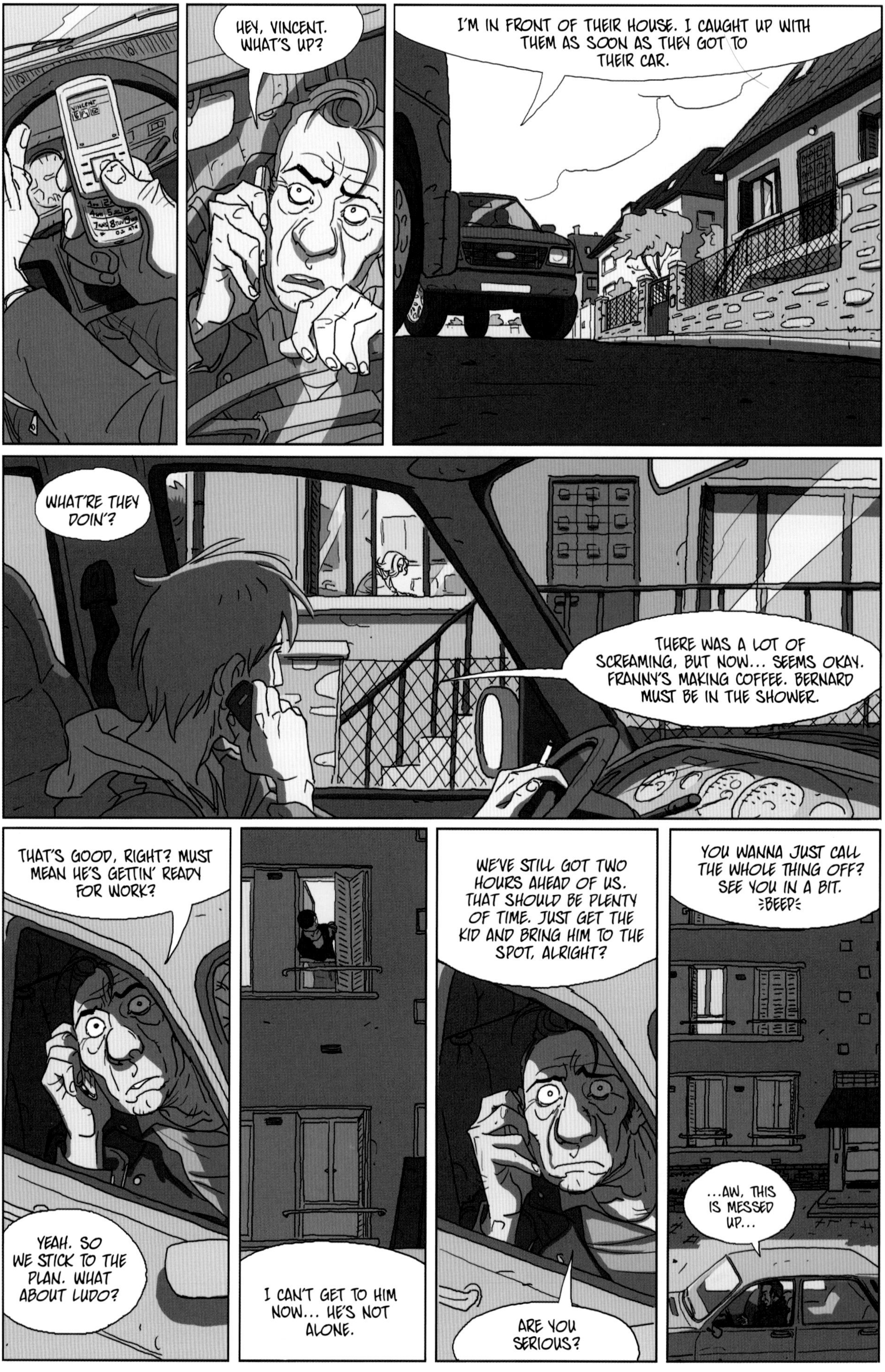
VINCENT
HEY, VINCENT. WHAT'S UP?
I'M IN FRONT OF THEIR HOUSE. I CAUGHT UP WITH THEM AS SOON AS THEY GOT TO THEIR CAR.
WHAT'RE THEY DOIN'?
THERE WAS A LOT OF SCREAMING, BUT NOW... SEEMS OKAY. FRANNY'S MAKING COFFEE. BERNARD MUST BE IN THE SHOWER.
THAT'S GOOD, RIGHT? MUST MEAN HE'S GETTIN' READY FOR WORK?
YEAH. SO WE STICK TO THE PLAN. WHAT ABOUT LUDO?
I CAN'T GET TO HIM NOW... HE'S NOT ALONE.
WE'VE STILL GOT TWO HOURS AHEAD OF US. THAT SHOULD BE PLENTY OF TIME. JUST GET THE KID AND BRING HIM TO THE SPOT, ALRIGHT?
ARE YOU SERIOUS?
YOU WANNA JUST CALL THE WHOLE THING OFF? SEE YOU IN A BIT.
≷BEEP≶
...AW, THIS IS MESSED UP...

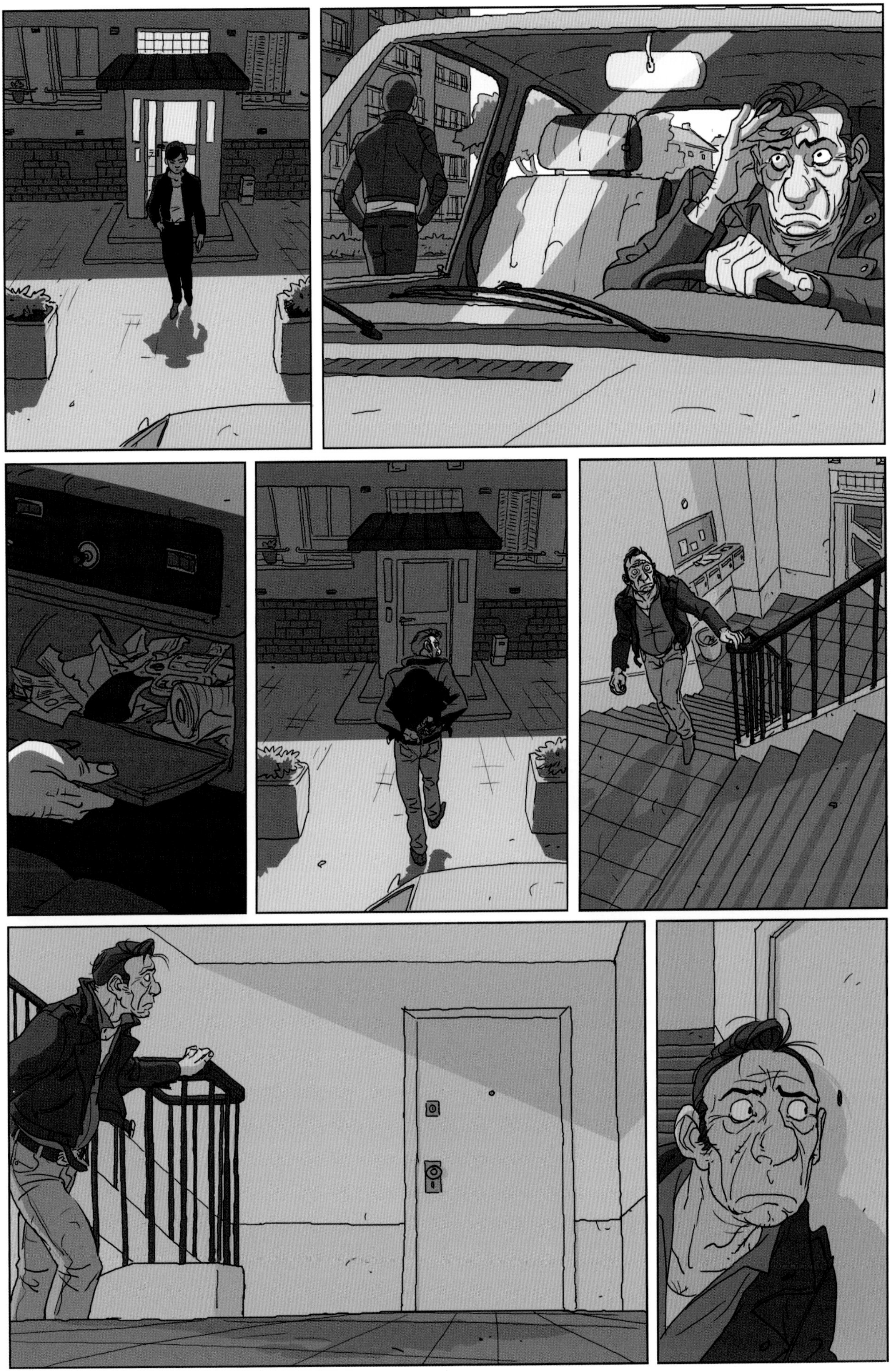

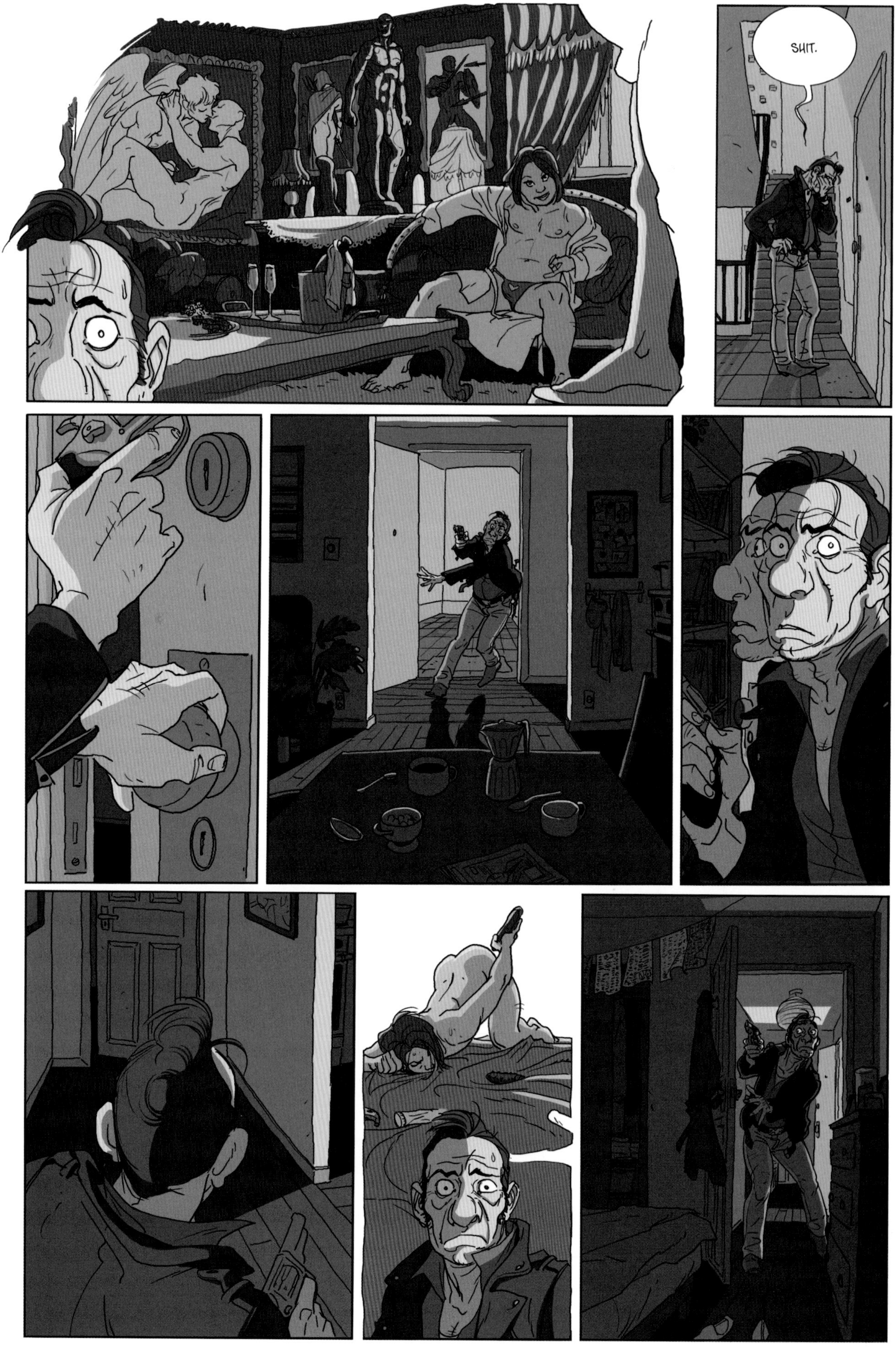
SHIT.

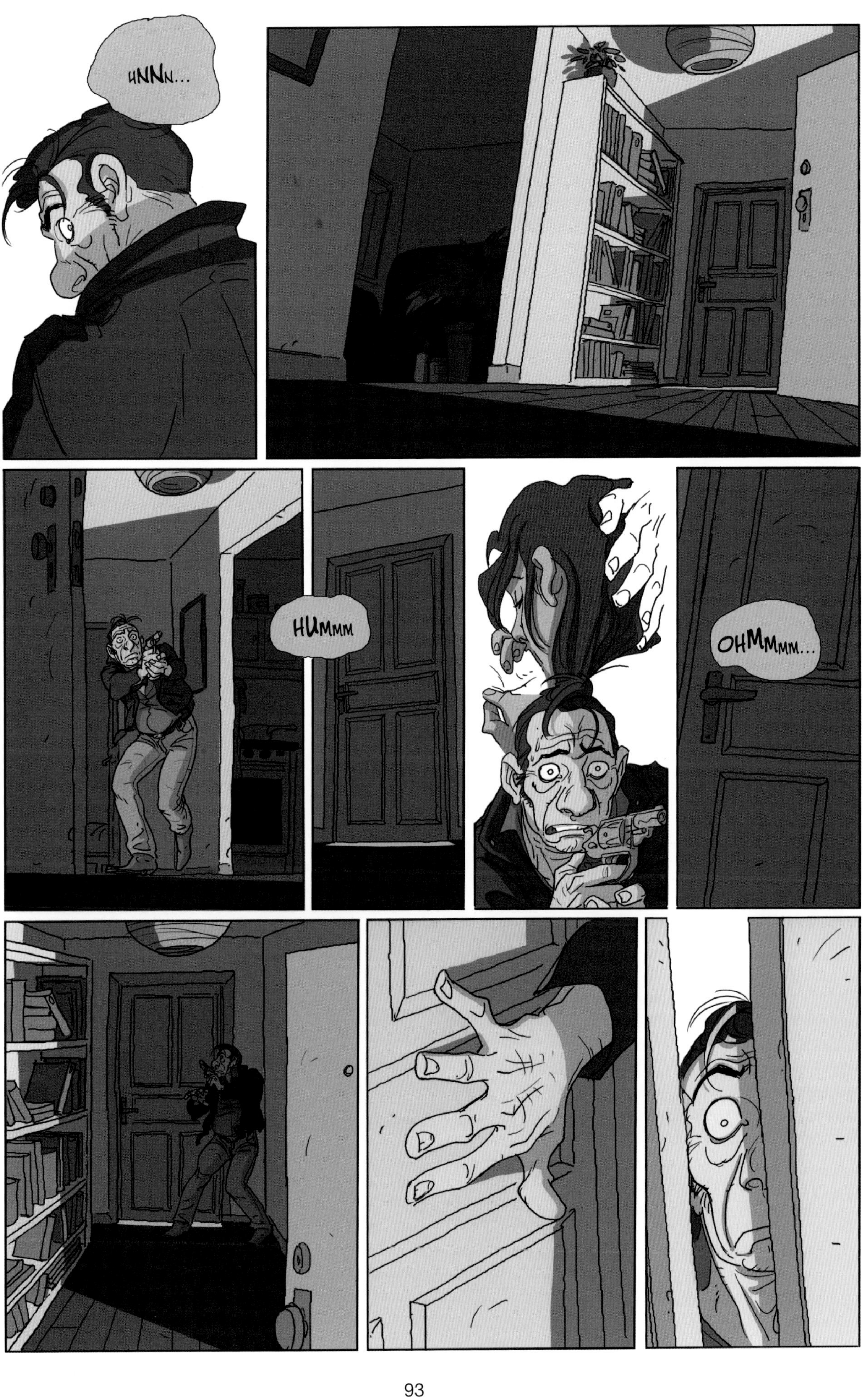
uNNn...
HUmmm
OHMmmm...

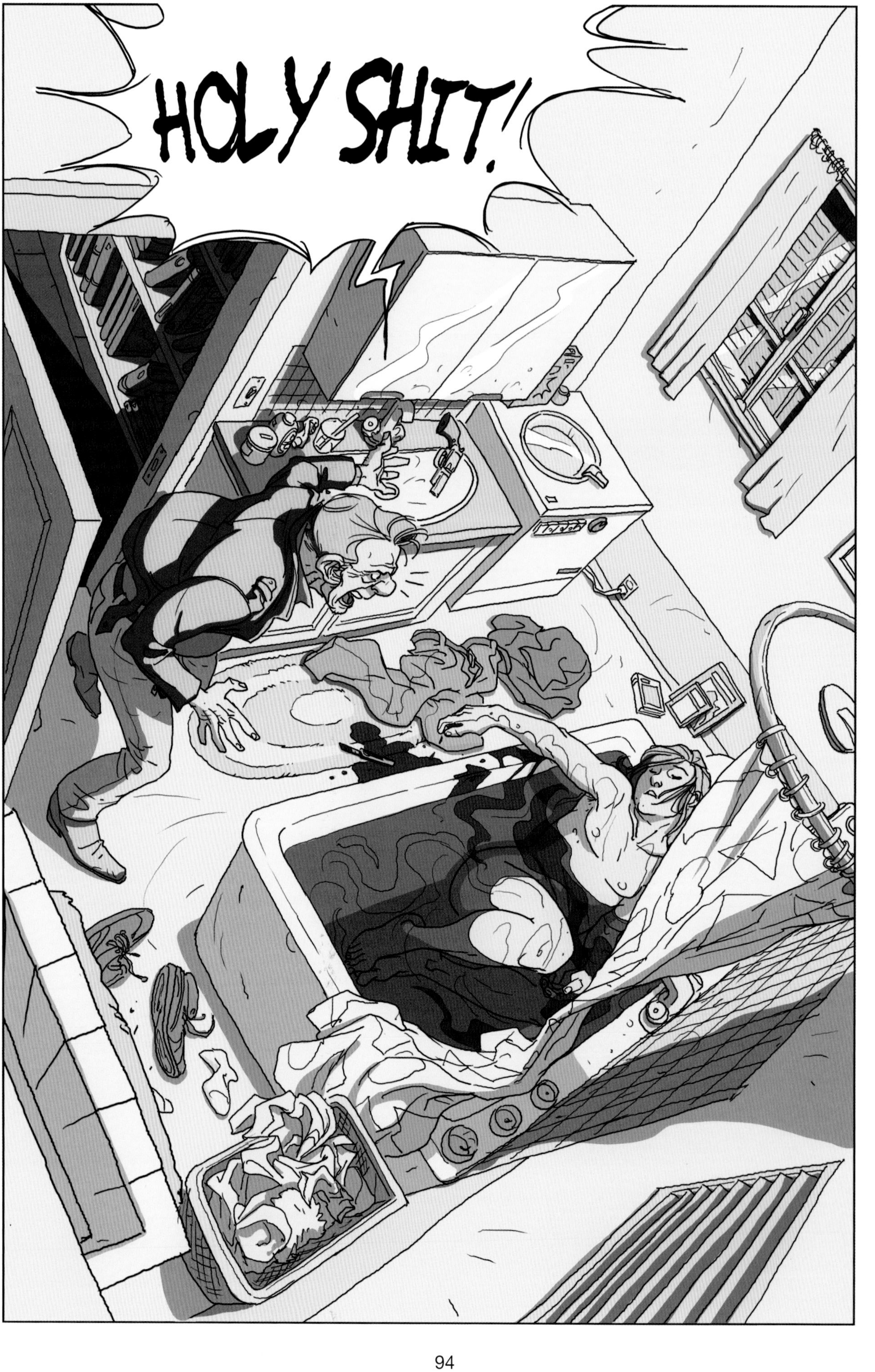
HOLY SHIT!

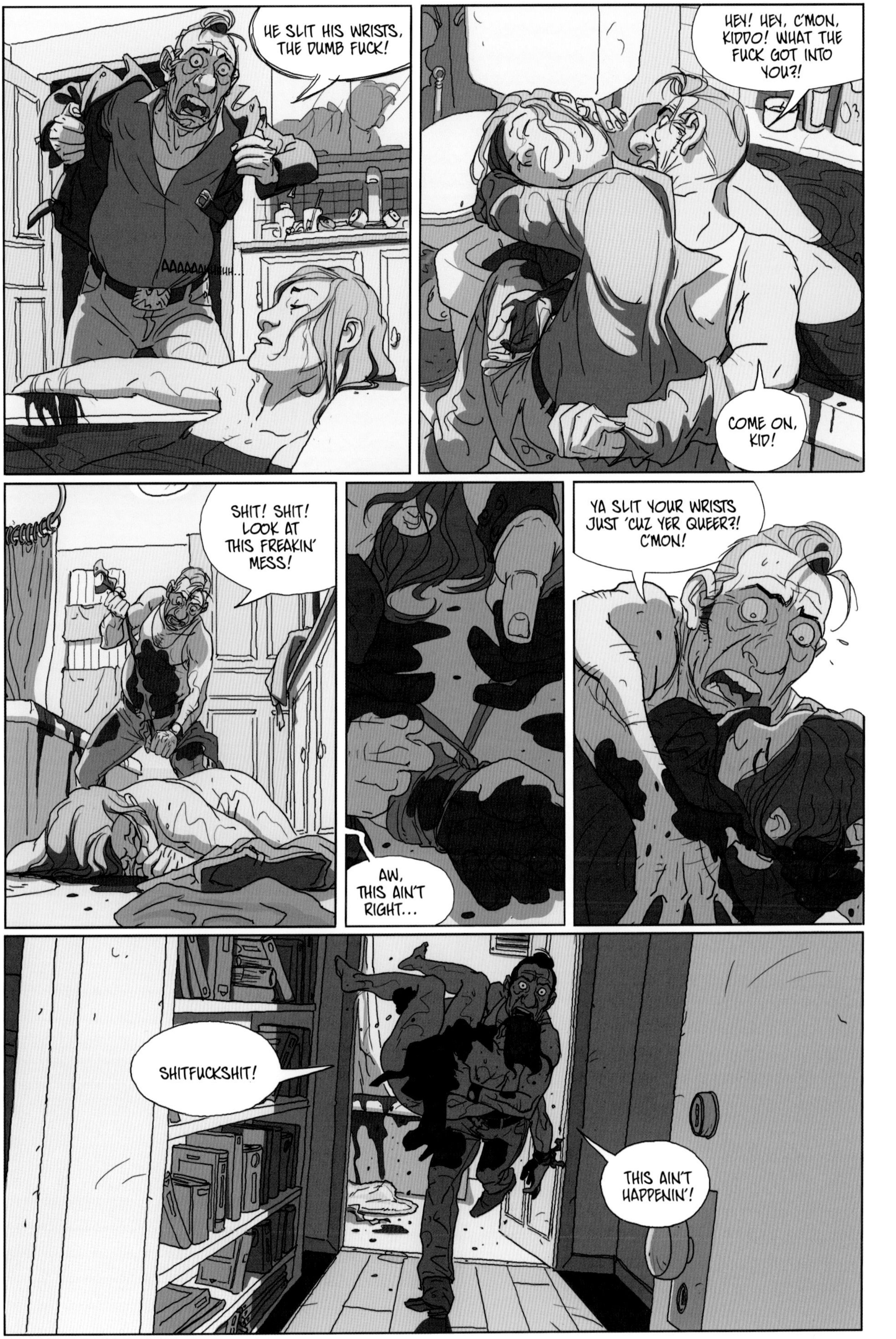
HE SLIT HIS WRISTS, THE DUMB FUCK!
AAAAAAHHHHH...
HEY! HEY, C'MON, KIDDO! WHAT THE FUCK GOT INTO YOU?!
COME ON, KID!
SHIT! SHIT! LOOK AT THIS FREAKIN' MESS!
AW, THIS AIN'T RIGHT...
YA SLIT YOUR WRISTS JUST 'CUZ YER QUEER?! C'MON!
SHITFUCKSHIT!
THIS AIN'T HAPPENIN'!

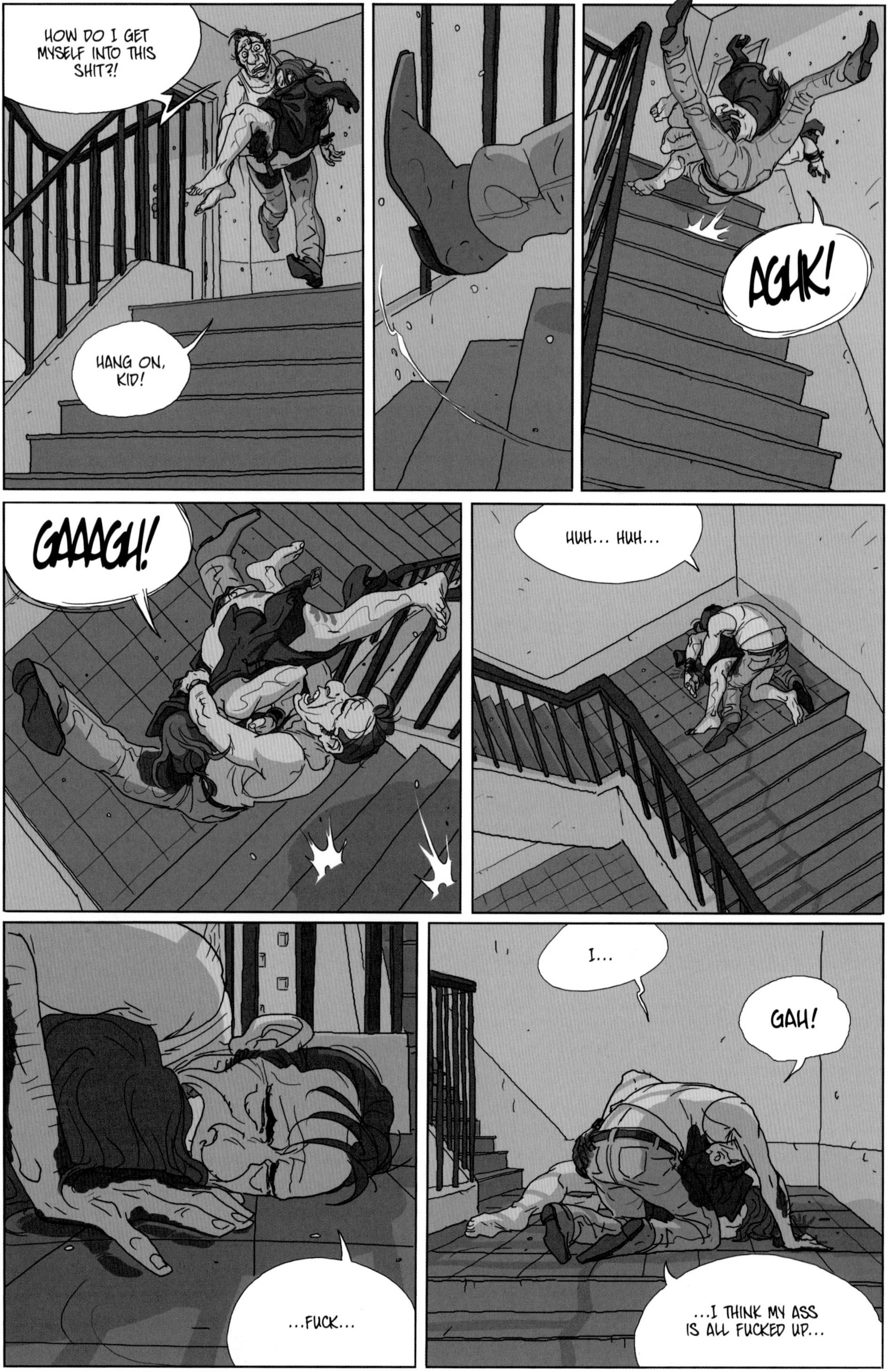
HOW DO I GET MYSELF INTO THIS SHIT?!
HANG ON, KID!
AGHK!
GAAAGH!
HUH... HUH...
...FUCK...
I...
GAH!
...I THINK MY ASS IS ALL FUCKED UP...

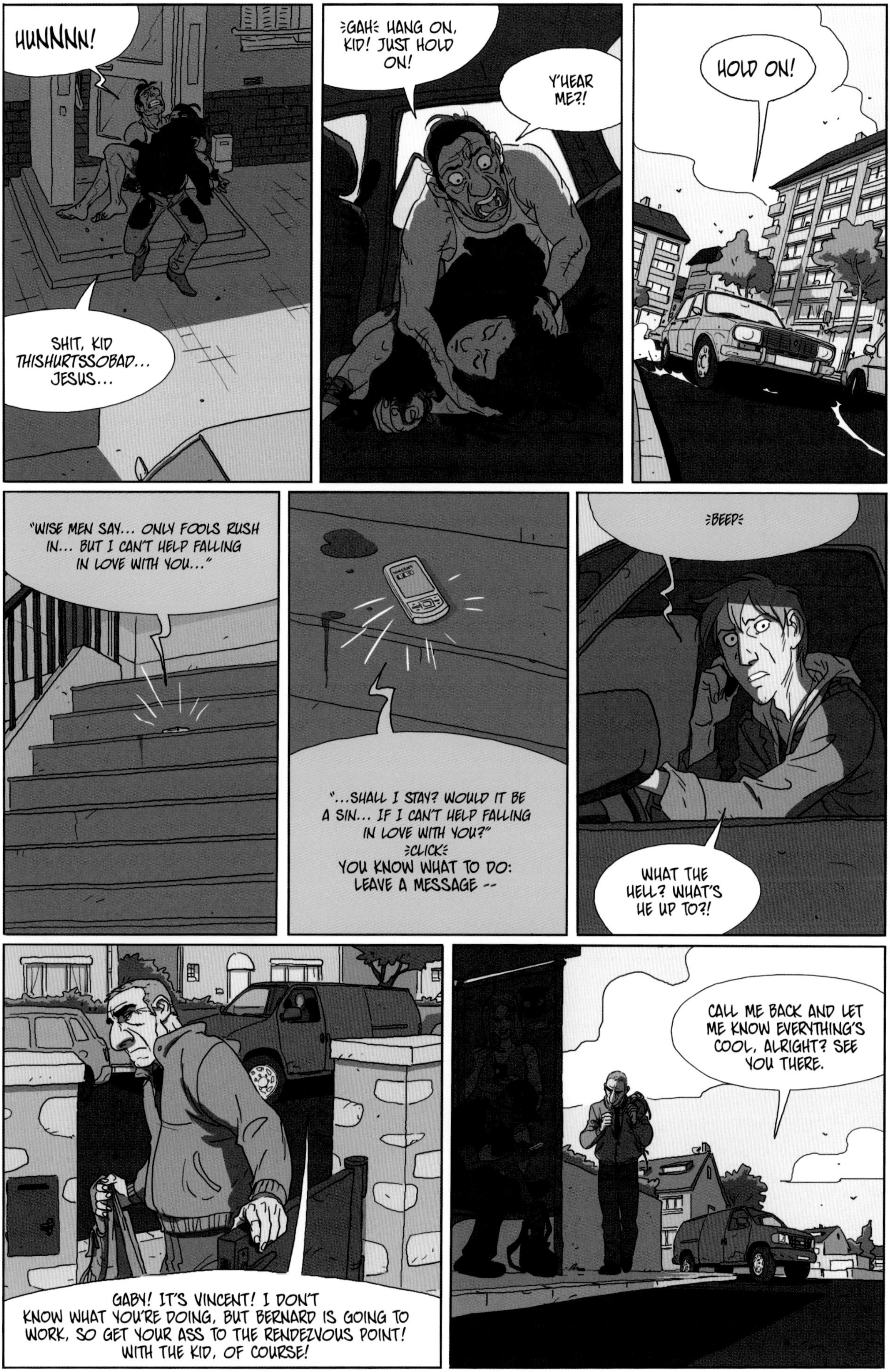
HUNNNN!
SHIT, KID THISHURTSSOBAD... JESUS...
≡GAH≡ HANG ON, KID! JUST HOLD ON!
Y'HEAR ME?!
HOLD ON!
"WISE MEN SAY... ONLY FOOLS RUSH IN... BUT I CAN'T HELP FALLING IN LOVE WITH YOU..."
"...SHALL I STAY? WOULD IT BE A SIN... IF I CAN'T HELP FALLING IN LOVE WITH YOU?"
≡CLICK≡
YOU KNOW WHAT TO DO: LEAVE A MESSAGE --
≡BEEP≡
WHAT THE HELL? WHAT'S HE UP TO?!
GABY! IT'S VINCENT! I DON'T KNOW WHAT YOU'RE DOING, BUT BERNARD IS GOING TO WORK, SO GET YOUR ASS TO THE RENDEZVOUS POINT! WITH THE KID, OF COURSE!
CALL ME BACK AND LET ME KNOW EVERYTHING'S COOL, ALRIGHT? SEE YOU THERE.

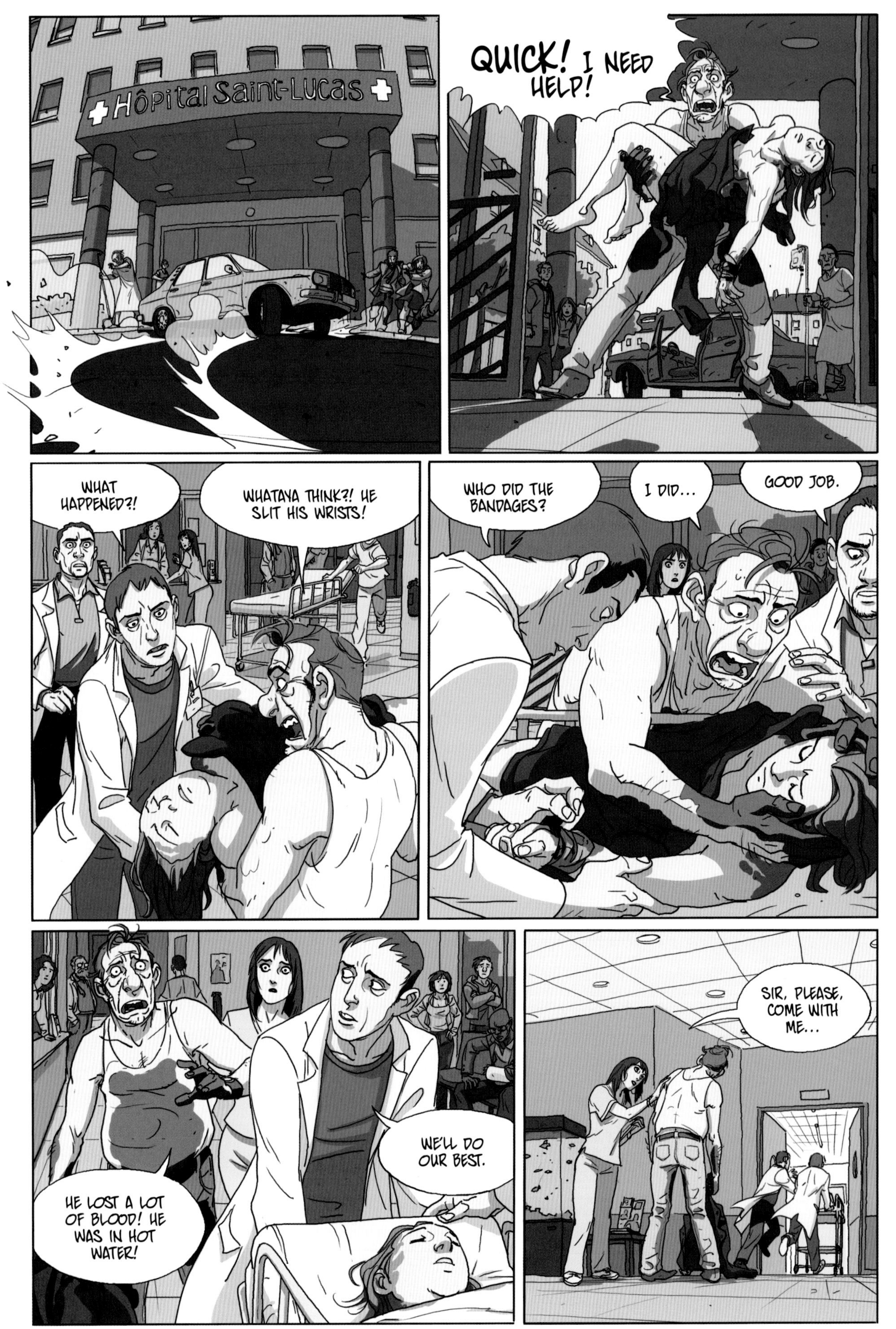
Hôpital Saint-Lucas
QUICK! I NEED HELP!
WHAT HAPPENED?!
WHATAYA THINK?! HE SLIT HIS WRISTS!
WHO DID THE BANDAGES?
I DID...
GOOD JOB.
HE LOST A LOT OF BLOOD! HE WAS IN HOT WATER!
WE'LL DO OUR BEST.
SIR, PLEASE, COME WITH ME...

WE NEED TO FILL OUT SOME PAPERWORK. HAVE A SEAT OVER THERE. WHAT'S THE BOY'S NAME?

LUDO... LUDOVIC...

ARE YOU RELATED?

...YEAH, HE'S MY...

ER, NO.

YES.

NO.

GINNY, CAN YOU COME HERE FOR A MINUTE, PLEASE?

I'LL BE RIGHT BACK, SIR.

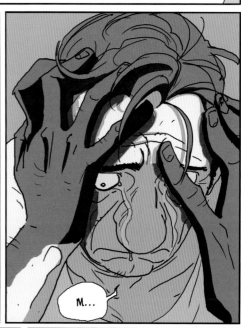

M...

MY SON...

...HE'S MY SON...

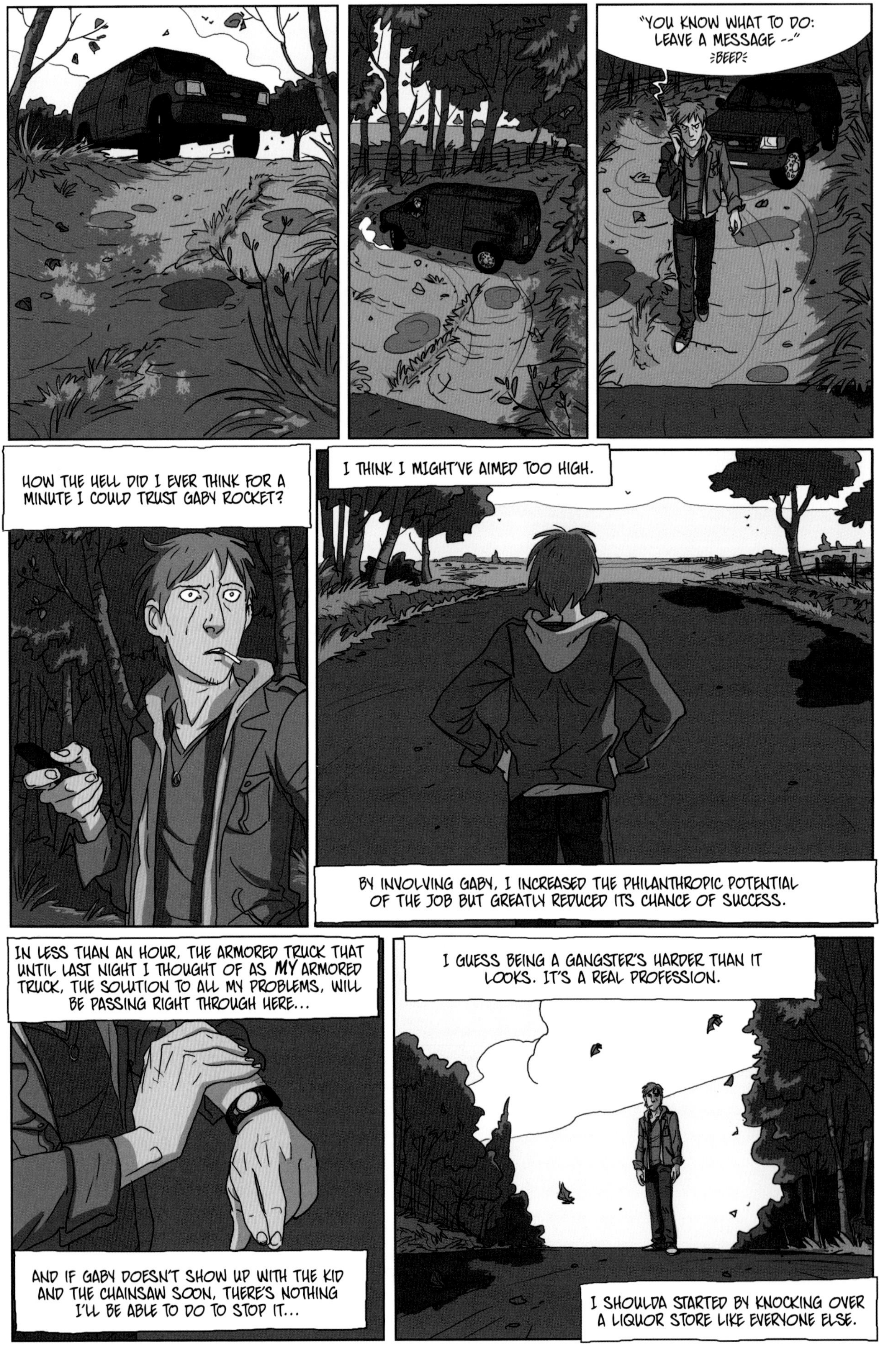
"YOU KNOW WHAT TO DO: LEAVE A MESSAGE --"
BEEP
HOW THE HELL DID I EVER THINK FOR A MINUTE I COULD TRUST GABY ROCKET?
I THINK I MIGHT'VE AIMED TOO HIGH.
BY INVOLVING GABY, I INCREASED THE PHILANTHROPIC POTENTIAL OF THE JOB BUT GREATLY REDUCED ITS CHANCE OF SUCCESS.
IN LESS THAN AN HOUR, THE ARMORED TRUCK THAT UNTIL LAST NIGHT I THOUGHT OF AS MY ARMORED TRUCK, THE SOLUTION TO ALL MY PROBLEMS, WILL BE PASSING RIGHT THROUGH HERE...
AND IF GABY DOESN'T SHOW UP WITH THE KID AND THE CHAINSAW SOON, THERE'S NOTHING I'LL BE ABLE TO DO TO STOP IT...
I GUESS BEING A GANGSTER'S HARDER THAN IT LOOKS. IT'S A REAL PROFESSION.
I SHOULDA STARTED BY KNOCKING OVER A LIQUOR STORE LIKE EVERYONE ELSE.

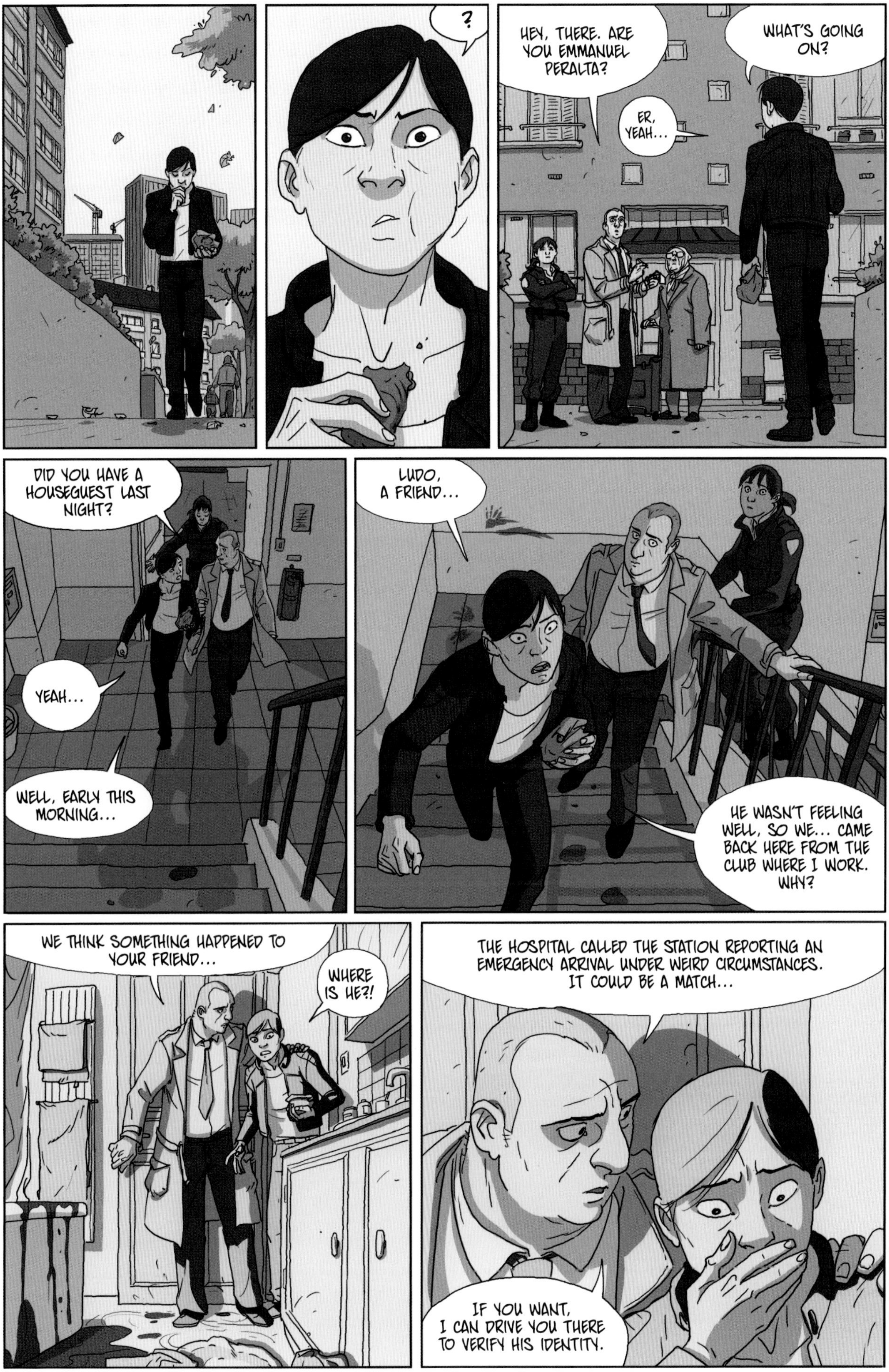
?
HEY, THERE. ARE YOU EMMANUEL PERALTA?
ER, YEAH...
WHAT'S GOING ON?
DID YOU HAVE A HOUSEGUEST LAST NIGHT?
YEAH...
WELL, EARLY THIS MORNING...
LUDO, A FRIEND...
HE WASN'T FEELING WELL, SO WE... CAME BACK HERE FROM THE CLUB WHERE I WORK. WHY?
WE THINK SOMETHING HAPPENED TO YOUR FRIEND...
WHERE IS HE?!
THE HOSPITAL CALLED THE STATION REPORTING AN EMERGENCY ARRIVAL UNDER WEIRD CIRCUMSTANCES. IT COULD BE A MATCH...
IF YOU WANT, I CAN DRIVE YOU THERE TO VERIFY HIS IDENTITY.

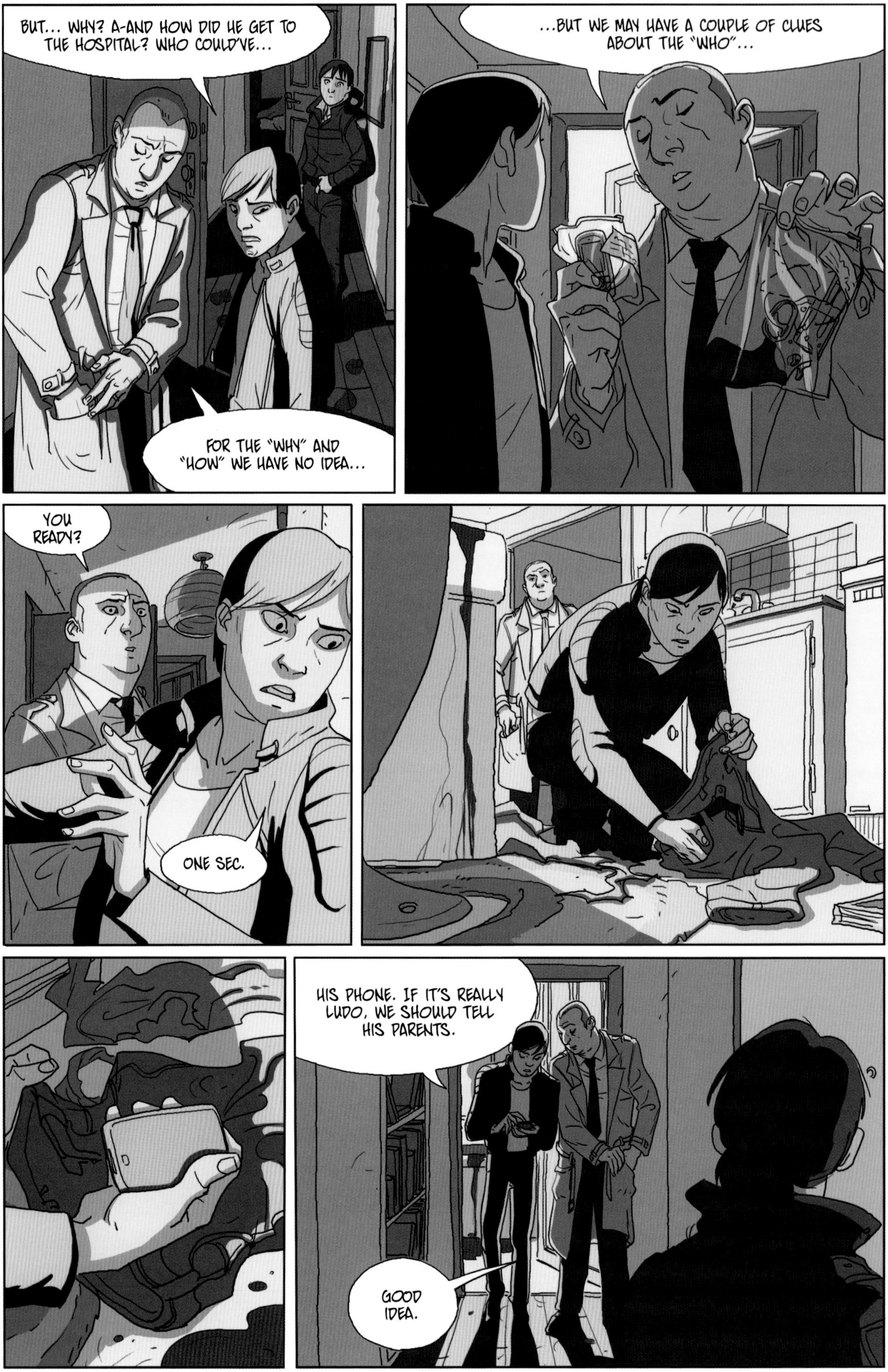
BUT... WHY? A-AND HOW DID HE GET TO THE HOSPITAL? WHO COULD'VE...
FOR THE "WHY" AND "HOW" WE HAVE NO IDEA...
...BUT WE MAY HAVE A COUPLE OF CLUES ABOUT THE "WHO"...
YOU READY?
ONE SEC.
HIS PHONE. IF IT'S REALLY LUDO, WE SHOULD TELL HIS PARENTS.
GOOD IDEA.

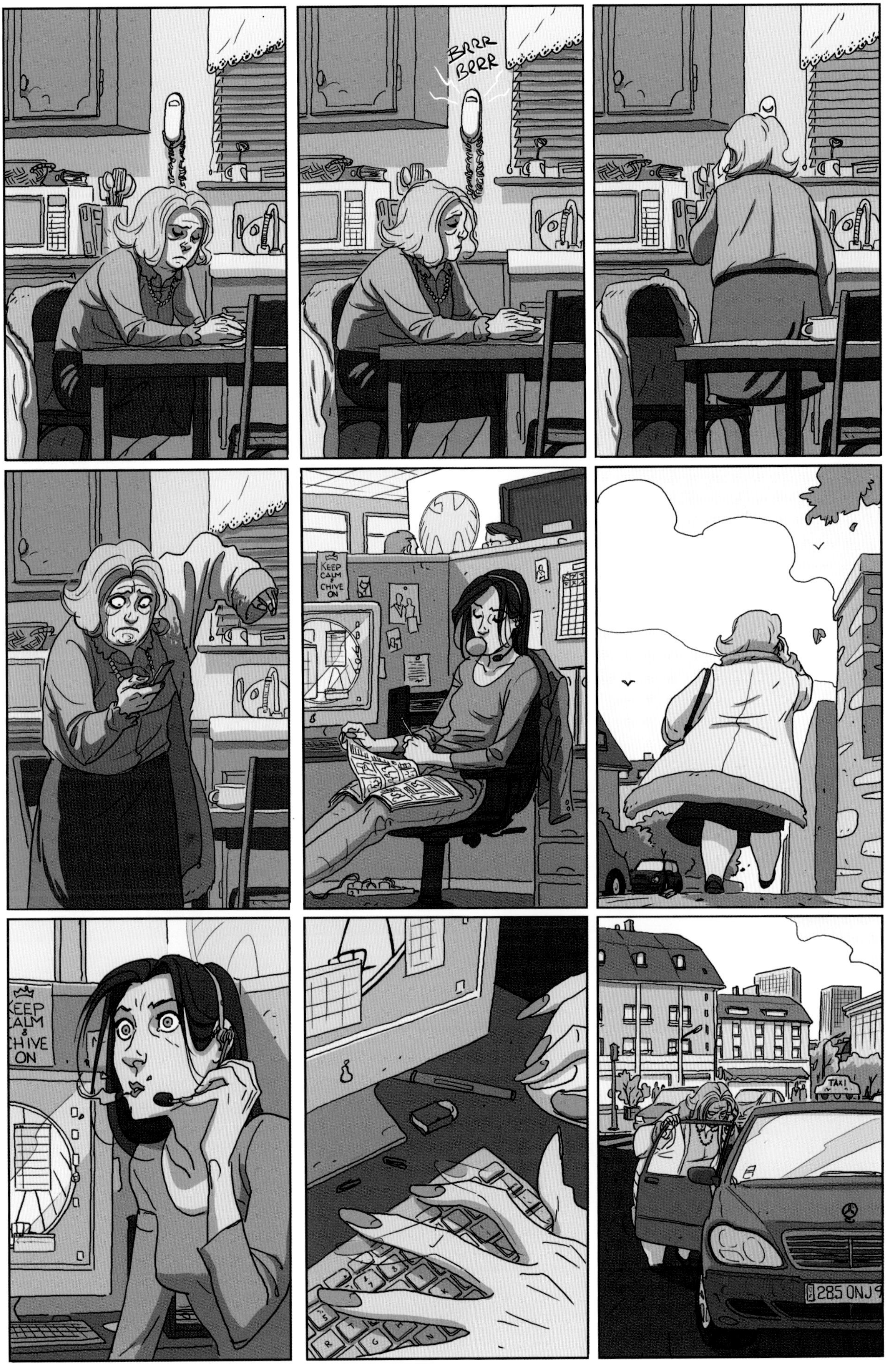
BRRR
BRRR
KEEP CALM & CHIVE ON
KEEP CALM & CHIVE ON
TAXI
285 ONJ 9

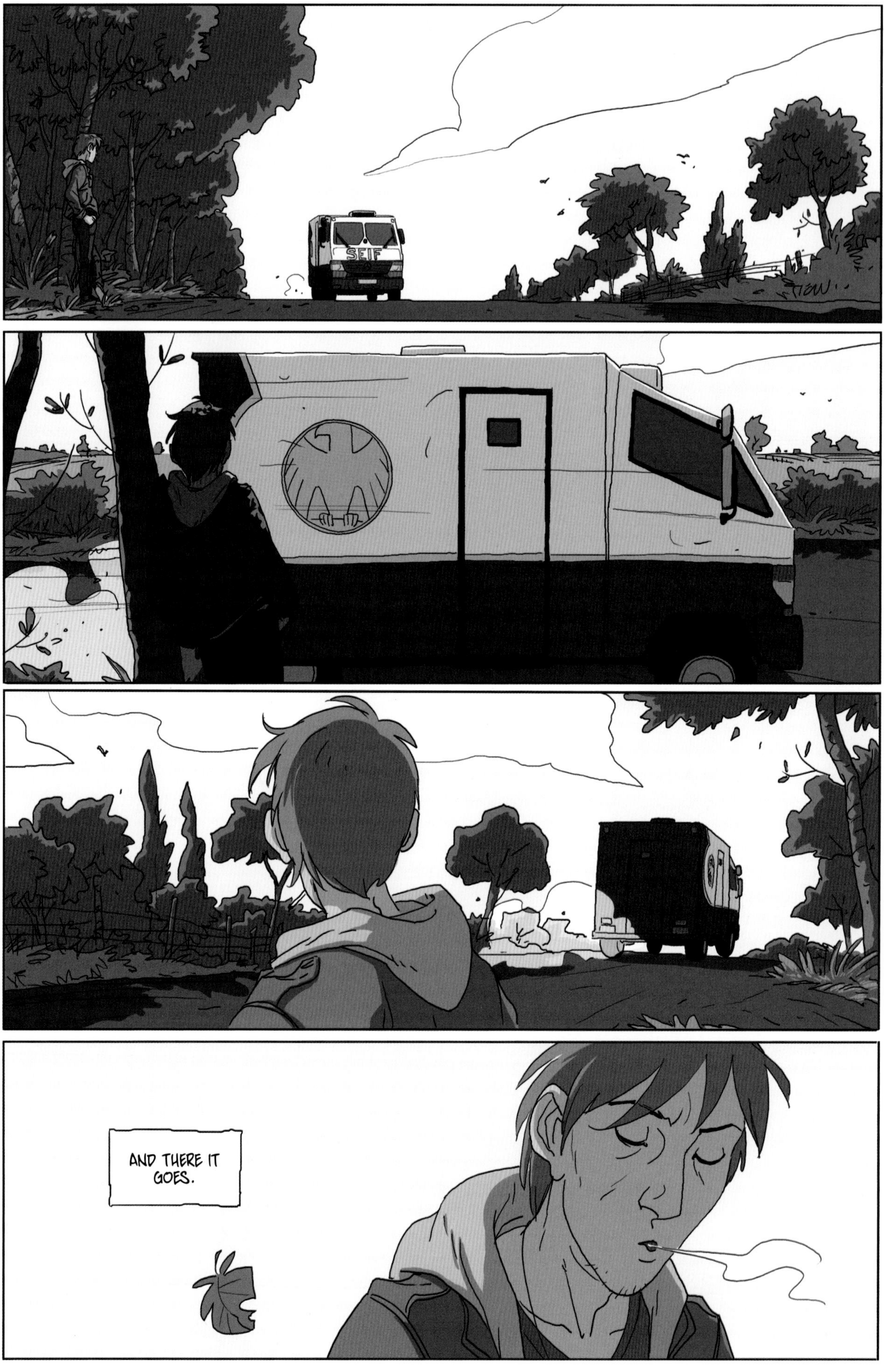
SEIF
AND THERE IT GOES.

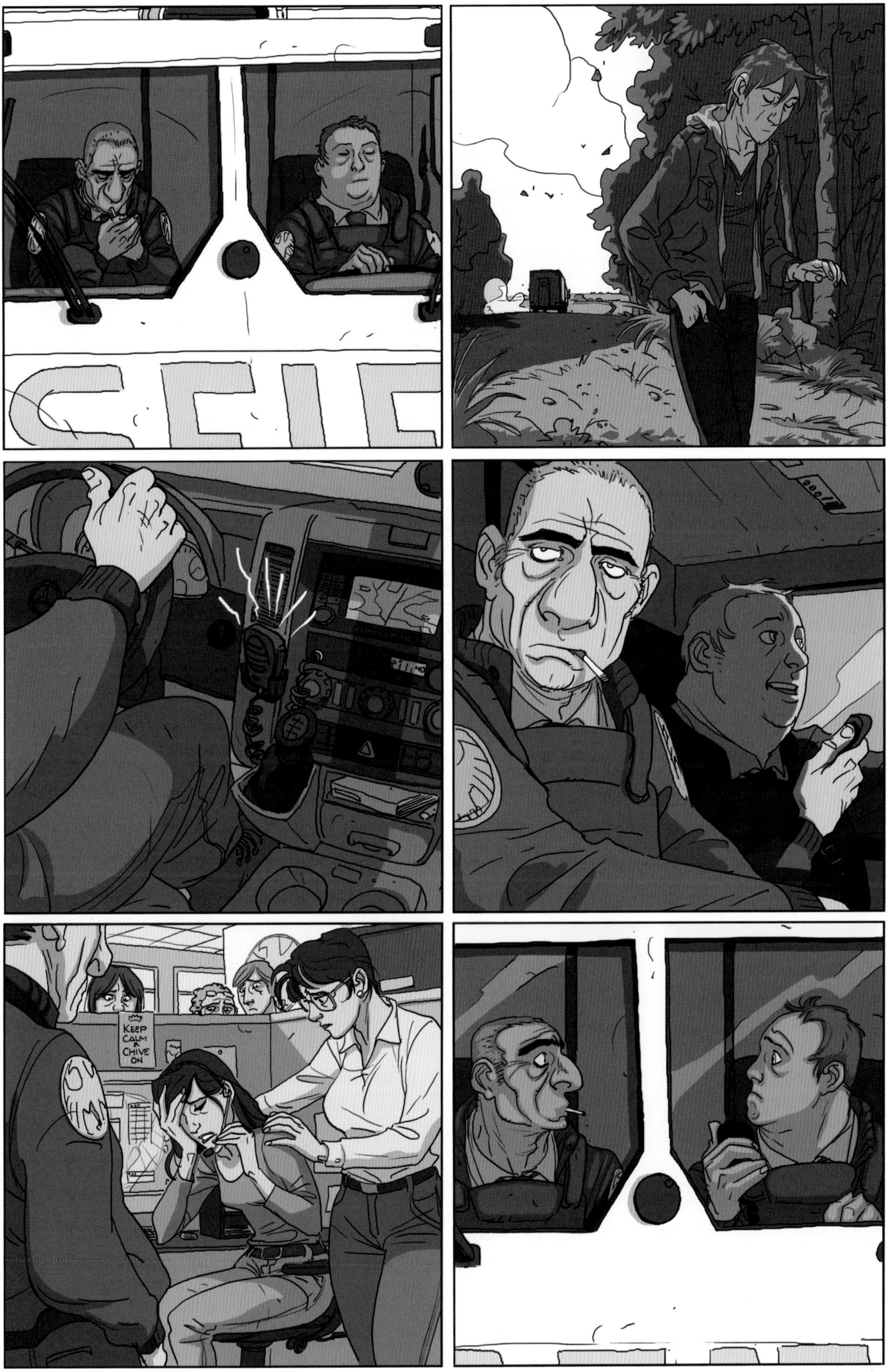
KEEP CALM & CHIVE ON

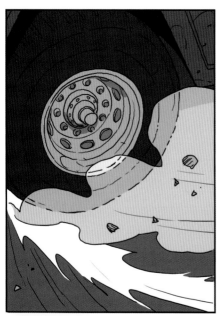

?

BERNARD! WHAT ARE YOU DOIN'?! WE CAN'T STOP HERE!

BERNARD!

BERNARD, COME ON, MAN!

BERNIE?

?!

106

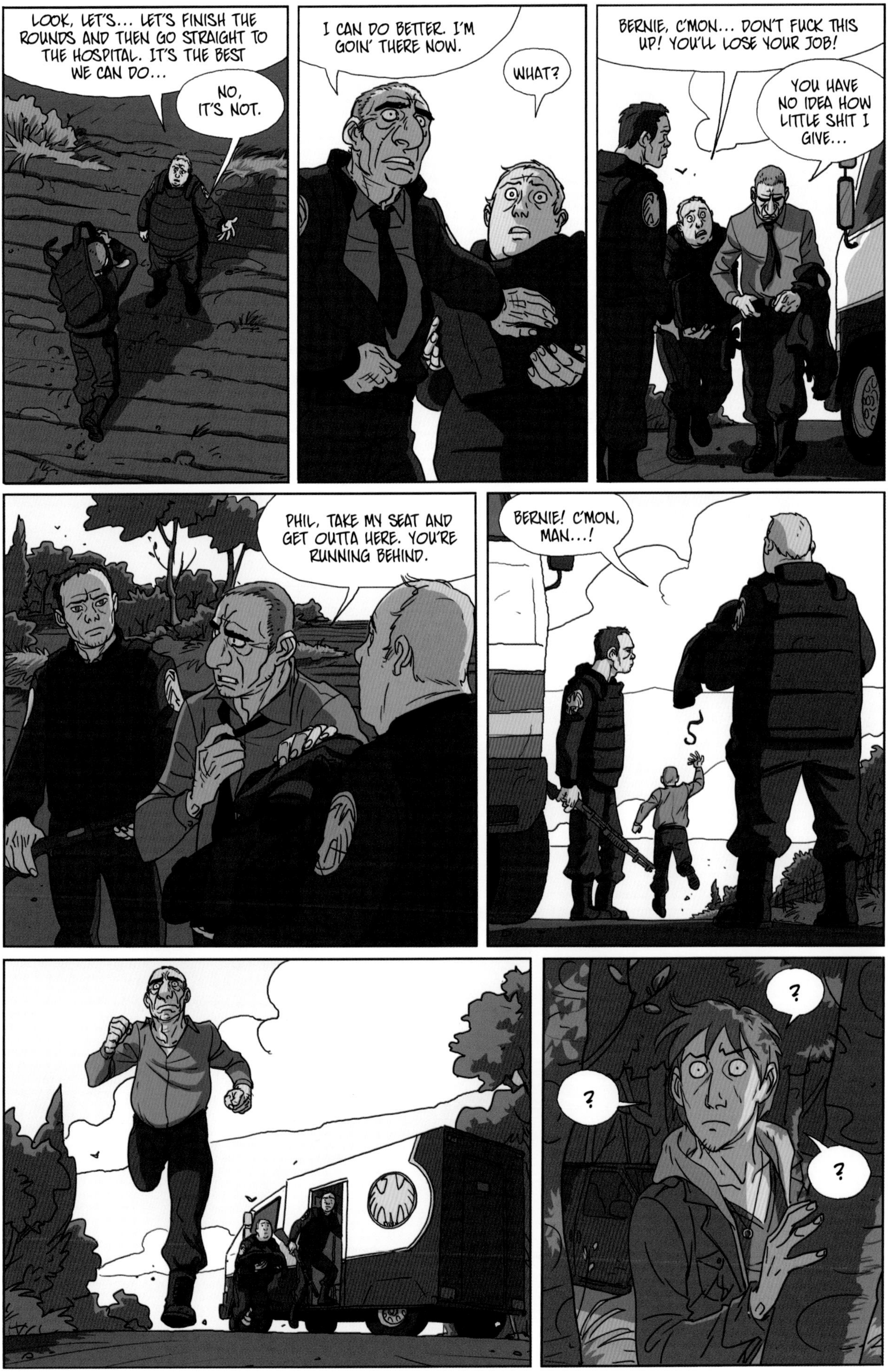

LOOK, LET'S... LET'S FINISH THE ROUNDS AND THEN GO STRAIGHT TO THE HOSPITAL. IT'S THE BEST WE CAN DO...
NO, IT'S NOT.
I CAN DO BETTER. I'M GOIN' THERE NOW.
WHAT?
BERNIE, C'MON... DON'T FUCK THIS UP! YOU'LL LOSE YOUR JOB!
YOU HAVE NO IDEA HOW LITTLE SHIT I GIVE...
PHIL, TAKE MY SEAT AND GET OUTTA HERE. YOU'RE RUNNING BEHIND.
BERNIE! C'MON, MAN...!
?
?
?

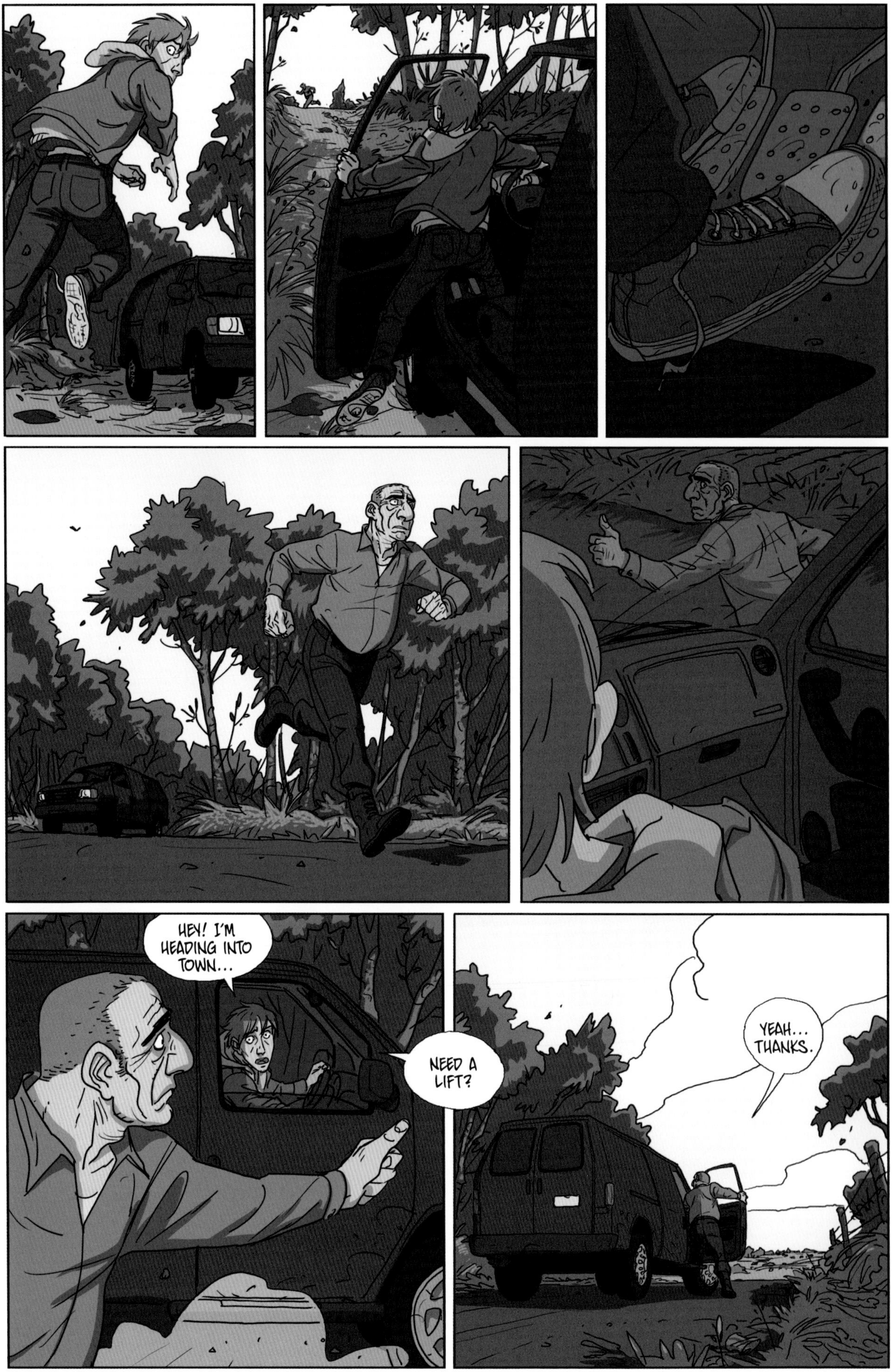
HEY! I'M HEADING INTO TOWN...
NEED A LIFT?
YEAH... THANKS.

YOU, AH... WANT ME TO DROP YOU OFF SOMEWHERE?

YEAH, NEAR SAINT LUCAS HOSPITAL, IF YOU DON'T MIND.

HOSPI... YEAH, SURE.

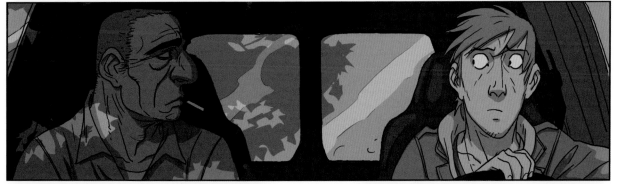

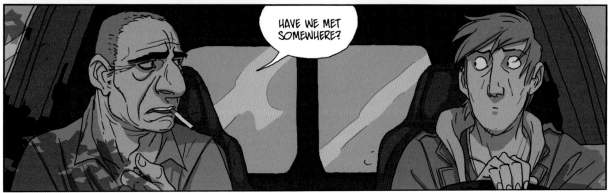

HAVE WE MET SOMEWHERE?

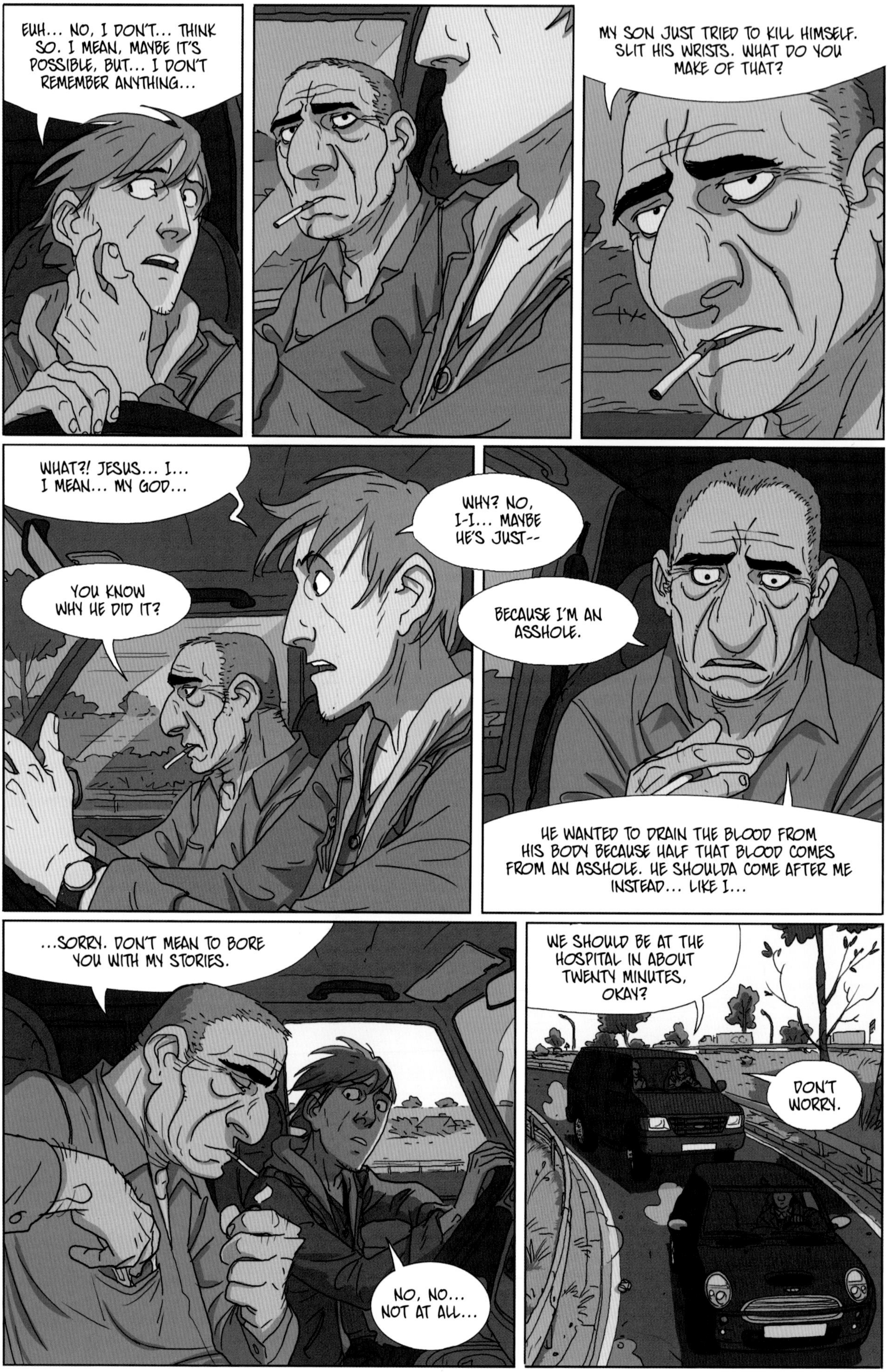
EUH... NO, I DON'T... THINK SO. I MEAN, MAYBE IT'S POSSIBLE, BUT... I DON'T REMEMBER ANYTHING...
MY SON JUST TRIED TO KILL HIMSELF. SLIT HIS WRISTS. WHAT DO YOU MAKE OF THAT?
WHAT?! JESUS... I... I MEAN... MY GOD...
YOU KNOW WHY HE DID IT?
WHY? NO, I-I... MAYBE HE'S JUST--
BECAUSE I'M AN ASSHOLE.
HE WANTED TO DRAIN THE BLOOD FROM HIS BODY BECAUSE HALF THAT BLOOD COMES FROM AN ASSHOLE. HE SHOULDA COME AFTER ME INSTEAD... LIKE I...
...SORRY. DON'T MEAN TO BORE YOU WITH MY STORIES.
NO, NO... NOT AT ALL...
WE SHOULD BE AT THE HOSPITAL IN ABOUT TWENTY MINUTES, OKAY?
DON'T WORRY.

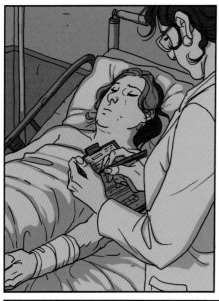

NO LUCK. THE GUY WHO BROUGHT HIM IN'S GONE.

TOC TOC

THEY LET HIM GO?!

THEY HAD NO REASON TO HOLD HIM. FROM WHAT WE COULD GATHER, HE'S ABOUT FIFTY YEARS OLD, WEARING BOOTS AND A BLACK LEATHER JACKET...

...AND HE LEFT A NAME: GABRIEL ROQUET. DOES THAT RING ANY BELLS?

NO...

NOPE.

HE SEEMED TO KNOW YOUR SON REALLY WELL. HE WAS PRETTY EMOTIONAL. ALMOST TRAUMATIZED. HE COLLAPSED IN TEARS WHEN WE TOOK YOUR BOY TO THE ICU. WE HAD TO GIVE HIM SOME ANTIDEPRESSANTS JUST TO CALM HIM DOWN...

THAT'S CRAZY! I LEFT LUDO FOR BARELY AN HOUR! JUST LONG ENOUGH TO GO BACK TO THE CLUB TO FINISH CLEANING UP! I STARTED A BATH FOR HIM AND THEN LEFT...

I GUESS WE'LL JUST HAVE TO WAIT FOR YOUR SON TO WAKE UP. MAYBE HE CAN EXPLAIN.

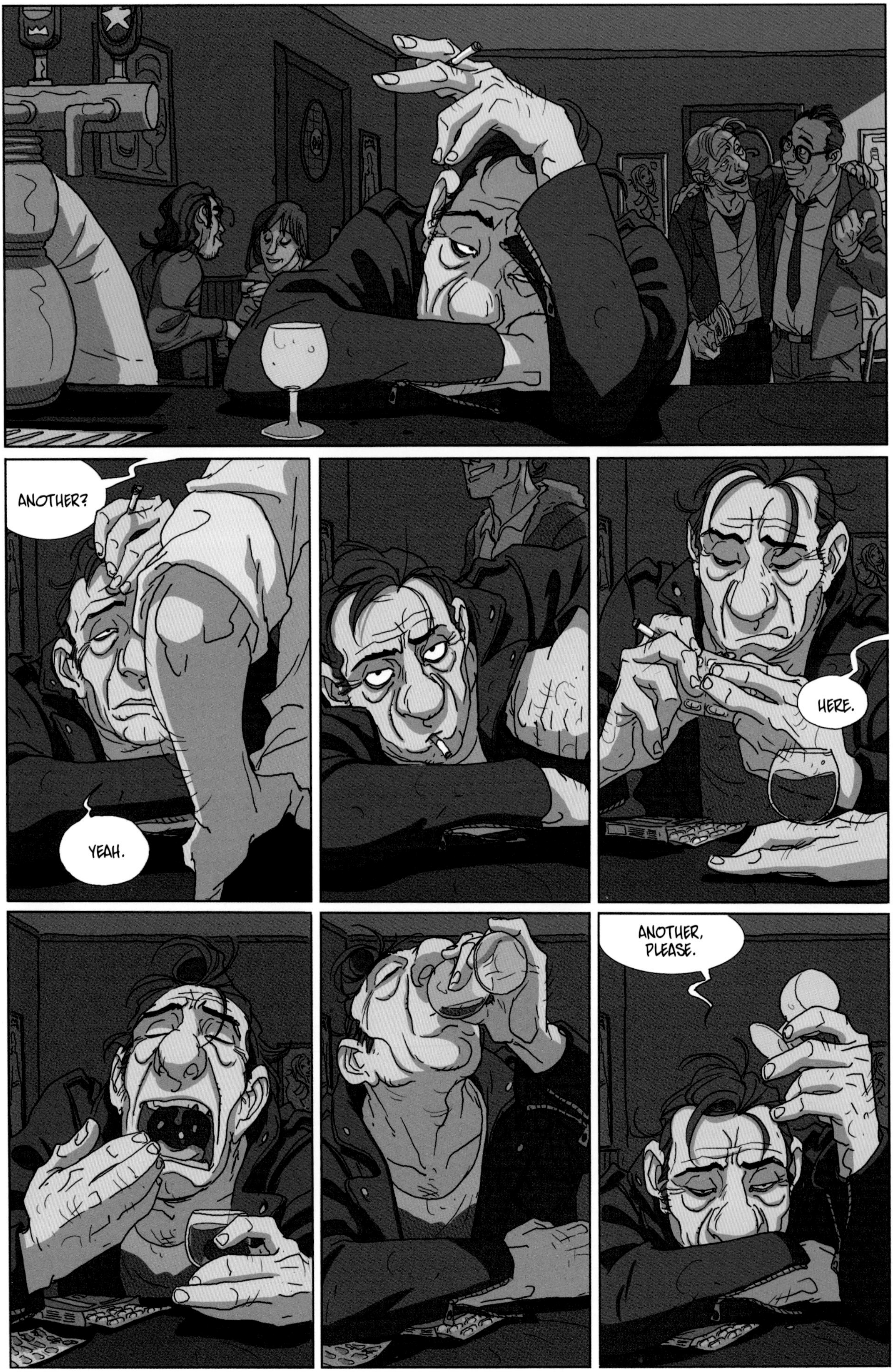
ANOTHER?
YEAH.
HERE.
ANOTHER, PLEASE.

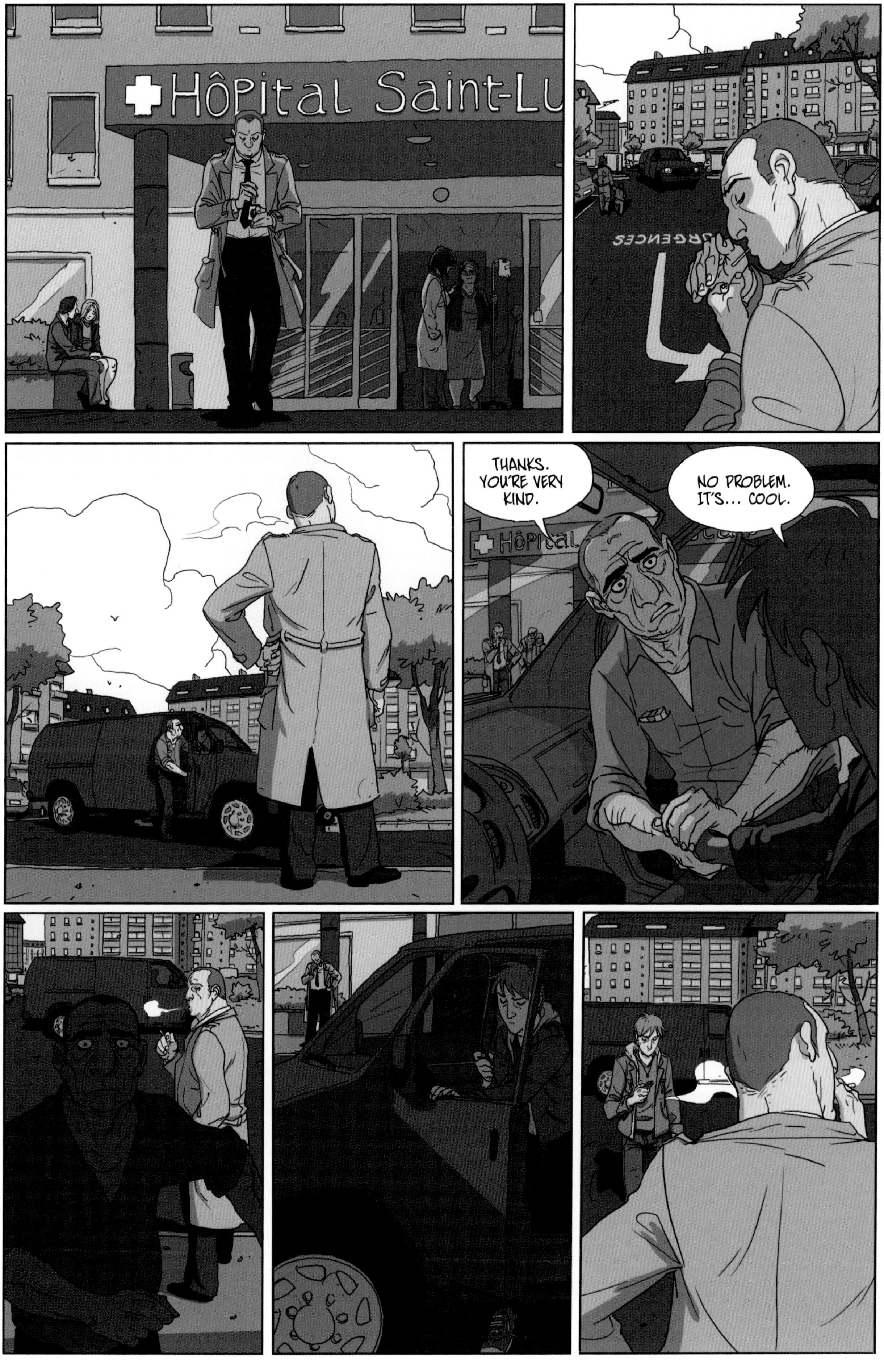
Hôpital Saint-Lu
THANKS. YOU'RE VERY KIND.
NO PROBLEM. IT'S... COOL.
Hôpital

CAN I BUM ONE OF THOSE?

YEAH, SURE.

"WISE MEN SAY... ONLY FOOLS RUSH IN... BUT I CAN'T HELP..."

"...FALLING IN LOVE WITH YOU..."

"...SHALL I STAY?..."

"...WOULD IT BE A SIN... IF I CAN'T HELP FALLING IN LOVE WITH--"

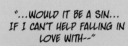

HEY, YOU WANT THAT CIGARETTE?

SIR?

HEY!

114

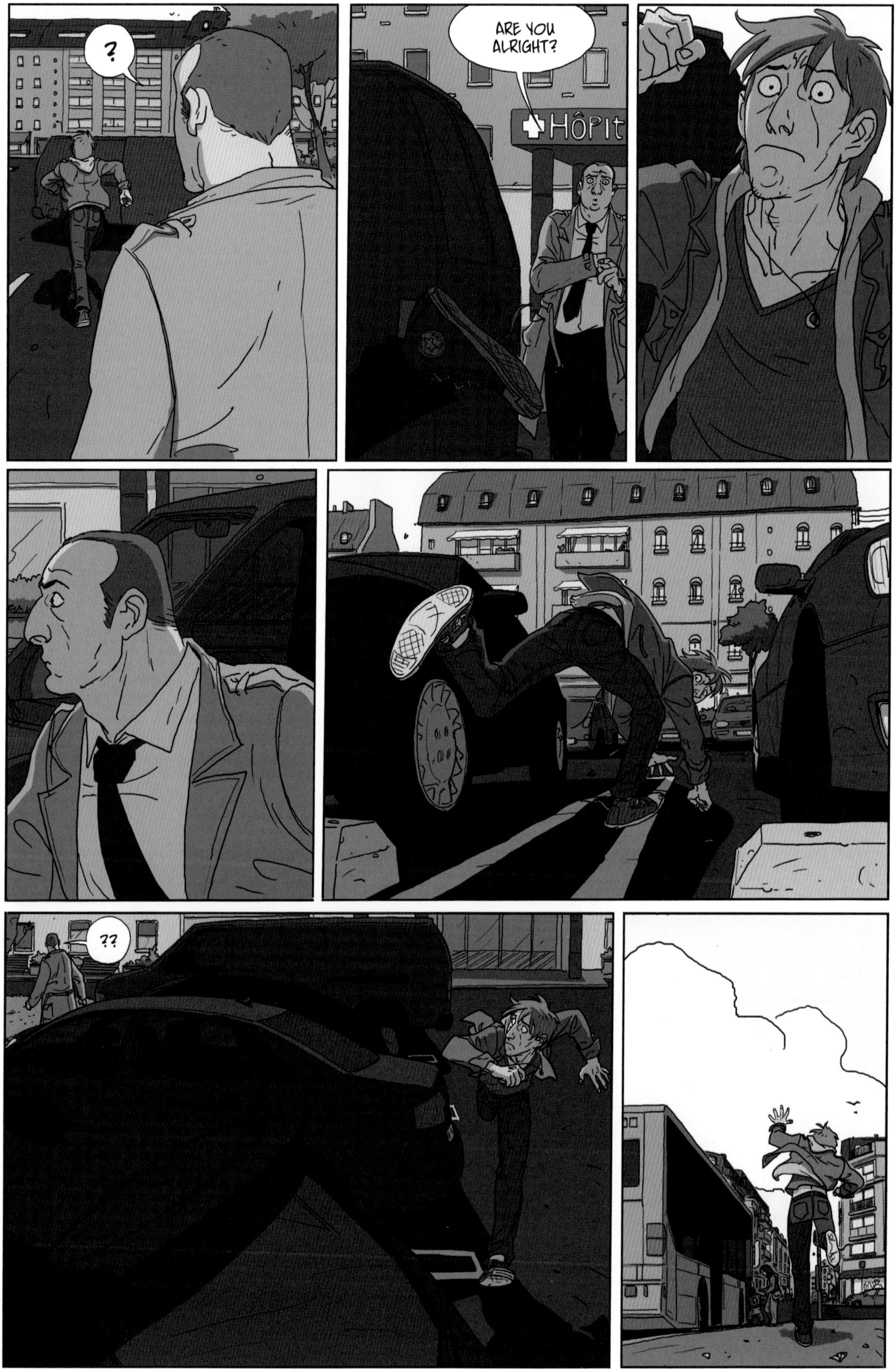
?
ARE YOU ALRIGHT?
HÔPIt
??

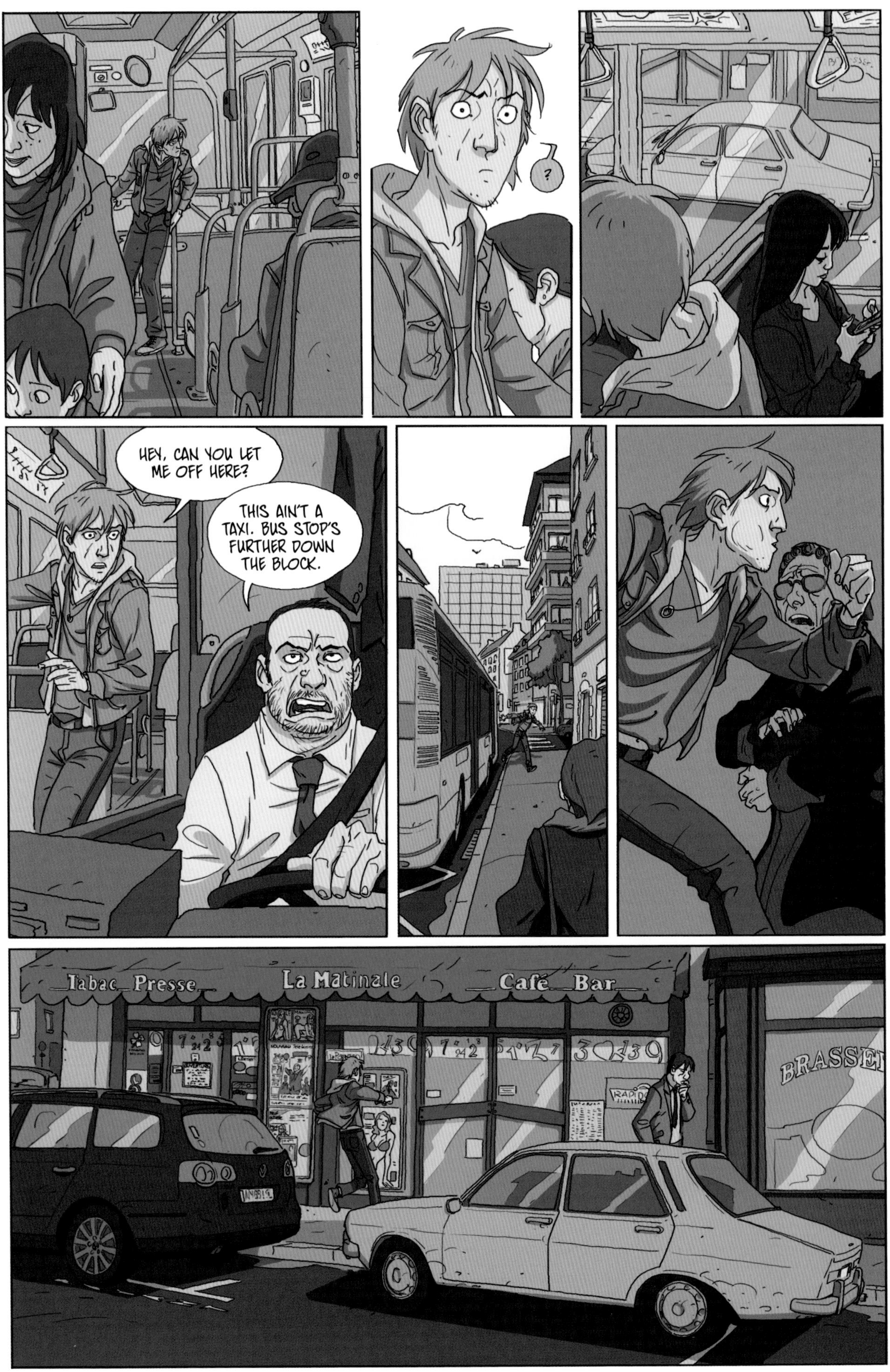
?
HEY, CAN YOU LET ME OFF HERE?
THIS AIN'T A TAXI. BUS STOP'S FURTHER DOWN THE BLOCK.
Tabac Presse
La Matinale
Café Bar
BRASSE

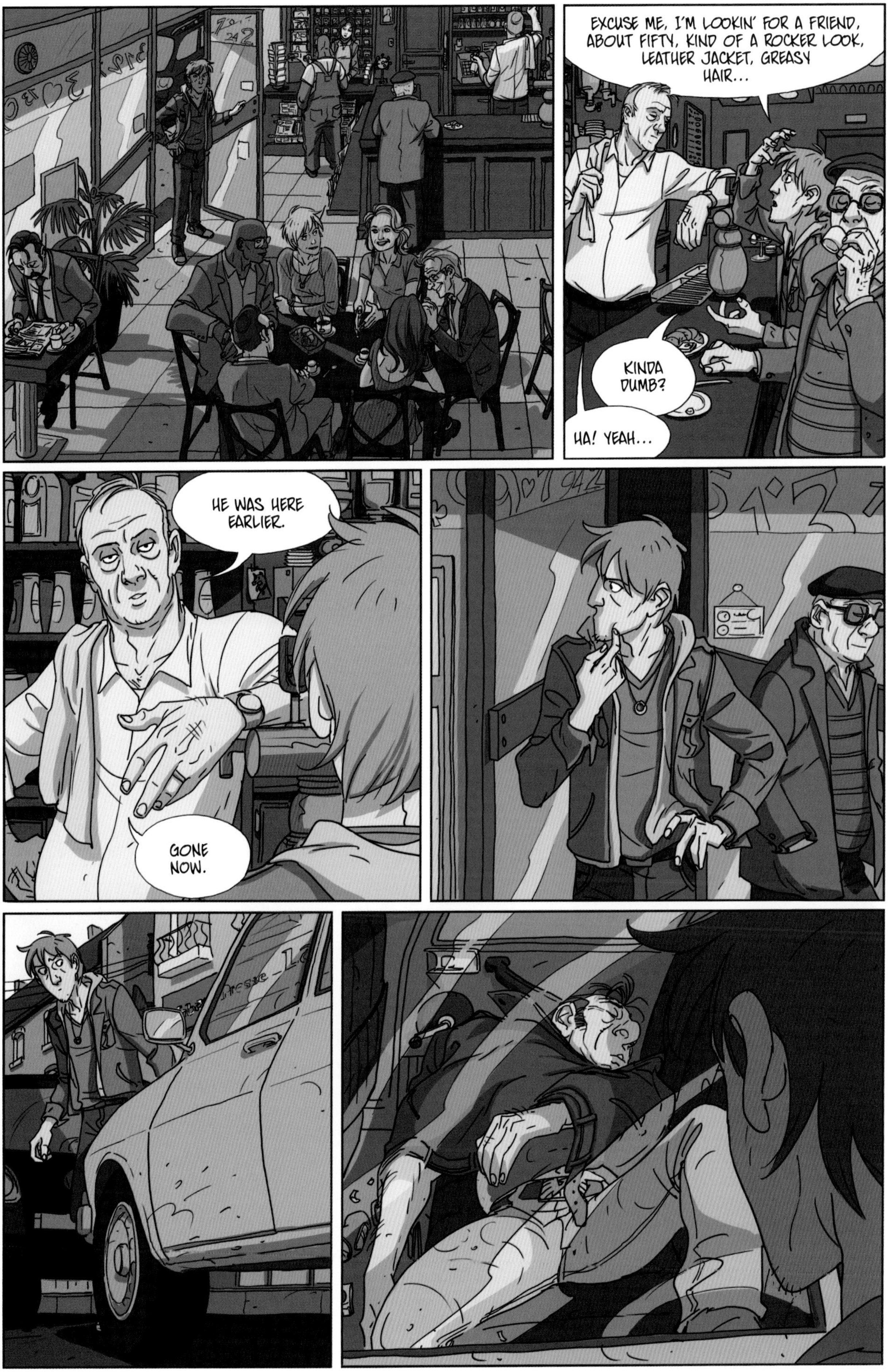
EXCUSE ME, I'M LOOKIN' FOR A FRIEND, ABOUT FIFTY, KIND OF A ROCKER LOOK, LEATHER JACKET, GREASY HAIR...
KINDA DUMB?
HA! YEAH...
HE WAS HERE EARLIER.
GONE NOW.

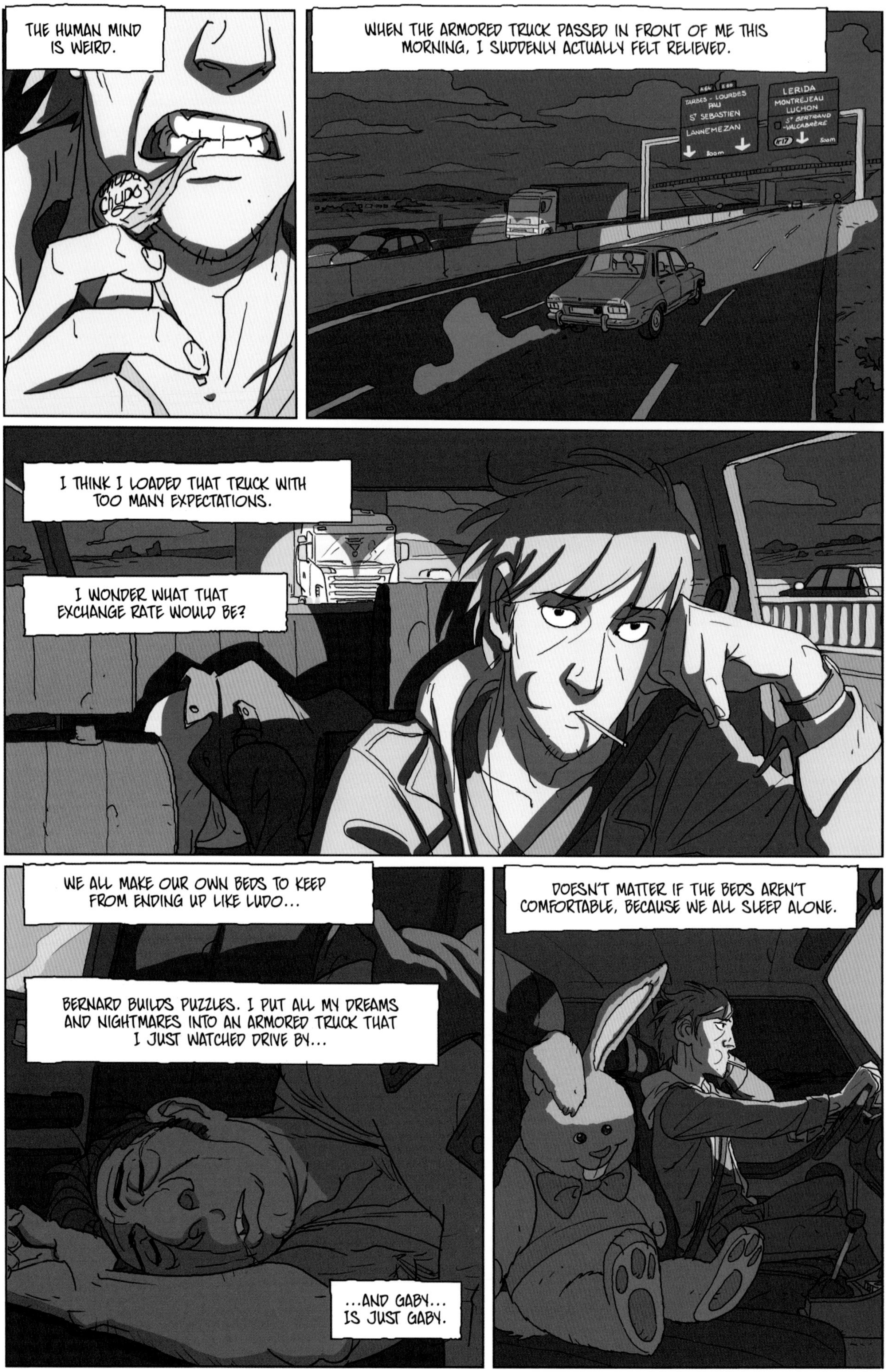
THE HUMAN MIND IS WEIRD.
WHEN THE ARMORED TRUCK PASSED IN FRONT OF ME THIS MORNING, I SUDDENLY ACTUALLY FELT RELIEVED.
I THINK I LOADED THAT TRUCK WITH TOO MANY EXPECTATIONS.
I WONDER WHAT THAT EXCHANGE RATE WOULD BE?
WE ALL MAKE OUR OWN BEDS TO KEEP FROM ENDING UP LIKE LUDO...
BERNARD BUILDS PUZZLES. I PUT ALL MY DREAMS AND NIGHTMARES INTO AN ARMORED TRUCK THAT I JUST WATCHED DRIVE BY...
...AND GABY... IS JUST GABY.
DOESN'T MATTER IF THE BEDS AREN'T COMFORTABLE, BECAUSE WE ALL SLEEP ALONE.

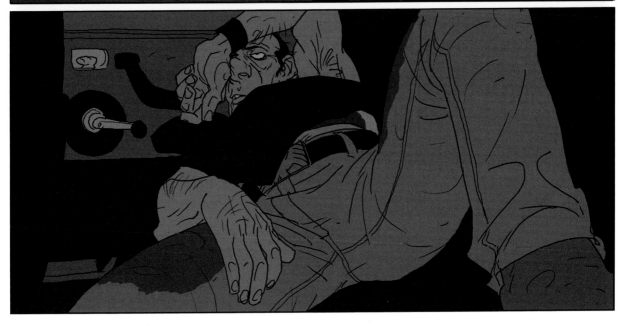

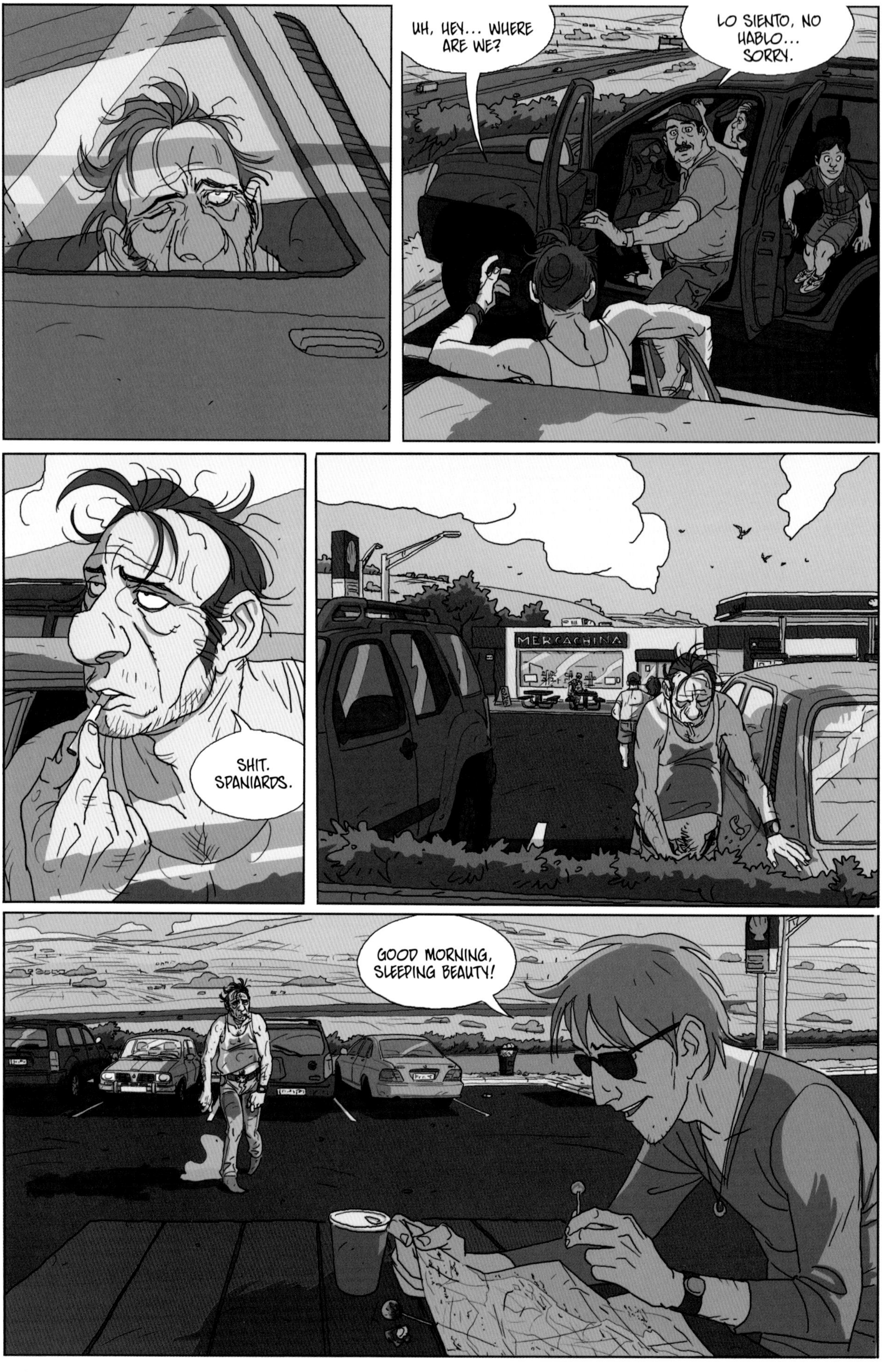
UH, HEY... WHERE ARE WE?
LO SIENTO, NO HABLO... SORRY.
SHIT. SPANIARDS.
MERCACHINA
GOOD MORNING, SLEEPING BEAUTY!

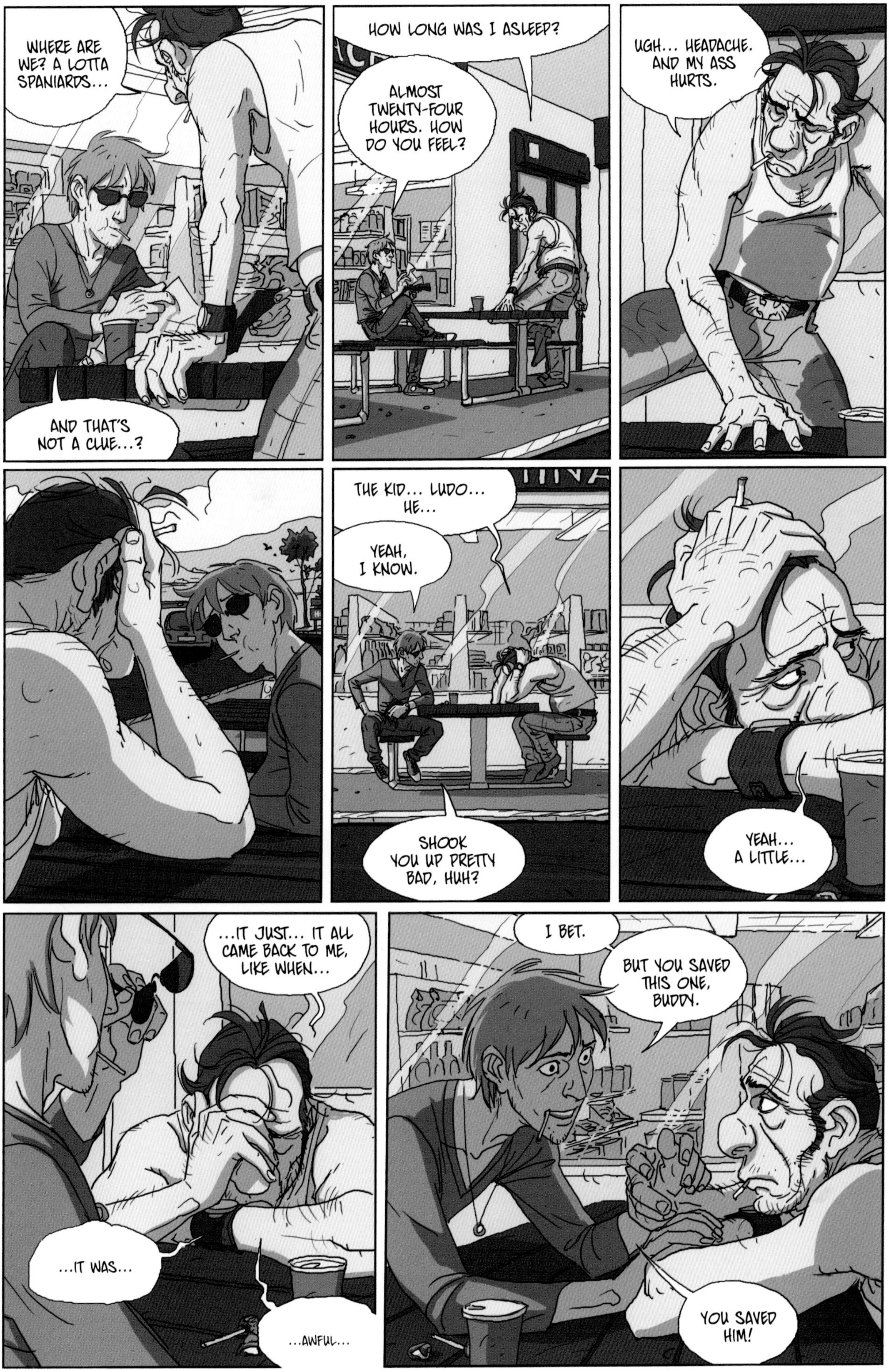
WHERE ARE WE? A LOTTA SPANIARDS...
AND THAT'S NOT A CLUE...?
HOW LONG WAS I ASLEEP?
ALMOST TWENTY-FOUR HOURS. HOW DO YOU FEEL?
UGH... HEADACHE. AND MY ASS HURTS.
THE KID... LUDO... HE...
YEAH, I KNOW.
SHOOK YOU UP PRETTY BAD, HUH?
YEAH... A LITTLE...
...IT JUST... IT ALL CAME BACK TO ME, LIKE WHEN...
...IT WAS...
...AWFUL...
I BET.
BUT YOU SAVED THIS ONE, BUDDY.
YOU SAVED HIM!

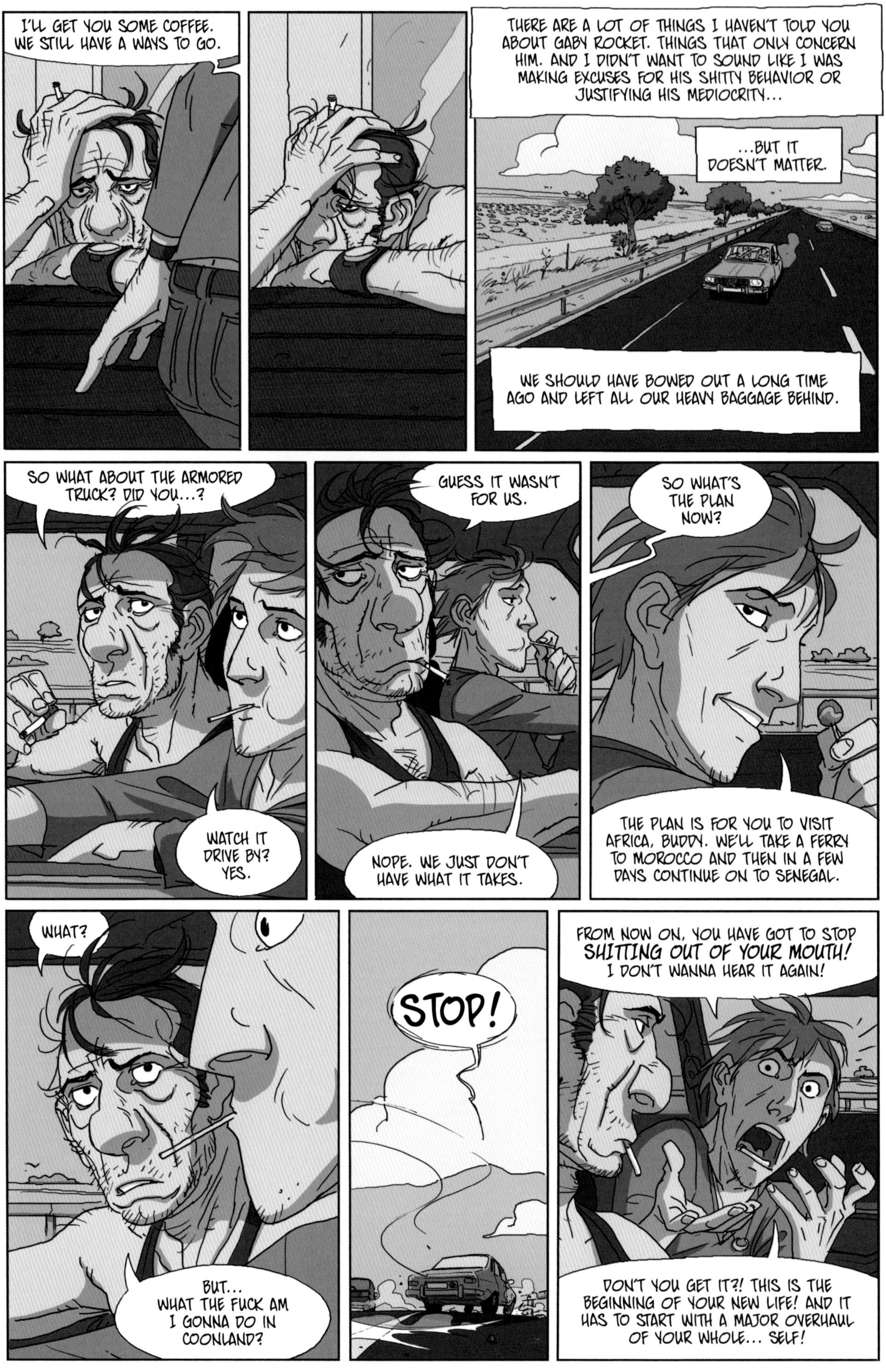
I'LL GET YOU SOME COFFEE.
WE STILL HAVE A WAYS TO GO.
THERE ARE A LOT OF THINGS I HAVEN'T TOLD YOU ABOUT GABY ROCKET. THINGS THAT ONLY CONCERN HIM. AND I DIDN'T WANT TO SOUND LIKE I WAS MAKING EXCUSES FOR HIS SHITTY BEHAVIOR OR JUSTIFYING HIS MEDIOCRITY...
...BUT IT DOESN'T MATTER.
WE SHOULD HAVE BOWED OUT A LONG TIME AGO AND LEFT ALL OUR HEAVY BAGGAGE BEHIND.
SO WHAT ABOUT THE ARMORED TRUCK? DID YOU...?
WATCH IT DRIVE BY? YES.
GUESS IT WASN'T FOR US.
NOPE. WE JUST DON'T HAVE WHAT IT TAKES.
SO WHAT'S THE PLAN NOW?
THE PLAN IS FOR YOU TO VISIT AFRICA, BUDDY. WE'LL TAKE A FERRY TO MOROCCO AND THEN IN A FEW DAYS CONTINUE ON TO SENEGAL.
WHAT?
BUT... WHAT THE FUCK AM I GONNA DO IN COONLAND?
STOP!
FROM NOW ON, YOU HAVE GOT TO STOP SHITTING OUT OF YOUR MOUTH! I DON'T WANNA HEAR IT AGAIN!
DON'T YOU GET IT?! THIS IS THE BEGINNING OF YOUR NEW LIFE! AND IT HAS TO START WITH A MAJOR OVERHAUL OF YOUR WHOLE... SELF!

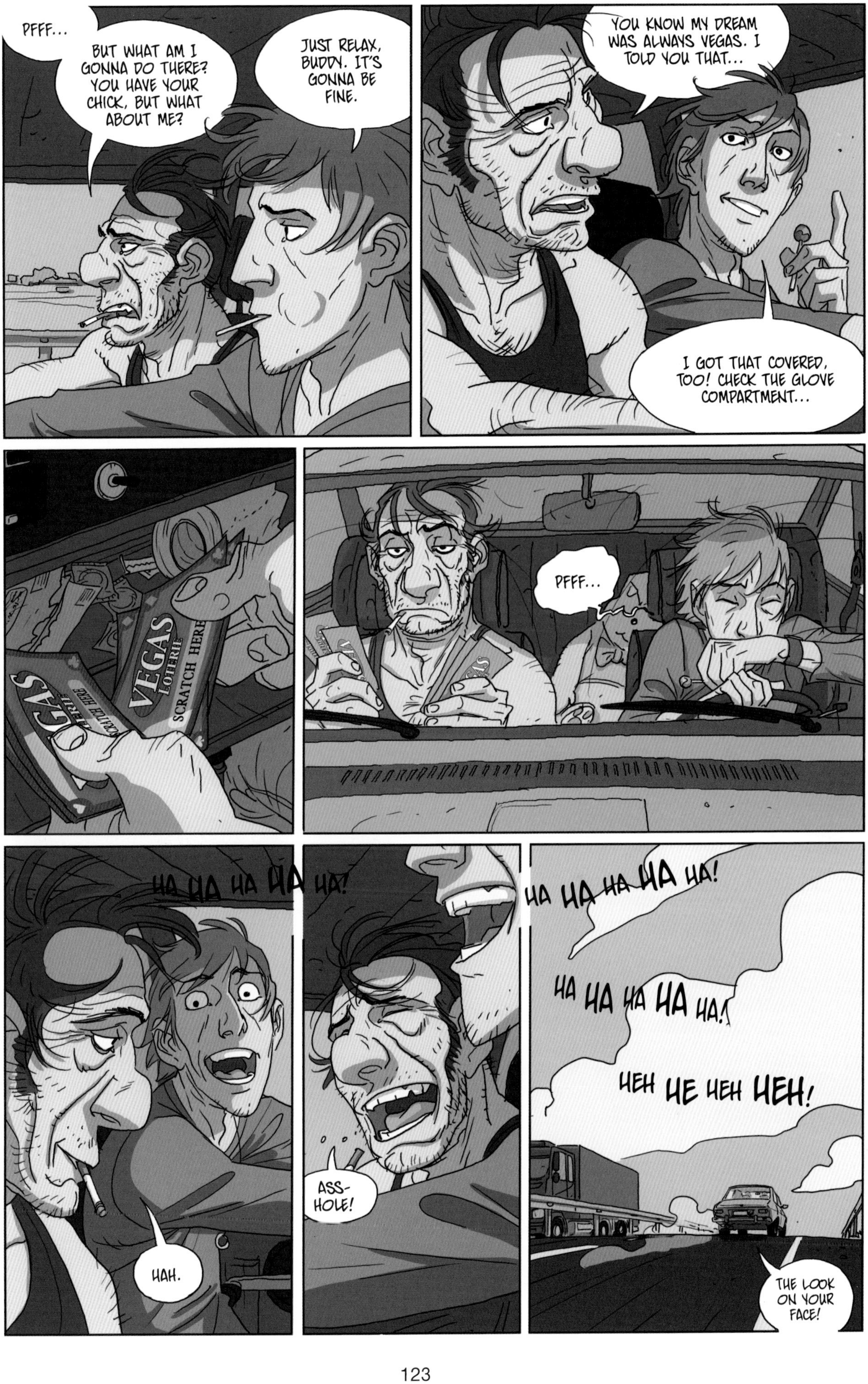
PFFF...
BUT WHAT AM I GONNA DO THERE? YOU HAVE YOUR CHICK, BUT WHAT ABOUT ME?
JUST RELAX, BUDDY. IT'S GONNA BE FINE.
YOU KNOW MY DREAM WAS ALWAYS VEGAS. I TOLD YOU THAT...
I GOT THAT COVERED, TOO! CHECK THE GLOVE COMPARTMENT...
VEGAS LOTERIE SCRATCH HERE
PFFF...
HA HA HA HA HA!
HAH.
ASS-HOLE!
HA HA HA HA HA!
HA HA HA HA HA!
HEH HE HEH HEH!
THE LOOK ON YOUR FACE!

THERE ARE SO MANY OTHER THINGS I COULD TELL YOU...

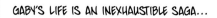

GABY'S LIFE IS AN INEXHAUSTIBLE SAGA...

THE STORY OF HIS DISCOVERY OF AFRICA WOULD MAKE *TINTIN IN THE CONGO* LOOK TAME...

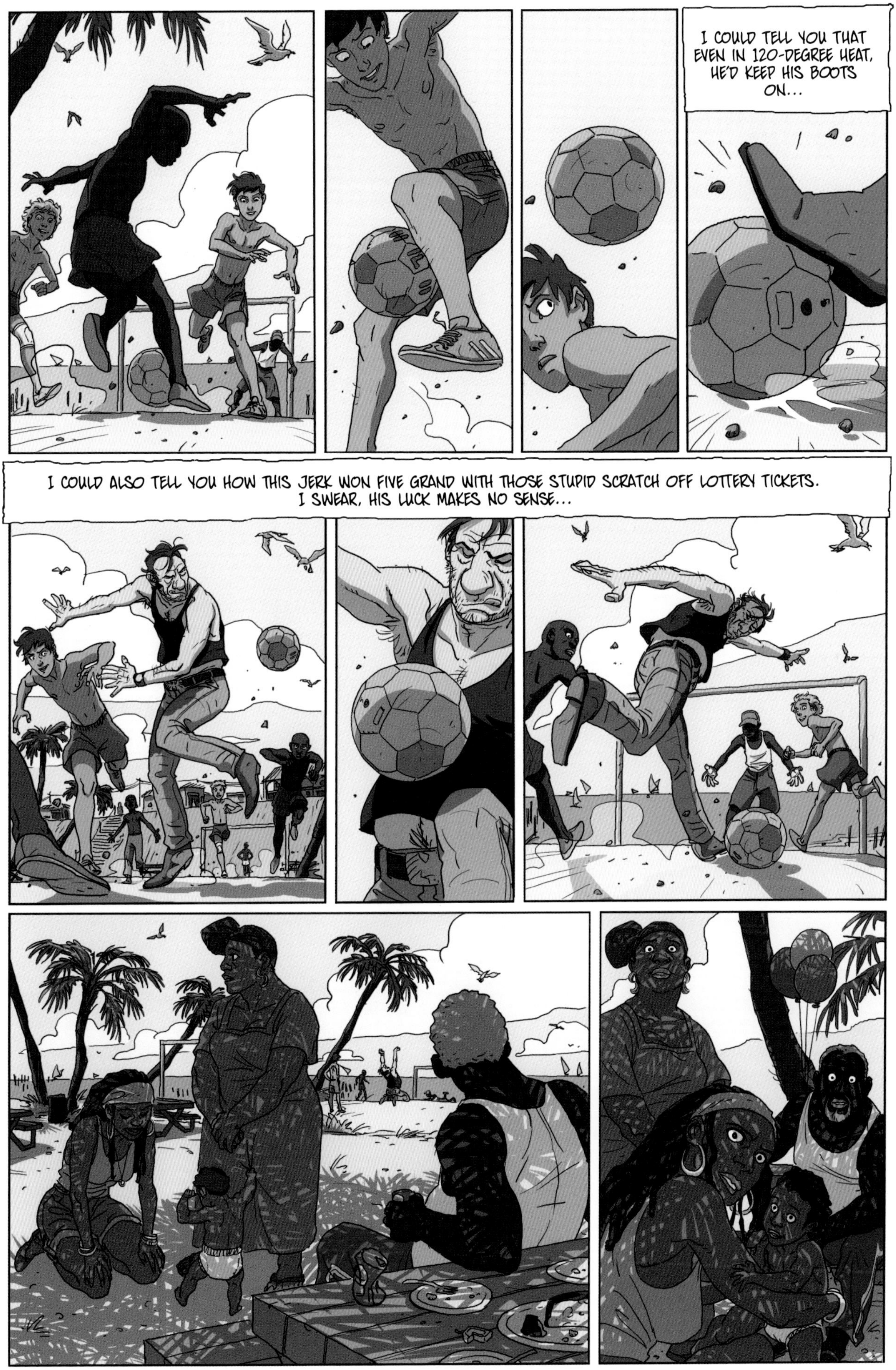
I COULD TELL YOU THAT EVEN IN 120-DEGREE HEAT, HE'D KEEP HIS BOOTS ON...
I COULD ALSO TELL YOU HOW THIS JERK WON FIVE GRAND WITH THOSE STUPID SCRATCH OFF LOTTERY TICKETS. I SWEAR, HIS LUCK MAKES NO SENSE...

YEAH, THERE'S A LOT MORE I COULD TELL YOU...

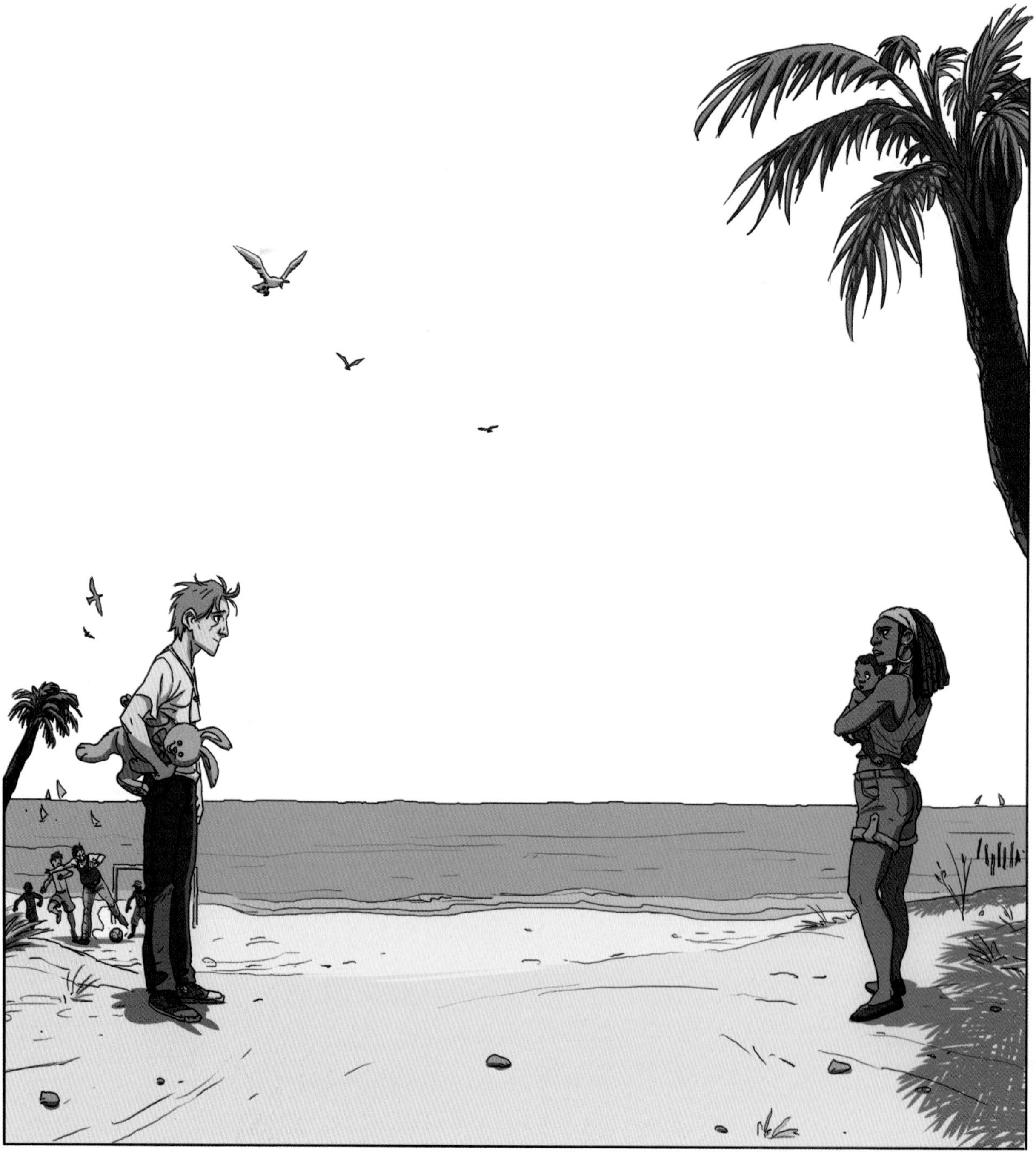

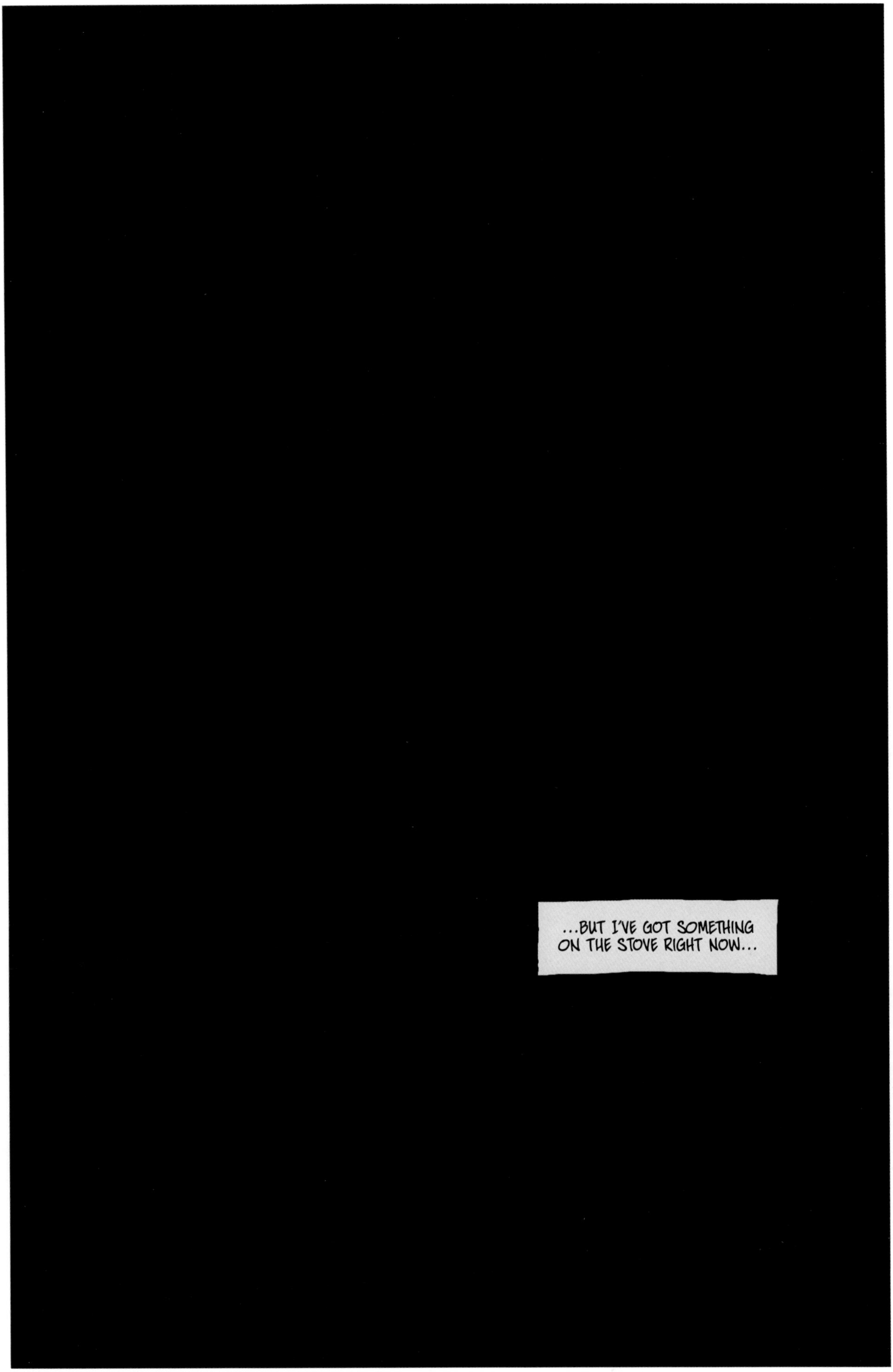
...BUT I'VE GOT SOMETHING ON THE STOVE RIGHT NOW...

Writer **Wilfrid Lupano** graduated from La Sorbonne with a literary baccalaureate and a degree in philosophy; not exactly what one would expect from a writer who draws the majority of his inspiration from role-playing games and bar life. But it was extensive interest and hours spent immersed in the storytelling routine of running role-playing games with his friends, and the reality of human life that surrounded them in the taverns in which they'd play these games that led him to writing as a career. Since his first creation, *Little Big Joe* in 2001, he has written over twenty different titles comprising over sixty volumes in total, and has won many awards and accolades for his more popular works, including *The Hartlepool Monkey*, *Curtain Call, A Sea of Love*, and *The Geezers*.

Artist **Rodguen** (born Rodolphe Guenoden) is a fifteen-year veteran at DreamWorks animation studio, having worked on many of their original 2-D features, such as *Balto, The Prince of Egypt*, and *The Road to El Dorado*, before cultivating their transition into 3-D with *Madagascar* and the *Kung Fu Panda* series. This is his first graphic novel.